SCHUMAN REPORT
ON EUROPE

STATE OF THE UNION 2013

Springer

Paris
Berlin
Heidelberg
New York
Hong Kong
London
Milan
Tokyo

SCHUMAN REPORT ON EUROPE

STATE OF THE UNION 2013

by the Robert Schuman Foundation
for Springer Verlag

Publication edited by
Thierry Chopin and Michel Foucher

Publication edited by Thierry Chopin and Michel Foucher
Translated by Rachel Ischoffen and Helen Levy

ISBN : 978-2-8178-0450-7 Springer Paris Berlin Heidelberg New York

© Springer-Verlag France, Paris, 2013
Printed in France SEPEC
Springer-Verlag France is a member of the group Springer Science + Business Media
Original title : *"Rapport Schuman sur l'Europe, l'état de l'Union 2013"*
© Éditions Lignes de Repères, 2013
3, rue de Téhéran - 75008 Paris
Site internet : www.lignes-de-reperes.com
ISBN : 978-2-915752-98-4

Cover design : Jean-François Montmarché
Illustration of cover : Ulrich Baumgarten via Getty Images

Translated by Rachel Ischoffen and Helen Levy

The State of the Union 2013, Schuman Report on Europe is a collective work created
on the initiative of the Robert Schuman Foundation according article 9
of law number 57-298 11th March1957 and article L.113-2 paragraph 3
of the intellectual property code.

This work has been published with the support of the Centre for European Studies.

"The Centre for European Studies" (CES) is the official think tank of the European People's Party (EPP) dedicated to the promotion of Christian Democrat, conservative and similar political values. For more information
consult: www.thinkingeurope.eu.

This publication receives funding from the European Parliament. The European Parliament and the Centre
for European Studies assume no responsibility for facts or opinions expressed in this publication or their sub-
sequent use. Sole responsibility lies with the author for this publication.

Table of Content

List of Maps

SCHUMAN REPORT ON EUROPE

State of the Union 2013

Publication edited by Thierry CHOPIN and Michel FOUCHER

Contributors to this book:

Josef Ackermann, Magali Balent, José Manuel Barroso, Joachim Bitterlich, Stefaan De Corte, Jean-Marc Daniel, Nicolas Delmas, Corinne Deloy, Javier Doz, Hugh Dykes, Alain Fabre, Jean-Pierre Filiu, Jean-Dominique Giuliani, Nicole Gnesotto, Jean-François Jamet, Pascale Joannin, Jean-Baptiste Laignelot, Alain Lamassoure, Mathilde Lemoine, Pascal Perrineau, Joseph Quinlan, Simon Serfaty, Gerald Stang, Ignacio Fernández Toxo, Henrik Uterwedde

The authors alone are solely responsible for the opinions expressed in the contributions to this book.

Contributors

Texts

Josef Ackermann

Chairman of the Board of Directors of Zurich Insurance Group since March 2012, after being its Vice-chairman for two years. After his doctorate, obtained in 1977, he joined Schweizerische Kreditanstalt (SKA). In 1990, he was appointed to the Executive Board of SKA and became its president in 1993. In 1996, he joined the Management Board of Deutsche Bank and, in 2002, he became its spokesman. From 2006 until May 2012, he was Chairman of the Management Board of Deutsche Bank Group.

Magali Balent

PhD in International Relations from the Graduate Institute (HEI, Geneva), she is currently project Manager in charge of external partnerships at the Robert Schuman Foundation. Specialist in European far right parties, she is a lecturer at Sciences Po Paris.

José Manuel Durão Barroso

He took office as President of the European Commission in November 2004 and was re-elected for another five-year term by the European Parliament in September 2009. He served as head of the International Relations Department of Lusíada University in Portugal from 1995 to 1999 and was a visiting professor at Georgetown University in the United States from 1996 to 1998. He was first elected to the Portuguese Parliament in 1985. He served as State Secretary for Home Affairs, State Secretary for Foreign Affairs and Cooperation, and Minister for Foreign Affairs in successive governments. In 1999, he was elected President of the Social Democratic Party (PSD) and became the leader of the opposition. He led the PSD to a coalition government in 2002 and served as Prime Minister until 2004.

Joachim Bitterlich

A German Ambassador (retired) and former diplomatic and security advisor to Chancellor Helmut Kohl. From 2003 to 2012, he was Executive Vice President International Affairs for Veolia Environment; from 2009 to 2012 he was Chairman of group activities in Germany. He is a board member of public and private institutions. Vice-President of the association Notre Europe-Institut Jacques Delors, he is also a Professor at the ESCP Europe Paris management school and co-founder of the Rhénan Club. He is a member of the Robert Schuman Foundation's Scientific Committee.

Thierry Chopin

PhD in Political Science from the School for Advanced Studies in Social Sciences (EHESS, Paris) he is currently Studies Director at the Robert Schuman Foundation. He is associate professor at the Conservatoire National des Arts et Métiers (CNAM). Visiting Professor at the Collège d'Europe (Bruges), he also teaches at Sciences Po and at the Mines Paris Tech. He is an associate expert at the Centre for International Studies and Research (CERI – Sciences Po). He is the author of many books on European issues including (with Jean-François Jamet and Christian Lequesne), *L'Europe d'après. En finir avec le pessimisme*, Lignes de repères, 2012.

Stefaan De Corte

Senior Research Officer at the Centre for European Studies (CES), he covers social, economic and energy issues. Before joining the CES, he was an economic policy advisor to the Belgian Minister of Foreign Affairs and the Vice-Prime Minister. Prior to that, he was a policy evaluation consultant. He is a commercial engineer and also has a master's degree in European Economics.

Jean-Marc Daniel

A former student at the Ecole Polytechnique and ENSAE (National School of Statistics and Economic Administration), he is an economist, a professor at the ESCP Europe management school and a course director at the Paris Ecole des Mines. He is also director of Sociétal magazine, a columnist for the Le Monde newspaper and a contributor on BFM radio. He is the author of the "Que sais-je?" issue on La politique économique (PUF) and of Histoire vivante de la pensée économique, (Pearson).

Nicolas Delmas

A graduate in European law from Paris II – Panthéon-Assas and Paris I – Panthéon-Sorbonne Universities, holder of a Master 2 degree in European Disputes, he now works with the Legal Advisor at the Permanent French Representation to the European Union, after initial experience with the legal sector of the European Affairs general secretariat (SGAE).

Corinne Deloy

A graduate of the Institute for Political Studies in Paris and holder of a DEA in Political Science from the University of Paris I-Pantheon Sorbonne, she has been a journalist on the *Nouvel Observateur* magazine and research manager at the CERI (Sciences Po International Studies and Research Centre) as well as general secretary of the Foundation for Political Innovation. She writes the European Elections Monitor for the Robert Schuman Foundation.

Javier Doz

Confederal Secretary of International Trade Union Action Comisiones Obreras (CC. OO.), he was previously General Secretary of CC.OO.'s Teaching Federation (1977-1989), deputy at the Parliament of the Autonomous Region of Madrid (1991-1995) where he was spokesperson for the Commission of Education and Culture, and for the Commission of Budget and Treasury in the Parliament. He has been member of CC.OO.'s Executive Committee since 1997.

Hugh Dykes

Stockbroker and financial consultant, he was previously MP for Harrow East (1970-97), and MEP (1974-1977). He was also adviser on EU affairs, chairman of the European Move-ment-UK (1990-95), Liberal Democrat Spokesperson for Foreign and Commonwealth Affairs (Europe) in the House of Lords (2005-10) and is currently Vice President of the British-German Association. He published with B. Donnelly *On the Edge: Britain and Europe*, Forumpress, 2012

Jean-Pierre Filiu

PhD in history, graduate from the Paris Institut d'études politiques (Sciences Po) and from INALCO (Langues O), he is a specialist of the Arab-Muslim world. A former delegate of the International Human Rights Federation in Lebanon in 1984, he drafted the first report about missing civilians during the conflict and testified on that at the United Nations Human Rights Commission. As a career-diplomat for two decades, he was posted in Jordan, Syria, Tunisia and the United States and was an adviser to the Minister Pierre Joxe (1990-1993) and to Prime Minister Lionel Jospin (2000-2002). He is now a university professor at Sciences Po (Paris), after teaching at Columbia (New York) and Georgetown (Washington). He is currently working on the Arab revolutions.

Michel Foucher

A geographer and diplomat, he teaches at the Ecole Normale Supérieure (Ulm). He is also Director of Studies and Research at the Institute for Higher National Defence Studies (IHEDN) and a member of the Robert Schuman Foundation Scientific Committee. He holds the applied geopolitics chair at the Collège d'études mondiales FMSH/ENS. He was Ambas-sador for France in Latvia, advisor to Hubert Védrine and director of the Policy Planning Staff of the French Foreign Ministry. He has published many books, including *L'Europe et l'avenir du monde*, éditions Odile Jacob, 2009 and *The Battle of Maps; a critical analysis of the visions of the world*, bilingual and interactive edition, ITunes, François Bourin Editeur, 2012.

Jean-Dominique Giuliani

Jean-Dominique Giuliani is the Chairman of the Robert Schuman Foundation. He was a director at the SOFRES and head of cabinet for Senate President René Monory (1992-1998). He has notably published *Un Européen très pressé* (Editions du Moment, 2008), *L'élargissement de l'Europe* (PUF "Que Sais-je?", 2004), *"Quinze + Dix", le grand élargissement* (Albin Michel, 2003), "Plaidoyer pour l'élargissement", "Atlas des nouveaux membres", *Note de la Fondation Robert Schuman*, n°11, 2002, and *Les 100 mots de l'Europe* (with J-P. Betbèze, collection PUF "Que sais-je ?", 2011). He co-directed the *Atlas perma-nent de l'Union européenne*, Lignes de Repères, 2012.

Nicole Gnesotto

Agrégée teacher of modern literature and Professor and chair of European Union ins-titutions and policies at the CNAM and vice-president of Notre Europe-Institut Jacques Delors, she is former Director of the European Institute for Security Studies. She is a spe-cialist in Europe and strategic issues and notably the author of *La politique de sécurité et de défense de l'UE – Les cinq premières années* (EUISS, 2005), *Le monde en 2025* (co-directed with Giovanni Grevi, Robert Laffont, 2007), *Notre Europe* with Michel Rocard (Robert Laffont, 2008) and *L'Europe a-t-elle un avenir stratégique?* (Armand Colin, 2011). She is a member of the white paper commission on defence and national security.

Jean-François Jamet

Jean-François Jamet is lecturer in European political economy at Sciences Po. A graduate from the Ecole Normale Supérieure, Sciences Po and Harvard, he worked as an economist at the World Bank and the European Commission. He is the author of *L'Europe peut-elle se passer d'un gouvernement économique?* (La Documentation Française, 2ᵉ édition, 2012), *L'Europe d'après. En finir avec le pessimisme* (with Thierry Chopin and Christian Lequesne, Lignes de Repères, 2012) and *Europe, la dernière chance?* (with Guillaume Klossa, 2011, Europe Promotion award). Since 2010, he has been the spokesman for EuropaNova.

Pascale Joannin

Pascale Joannin is General Manager of the Robert Schuman Foundation. Former auditor of the Institute for Higher National Defence Studies (IHEDN), she is the author of "L'Europe, une chance pour la femme", *Note de la Fondation Robert Schuman*, n°22, 2004. She also co-directed the *Atlas permanent de l'Union européenne*, Lignes de Repères, 2012.

Jean-Baptiste Laignelot

A graduate from Aix-Marseille III, Paris I, Paris IX and Noumea universities, Maître de Requêtes at the Council of State he worked in the legal department of the European Commission from 2006 to 2010, and then at the General Secretariat for European Affairs (SGAE) as a legal advisor from 2010 to 2012. He is currently legal advisor for France's permanent representation at the European Union.

Alain Lamassoure

Former French European Affairs Minister then Budget Minister, he is a former member of the European Convention. At present he is an MEP (European People's Party, EPP), Vice-President of the French delegation of the EPP group and Chair of the European Parliament's Budgets Committee.

Mathilde Lemoine

PhD in Economics from the Institute for Political Studies in Paris (Sciences Po) and a graduate of the University Paris Dauphine, Mathilde Lemoine is Director of Economic Studies and Market Strategy for HSBC France. She has also taught at Sciences Po since 1997, is a member of the National Economic Commission (CEN) and a company board member. Mathilde Lemoine has been a member of the Economic Analysis Council (CAE), the Commission for the Liberation of Growth and reporter for the Expert Conference on the Climate and Energy Contribution.

Pascal Perrineau

Pascal Perrineau is a University Professor at the Paris Institut d'études politiques (Sciences Po) and director of the Political Research Centre at Sciences Po (CEVIPOF associate at the CNRS). He works mainly on the vote, the far right in France and Europe and on new splits at work in the political systems on the European continent. He has recently published *Le choix de Marianne. Pourquoi et pour qui votons-nous?*, Fayard, 2012; (dir.), and *La décision électorale en 2012*, Armand Colin, 2013.

Joseph Quinlan

Fellow at the Center for Transatlantic Relations (CTR) in Washington DC and a Non-Resident Transatlantic Fellow with GMF. He is a leading expert on the transatlantic economy and well-known global economist. He regularly debriefs and advises senior U.S. Leaders of Congress on global economic/financial affairs on Capitol Hill, and has testified before the European Parliament on transatlantic trade issues. Every year, he publishes *"The Transatlantic Economy"*» (with Daniel Hamilton), CTR.

Simon Serfaty

Professor of US Foreign Policy at Old Dominion University in Norfolk, Virginia. Senior Fellow at the German Marshall Fund of the United States, and Zbigniew Brzezinski Chair (Emeritus) in Global Security and Geostrategy at the Center of Strategic & International Studies (CSIS) in Washington, DC. His most recent books include *La tentation impériale* (Odile Jacob, 2004), *Vital Partnership (Rowman & Littlefield, 2005), Architects of Delusion* (University of Pennsylvania Press, 2008), and *A World Recast: An American Moment in a Post-Western World* (Rowman & Littlefield, 2012).

Ignacio Fernández Toxo

From 1987 to 1995 he was General Secretary for the Metal Federation of Workers' Commissions (CCOO). From 1995 to 2004, he was voted General Secretary of the Metal-lurgical and Mining Federation of the CCOO, after the merger between the metal and mining industry federations. In 2004 he was elected a member of the confederate executive commission of the CCOO, at the 8th Congress of this body and appointed Secretary for trade union action and sector policies. In 2008 he was elected General Secretary of the trade union confederation of workers' commissions. In May 2011, he was elected President of the European Trades Union Confederation (ETUC).

Henrik Uterwedde

After his studies of Political Science and Economics in Berlin and Paris, he joined the Deutsch-Französisches Institut (dfi) in Ludwigsburg (Germany) as a researcher. He has been deputy director of the dfi since1996. He is a honorary professor at the University of Stuttgart and, since his habilitation, associated professor at Osnabrück University. Numerous publications (mostly in German and French, some in English): French politics, society and economics, Franco-German relations, French and German economy and economic policy compared. He has notably published *Länderbericht Frankreich* (co-dir., 2012).

Statistics

Alain Fabre

A graduate from the Paris Institut d'études politiques (Sciences Po), with a master's degree in political sciences and business law and a DESS in banking and financial law, he began his career as an economist at the Banque de France (1988-1991). He taught economics at Sciences Po (1989-1992). After joining the Caisse des Dépôts et Consignations, he continued his career with the Compagnie Financière Edmond de Rothschild (1992-1999). In 1999, he set up Victoria & Cie, a financial consulting firm for businesses.

Gerald Stang

A graduate from the School of International and Public Affairs (SIPA) at Columbia University and from the College of Engineering at Saskatchewan University, he specialises in democratic institutions in developing States and in long-term strategic prospects in the field of international relations. In 2012 he was a visiting researcher at the Institut européen d'études de sécurité.

Maps

Pascal Orcier

A graduate of the Ecole Normale Supérieure (ENS Lyon), agrégé and PhD in geography, he is a specialist of the Baltic and a researcher at the University of Lyon III. He is the author of the *"Atlas: La Lettonie en Europe"* (Zvaigzne ABC/Belin 2005) and contributor to various books which have been published since.

I

The European Union and the economic crisis: between defending national interests and progress towards integration

Europe, towards recovery?

Jean-Dominique GIULIANI

We have lost count of the pessimistic forecasts about the European Union, made by the most eminent experts over the last four years! Renowned economists, some Nobel Prize winners, financial analysts of all kinds – how many of them were clearly mistaken in announcing the end of the euro, the default and exit of Greece and the end of the European Union. They have all been belied by the facts.

In the same way that we wanted to revive a so-called Mayan calendar announcing the end of the world on 21st December 2012, all of these eminent personalities, employing their usual methods of assessment, rather hastily judged a European Union, which they do not know very well.

Over time European integration has been buffeted from all sides and is resisting – current world changes, which are upsetting the established order and balances of power; the criticism of the sceptics, who have compared it to other models, although it is unique in world history; attacks by the markets, even the speculators, who are sheep by nature and whose depth of analysis has never impressed anyone. Europe, which is above all a political project, manages crises in its own way, implementing political decisions even if sometimes they are slow and somewhat unclear – and never just with the aid of technical or financial formula.

So it can be proud of having politically overcome the first real challenge to its existence. Everyone now seems to have understood that it is hazardous to forecast the disappearance of the euro and European integration. In many respects the European Union should be considered as irreversible, because in the eyes of the Member States of Europe, it cannot be replaced. In spite of its apparent hesitation, as it faced the turbulence of the crisis, it has managed to rise to the challenge.

The crisis originated elsewhere; it crossed the Atlantic because incomplete Europe delayed on the long path towards unity. The Europeans have stepped up the pace of integration and 2013 is now auguring better to face an international environment, which is unstable to say the least.

An unpredictable international environment

This is probably the mark of an extremely curious time. It has been called a period of "transition", in the hope that a new world order will soon emerge for the duration. We were familiar with the old order, that of the Cold War and its rules and fragile balances of power. We no longer understand the developments in a world in which codes change faster than human thought. Technological, economic and therefore political and social changes ongoing in the world seem to be running riot; and they especially seem to be endless. We cannot be sure that the situation will become stable again in the near future. The crisis is not just a bad time to overcome before the return of calm. It might last - in the shape of permanent challenges to situations we have taken for granted so far. Those who are expecting to take advantage of world growth are mistaken. It is via internal reform that the Union and its Member States will illustrate their ability to adapt to a constantly changing world.

We are not about to enter a period of restored world order which is predictable and stable long term. In the recent history of international relations these periods have generally come after major conflict but this is not the case here. We might have to live with the anxiety of uncertainty for a long time to come. Arising from the crisis in Europe this merges with the fear of decline. This has led to a negative mood, loss of confidence, a feeling of gloom which is belied by statistics however. With 7% of the world population, the Union creates over 20% of its wealth; it is still the leading consumer market and the world's leading trade power which – intra-community trade included – concentrates 40% of world trade. Hence it still has a great many assets. A rapid overview of the world helps us establish a comparison.

Japan is struggling to emerge from a long period of stagnation marked by deflation, the US, in spite of its formidable capacity, is facing challenges of size with a colossal debt that has become a political stake - the era of "growth through spending" seems to be over. Even the emerging countries, which for a long time were dizzy with their catch-up growth, are now being forced to redirect their efforts towards their own citizens. China is entering a period of political instability, which will certainly influence its economic performance. Although a world war does not seem to be looming for the time being there are many areas of tension, - and even geographically contained conflict. This is leading to uncertainty about international stability. The Near East and Iran legitimately feature at the top of this list of concerns.

The international agenda will involve Europe again. It has to prepare itself for this.

Comfortably established thanks to European integration in societies in which solidarity, the rule of law and growth seem to be the norm, Europeans seem to have slipped into the slumber of facility. The size of the task ahead is immense if the European continent is to guarantee its - still eminently enviable - situation, long term. But Europeans might be well advised to anticipate other future changes in technology, economic power struggles, social organisation, because the criteria of efficacy in the 21st century might very well lie in their adaptability to change.

Work is underway to adapt the Union to the new world even if a great deal still has to be done.

A new Europe?

The Union has changed more in four years than since its creation and a little hindsight reveals this to us. It has mobilised unequalled financial clout in response to the crisis, committed to reforms that were unthinkable to date, and saved some of its struggling Members.

If we add the direct aid granted to States in difficulty (€400 billion), the European Central Bank's loan facilities (LTRO: €1000 billion), and its purchase of public debts (€200 billion), the rescue of the banks and the national rescue plans, the Union and its

Member States have, directly or indirectly, mobilised funds well over the equivalent of three Marshall plans[1]. From the beginning of the crisis in October 2008 to the end of 2011 State aid granted to the financial sector and to the real economy to overcome the crisis has, according to the European Commission, totalled €1,700 billion[2]. No other political entity in the world could have provided as much in order to counter the crisis. Of course the Union's Member States achieved this via cooperation and mainly according to an intergovernmental method, but this joint effort would not have been possible without the European Union. Of course we might criticise the decisions that have been taken and the way they were drafted - slowly, after debate and negotiation - but no one would have thought, even ten years ago, that this was possible, since the rules it had set itself in the European treaties were so cautious.

Moreover it engaged reforms that were unthinkable just a little while ago. It is has created a European Monetary Fund, the European Stability Mechanism, organised true budgetary union with the "six pack" and the Fiscal Compact and has laid the foundations of Banking Union. In response to the world crisis European integration has accelerated. It has done so at its own pace, which has forcibly been slow and sometimes erratic, since a genuine Economic and Budgetary Union has to be built with 27 or 17 Members based on extremely individual national systems. 2012 witnessed the completion of a great deal of work that was desired and undertaken as soon as the turbulence started in 2009. All of the institutions have contributed. The European Council *via* the Heads of State and government, the Parliament and the Commission have adopted new texts that strengthen budgetary discipline, the coordination of economic policies and encourage structural reform. The European Central Bank and its President, Mario Draghi, have succeeded in defusing the attacks made against the euro. Their declarations and decisions have brought calm and saved the financial circuits from implosion.

The Budgetary Treaty entered into force on 1st January 2013 although it was the focus of criticism and opposition, particularly in France. The Bundestag, in which observers wrongly see the only real democratic power in Europe, ratified all of the aid plans granted to the States in difficulty with a two third majority of their votes. This belied the negative clichés and opinions about the direction of Germany's European policy, which the Constitutional Court has deemed compatible with its Fundamental Law. The principle of the support measures to growth was approved under pressure from France, Italy, Spain and some of the major financial institutions (IMF, OECD) and was implemented by the Parliament and the European Commission. Furthermore the Union made significant progress in terms of its integration. It was re-directed, as a priority, towards finding a solution to the crisis via the introduction of a tax on financial transactions, an Act for the Single Market and the European patent.

In spite of evident political difficulties the Member States have committed to unprecedented structural reforms. Greece, Portugal, Ireland, all three beneficiaries of the Union and IMF's support plans, have accepted spectacular cuts in their public spending, reforms to their labour markets and the draconian management of their budgets. Spain, Italy and Slovenia, which were then affected, have made significant efforts in terms of their competitiveness. France, in spite of a presidential campaign and political alternation, seems to have taken the same direction, although we still have to see the results of this. Every time, in each of the Member States, governments have risked recession (-20% of the GDP in Greece in four years), social difficulties and of being unpopular, in order to put their economy back on the right tracks. In spite of the seriousness of some situations and braving protest movements, they have remained focused, constantly talking and

---

1. A "Marshall Plan" would represent 1 000 billion $ today
2. http://ec.europa.eu/comm/competition/state_aid/studies_reports/studies_reports.html

working together with Europe. The populations which have voted – the Greeks, Dutch and the Italians have made an unexpected show of wisdom. They have contributed in their way by choosing to support or bring to power pro-European political parties – in other words by acknowledging the merits of their policies. We can always try to disparage "old Europe" for its vacillation, its failures and its protests but nowhere else would changes like this have been possible without a revolution. In Europe everything has been achieved democratically and legitimately by the votes of the people or their parliaments.

No other political entity in the world has reformed its governance as Europe has. It certainly does not deserve the sarcasm of its rather hasty critics. The Nobel Peace Prize was quite rightly attributed to it, as if there had been a call to judge it and the achievement of its goals long term.

How can anyone say that European integration has not responded to the crisis? In reality the criticism targeted against it is rather more the illustration of external ignorance, internal fatigue, even a fashion of a decline in European morale in the face of the crisis. Rather than undertaking a serious, dispassionate analysis, Europe's critics believe all of this reveals the decline of Europe.

The challenges that still lie ahead

Future challenges to Europe will probably arise from developments in the international situation, but they involve rather more its functioning and internal developments and more generally its democratic dimension.

This is because events are not anticipated in Europe. It is still inward looking and constantly examining and questioning the way it functions as and when international crises occur – but these show that it is involved in everything that happens in the world. The Israeli-Palestinian conflict, Iran, the Arab revolutions, the war in Afghanistan and Libya, the conflict in West Africa, have revealed a Europe, with a voice weakened by division, and yet at the same time it has been called upon to participate to the full in all of these situations. Some say that it has exited the main international arena and is no longer considered by the main players. This is largely untrue, but it is the feeling that it gives. However doesn't the conduct of the international economy demand a strong Europe which defends and promotes its own message and provides added value to the international stage? Its own interests – in the areas of energy, the economy and politics now require urgent action.

After all Europe's modernity, which means that it prefers the peaceful settlement of disputes to confrontation, its generous development aid policies, its example of the pacification of a continent, the democratic nature of its members and its institutions, its commitment to Human Rights, the Rule of Law and Democracy, its idea of solidarity, all typify the strength of a specific message to the world. We would like to hear it being voiced. In the immediate future this will be necessary in the Near East, in regard to Iran, Africa and even Asia.

It has to recover its pride and influence by surpassing its internal divergence, otherwise it will simply be the instrument of policies undertaken by others. To do this it must first be aware of what it represents, with its economic strength, its message and all of the diplomatic tools at its disposal, including true military capabilities. It must be imaginative, and not focus just on method but rather on results. What does it matter that it progresses under the pressure of some of its members in some areas and not in others?

Of course its growth deficit and the confidence crisis, which it is suffering, have done nothing to restore its image, whilst only ten years ago it raced ahead in the world economic league. It has concentrated on its own internal problems at a time when, with the tools it had acquired with the Lisbon Treaty, it should have been looking to the world stage.

This has had considerable effect on the necessary response given to the public debt crisis. In the solutions put forward the much criticised Franco-German couple has again proven indispensable. It has been the active, often innovative engine, of joint response and the artisan of inevitable, difficult compromise. Political alternation in France, as with each change in majority with one country or another, has caused problems. The path towards privileged cooperation has to be recovered without which the Union will not move forwards. This will be one of the challenges in 2013. It is also a matter of urgency.

The way the Union is governed has been severely criticised. The way it is run, its rules, even its institutions have been denigrated, because it is true that Europeans make the terrible mistake of engaging in interminable institutional debate. In reality it is has been institutional practice that has seemed poorly adapted to times of crisis. Equipped with the institutions reformed by the Lisbon Treaty the Union's political actors have not used them to the full and have even misinterpreted the rules.

The common diplomatic service is a long term project, judged according to the short term of crises and surprises. It has not been convincing. Could it have been otherwise?

The European Commission, which is poorly equipped and often challenged by the States, has not distinguished itself by dint of its creativity and has been paralysed for fear of displeasing the Member States. The latter have used the crisis to assume a more national rather than a collective attitude.

But more than this, the Union's institutional players have lacked clear political determination. With its four Presidents – of the European Council, the Commission, the alternating Presidency and the European Parliament, citizens find it difficult to decide who is who, especially when all four want to have their say and jostle with each other for the limelight. The countries of the eurozone, which have been allowed to organise together in a central core - the Union's pioneers - have been slow to move forwards to give the Eurogroup any real weight.

These institutional shortfalls have damaged the Union's image and above all its communication, but they have not prevented the achievement of results mentioned earlier. Of course it is difficult for each of us, for citizens, as well as experts, to forge a path in the confusion of competences and spurious declarations. It is urgent therefore to bring order to Europe, firstly by deploying and expressing even greater common political determination and possibly later by reforming the Treaties.

The British attitude has revealed itself to be one of the biggest challenges that the Union has had to face. Taking advantage of the present difficulties and affected by a form of national withdrawal, which has also been seen in other Member States, the United Kingdom has clearly asked for the renegotiation of the treaties which link it to the Union. It is even questioning its membership of Europe. "Multi-speed Europe" has made a comeback, or rather "ad hoc Europe" than differentiated Europe. This is a formidable challenge indeed. Can the Union accept such an opportunistic and so contrary an attitude? Is this not a "Pandora's Box" that may give ideas to other "retrogrades"? How should this be expressed in the treaties and the harmonious functioning of a Union which is already struggling?

Similarly motivated and encouraged by an egotist national withdrawal, there are a growing number of secessionist regions: Catalonia, Flanders, Scotland ... all say they want to be independent and yet remain in the Union. In application of article 4 of the Treaty on the European Union, the Union *"shall respect their essential State functions, including ensuring the territorial integrity of the State, maintaining law and order and safeguarding national security"* and the common institutions have, for the time being, been extremely cautious. Will they be able to let this hope of harmonious secession grow for long without risking the emergence of more claims and the transformation of the Union's map into an unstable puzzle?

These developments go together with a sharp rise in populism on the continent. Exacerbated by the economic crisis, egoism is destabilising governments and influencing political debates. Rather than having an open, dynamic, combative, determined Europe they prefer withdrawal. They are restricting fragile governments and are opening the way to racist, xenophobic excesses that are always possible on the "warring continent".

Finally one of the greatest difficulties at present is to convince citizens about European integration. The enthusiasm of the first years has given way to the trivialisation of the European dimension. Then, as integration has progressed and world developments have made it necessary to take fundamental decisions over the transfer of competences, the time has come for eurosceptic revolt. This has been overcome in the main, but it has given way to deep scepticism regarding European efficiency[3]. Public opinion is losing confidence and finds it difficult to understand Europe's added value in the crisis even though people are still greatly attached to it; the national elites are glad that they are no longer being ignored – in their opinion, humiliated – by the European administrations and have found an opportunity for revenge in the crisis. At first the structural reforms had a negative effect on employment and living standards but their benefits are now emerging. Will European leaders have the courage and strength to resist the protest movements that have been caused by the temporary challenge made to people's acquis? Will the European elections of 2014, the year in which growth will probably return to Europe, provide an opportunity for a "grand democratic debate" about the recovery and continuation of the European project? It will be necessary because European unification is not just a technical or even a diplomatic path. Above all the European project is a political one and must therefore involve political decision makers as well as the people, the only ones who are legitimate in Democracy.

---

3. http://ec.europa.eu/comm/competition/state_aid/studies_reports/studies_reports.html

Political Union: from slogan to reality

Thierry CHOPIN

With the crisis vital debate about the future of European integration has arisen. However in spite of growing citizen mistrust with regard to the European institutions, the reforms that are underway carefully avoid fundamental political issues: how can we simplify the European decision making process so that it is more transparent and readily understandable for the citizens? How can we strengthen the democratic legitimacy of the decisions taken, which for the time being are mainly the result of a technocratic, diplomatic process?

Federation, Political Europe, Political Union: what does this mean?

In just a few months, due to the effects of the euro crisis the issue of "Political Union" has finally been transferred from the academic arena[1] to the political agenda[2]. Under the pressure of the crisis the issue of "Political Europe" has returned to the heart of public debate in the shape of a call for progress towards "budgetary federalism" and even "political union". Projects like this, although desirable, suppose however a certain amount of caution and a certain number of conditions if we are to prevent them becoming abstract slogans, as it has been the case with Political Europe and Federal Europe which only leads to further disillusion.

When on 12th May 2000 Joschka Fischer delivered a speech at the Humboldt University on the future of the European Union he pleaded in support of the European "federation" which Robert Schuman had already called for in the 1950's. For his part

---

1. On this issue see the work by S. Hix, including *What's wrong with the European Union and How to Fix it?* (Cambridge Polity Press, 2008); we might also refer to T. Chopin, "The Limits of the Functionalist Method : Politicisation as an Indispensable means to Settle the EU's Legitimacy Deficit", in O. Cramme (ed.), *An EU "Fit for Purpose in the Global Age"*, Policy Network, Eliamep, London School of Economics, vol. 1, 2009 and with L. Macek, "Après Lisbonne, le défi de la politisation de l'Union européenne", in *Les Etudes du CERI*, n°165, Centre d'Etudes et de Recherches Internationales, Sciences Po, 2010.

2. See for example S. Goulard and M. Monti, *De la démocratie en Europe*. Flammarion, 2012.

Jacques Delors' idea, which defined Europe as a "federation of Nation-States"[3], was so successful that for a time it became the political catchword, or conversely a taboo being used as a foil.

However it is not about having an "ideological" approach to the federation, it is rather more a question of demystifying it and deeming federalism simply as a means of organising powers, based on the principle of the distribution of competences between various levels of government. The problem lies in that the dominant doctrine quite wrongly assimilates federalism with the Federal State[4]. But the concept of the State is problematic and is not of much use in European affairs: the Union is not a State and the distribution of respective State and other administrative competences are contested. European integration has been built on the rejection of granting the Union sovereign prerogatives – as early as 1954, with the rejection of the European Community of Defence; France refused the constitution of European defence – because of the States' protection of their sovereignty. The Union is now devoted to tasks of redistribution (CAP, cohesion policy) which cause appropriation disputes.

However on a less theoretical and a more empirical level it is easy to see that the European Union already has federal tools: one currency for the Eurozone, one central bank, a budget, a civil service and a Parliament elected by direct universal suffrage, just to name a few. Moreover, and in spite of the failure of the treaty establishing a Constitution for Europe, which at first led to an obvious wish on the part of the national political elites to relinquish all reference to any kind of "federal" future for European integration, by a sort of a trick of history, the current crisis is forcing the federalisation of the European economic policy: implementation of the European Stability Mechanism (ESM); strengthening of the European Central Bank (ECB), a federal institution 'par excellence'; strengthening of economic governance mechanisms ("*six-pack*", "budgetary pact", "*two pack*"), are all elements that define genuine budgetary federalism, which is now vital if we are to overcome the crisis[5]. With this in view we can easily see the double drawback that lies in the unfortunate expression of "the federal leap": its anxiety generating nature (because it sounds like the "leap into the unknown", which is never reassuring) and the gap between it and the reality of the European Union, which is of a federal nature.

However, if the idea of federation might be applied to a certain degree to the Union[6], we have to note that the choice of the word itself is far from being shared by all Member States and they cannot even be pronounced, nor are they acceptable in some places. Some Member States – like Germany and Belgium – are at ease with this political idea because their contemporary political and judicial culture is based on a system of shared competences which form the heart of the federal idea; conversely, and also for cultural reasons, it is an absolute taboo in France since it is incompatible with the "obsession for unity" on the part of the authorities in office - so typical of French political and administrative centralisation; in the UK the term is even deemed a swear word (the "f-word"); in other Member States, notably in Central and Eastern Europe, the idea echoes submission to the USSR, which stood as a federation (whilst its political form was naturally closer to that of an empire). For many countries in the Western Balkans the use of the word is problematic and conjures up the history of the Yugoslav Federation.

---

3. Cf. G. Ricard-Nihoul, *Pour une Fédération européenne d'Etats-nations. La vision de Jacques Delors revisitée*, éditions Larcier, coll. « Essais », 2012.

4. Against this dominant theory read the work by O. Beaud, *Théorie de la Fédération*, Presses universitaires de France, 2007.

5. Cf. J. Pisani-Ferry, *Le réveil des démons. La crise de l'euro et comment nous en sortir*, Paris, Fayard, 2011 ; see also, P. Artus and I. Gravet, *La crise de l'euro. Comprendre les causes. En sortir par de nouvelles institutions*, Armand Colin, 2012, chap. 3.

6. See O. Beaud, « Peut-on penser l'Union européenne comme une Fédération ? », in F. Esposito and N. Levrat (eds), *Europe : de l'intégration à la fédération*, Institut européen de l'Université de Genève, Bruylant, 2010, p. 71-103.

For its part the expression "Political Europe" is ambiguous and even contradictory[7]. On the one hand Political Europe conjures up a "federalist" ideal that aims to go beyond national sovereignties to the benefit of community institutions that are supposed to guarantee a common European interest, starting with the European Commission. On the other it conjures up the determination of some States, notably France – of maintaining and consolidating a world position marked by a strategy of differentiation and even sometimes of opposition, vis-à-vis the USA and which goes together with a discourse on national exception. From this second standpoint the States, and more specifically the "main capitals" (Berlin, London, Paris) – have to play a leading role which contributes to the primacy of intergovernmental logic and the pre-eminence of the Council over the Commission.

The confusion over political vocabulary in terms of European issues can lead to harmful misunderstandings. In the economic area, to quote just one topical example, it affects thought about the reform of the Union's economic governance. The proposal of "economic governance"[8] finds much less of a consensus than at first it would appear whereas it pinpoints the real issue: the need for clarification, simplification and legitimisation of the European economic policy. But the fractures which this debate causes are the same as those which run through national political cultures in Europe. "Government" is synonymous to politicisation and interventionism in France, conjures up the idea of independently implemented rules in Germany and raises the spectre of a Federal State in the UK and in Central Europe. Since they cannot agree on a common design for their political and economic system, i.e. in reality for federalism – the Member States cannot agree on a common government and ultimately on a collective management of European public goods (macro-economic stabilisation policy, climate and energy, European defence, etc.)[9]. And yet not only is an agreement like this now necessary but it is a matter of urgency!

Political Union: a priority

For the last four years priority has been given to settling the economic crisis and at first this was understandable. To recover sovereignty over the markets and thereby the ability to decide over their future, European States, notably those in the Eurozone – understood that they had to form a more coherent entity. Hence stricter common rules have been adopted in budgetary matters and the European Stability Mechanism (ESM) has entered into force; furthermore the project for banking union has moved forwards over the last few months.

During the European Council of December 2012 Herman van Rompuy presented a roadmap for the achievement of real economic and monetary union[10], drafted together with the Presidents of the European Commission, the European Central Bank and the Eurogroup. The economic strategy was clarified: on the one hand macro-economic and financial supervision should be exercised Europe-wide with the necessary corrective tools

---

7. We owe it to N. Gnesotto for having highlighted this contradiction in « L'Europe politique a-t-elle un avenir ? », in N. Gnesotto and M. Rocard,(dir.), *Notre Europe*, Paris, Robert Laffont, 2008.

8. Cf J-F. Jamet, *L'Europe peut-elle se passer d'un gouvernement économique ?*, La documentation française, 2ᵉ édition, 2012.

9. On this point see work by S. Collignon on "The European Republic" and notably *The European Republic. Reflections on the Political Economy of a Future Constitution*, Bertelsmann Foundation, 2003 and also (with C. Paul), *Pour la République européenne*, Odile Jacob, 2008.

10. *Towards a Genuine Economic and Monetary Union*, 5ᵗʰ December 2012; also refer to the conclusions of the European Council of 13ᵗʰ and 14ᵗʰ December 2012 – http://www.consilium.europa.eu/uedocs/cms_data/docs/pressdata/fr/ec/134364.pdf

in order to be credible and effective; on the other hand the Eurozone should have its own means to prevent and settle the crises, which one State alone would not be able to withstand. This long-awaited clarification is indeed very welcome. Now we might hope that the Member States will subscribe to it and rapidly implement the recommendations contained within this report. Indeed we have too often seen the announcement of measures during European Councils taking months to enter into force due to a lack of agreement on the means to achieve their implementation.

Given the increasing federalisation of decisions regarding economic policy European citizens are still confused however.[11] The polls highlight a worrying decrease in citizen confidence vis-à-vis the main European institutions (see map)[12]. Hence, just as the European institutions are extending their competences and are being called to take decisions in sensitive areas that affect the very heart of democratic sovereignty they no longer seem to enjoy adequate legitimacy capital.

Given the transfer of competences that these common measures imply the issue of political union cannot be avoided. European decisions have to enjoy adequate legitimacy in the eyes of the citizen and decision making mechanisms must be sufficiently simple and clear for them to be effective and transparent. Without this, economic union will not receive citizens' support and questions will continue to be raised about the political vision which justifies European decisions and therefore their legitimacy. No Member State is now in a position in which its citizens "blindly" trust their elites to manage optimally their best interests in European matters. Citizens want to have their say. This has been clear for several years, and it is all the more so with the crisis. If we ignore the need for a clear political contract, economic integration as a whole will be weakened and even threatened.

Furthermore no European decision maker challenges this. Debate is ongoing in several Member States – it has notably been started at the highest level in Germany[13]. We should also stress the political importance of the report signed in September 2012 by the Foreign Ministers of eleven EU Member States[14]. It might be considered as the first bid to formalise a project for "political union". Thought has been launched on a European level as part of the task given to the "Group of 4" (Herman van Rompuy, José-Manuel Barroso, Mario Draghi and Jean-Claude Juncker) but political union is the poor relation in this debate for the time being and is the focus of very few detailed proposals. There is a notable exception to this however without giving a definite timetable: the Commission's recommendation for a common external representation for the Eurozone. Hence the Eurozone would speak with one voice within the international organisations such as the IMF for example[15].

Furthermore, thought on this issue does not seem to be very structured. Angela Merkel seemed to say that she wanted to have a new Convention[16] and Mario Draghi, President of the ECB deemed that "those who believe that only true federation could be sustainable are expecting too much"[17] whilst conversely José Manuel Barroso, President of the European Commission has spoken in support of a "democratic federation of

---

11. Cf. T. Chopin and J.-F. Jamet, « L'Europe sans les Européens », *Libération*, 14th December 2012.

12. Eurobarometer Standard 79, december 2012.

13. See Ulrike Guérot, "The Euro Debate in Germany : Towards Political Union?", European Council on Foreign Relations, ECFR, 5 september 2012.

14. Cf. Final Report of the Future of Europe Group of the Foreign Ministers (Austria, Belgium, Denmark, France, Italy, Germany, Luxembourg, The Netherlands, Poland, Portugal Spain) 17th September 2012 - http://www.msz.gov.pl/files/docs/komunikaty/20120918RAPORT/report.pdf

15. Cf. A Blueprint for a Deep and Genuine EMU. Launching a European Debate, European Commission, 28th November 2012.

16. Cf. "The Future of Europe: Merkel Pushes for Convention to Draft New EU Treaty", *Spiegel Online International*, 27th August 2012.

17. *Die Zeit*, 29th August 2012.

Nation-States."[18] In addition to this, whilst many taboos are melting away regarding the future of European integration, debate over the political and democratic dimension of the reform of the European institutions is lacking in many Member States, notably in France. Beyond all the discourses, nothing is happening. Angela Merkel and Michel Barnier have spoken in support of the election of the President of the European Commission by universal suffrage; Jean-Claude Trichet has recommended the creation of a post of Eurozone Finance Minister[19] but everyone is putting these innovations off to the future, and even further, which avoids having them to make a commitment.[20]

The leaders of Europe can no longer manage urgency and at the same time put off their more ambitious ideas until later. This is particularly true in France which is still feeling the after effects of 2005, with each party fearing division over the reform of the European institutions. But this is a mistake because both the supporters of the "yes" and the "no" mainly shared the same goal of wanting to make Europe more democratic.

On the contrary, it is time to open up this debate without conditioning it according to the content of the policies themselves. This is a mistake made by the van Rompuy Report. Europe should not be more democratic and clearer because it takes integration further. It should be more democratic and clearer because it is good for the Union and the Eurozone whatever the perimeter of its competences. The extension of competences alone is enough to make the present deficits in legitimacy and clarity even greater. We have no time to waste.

"Political Union": it is no longer a matter of when but how

Beyond this the project of European "Political Union" demands real progress which will be possible as soon as political will is tangible. This is why we presented a report to the European Council detailing pathways and the conditions for their implementation.[21]

On 10th December 2012 the Nobel Peace Prize was formally awarded to the three leaders of the European Union: the presidents of the European Council, the European Commission and the European Parliament. This polyarchy at the head of the Union alone symbolises the political complexity from which Europe suffers, both within and outside of its borders. In a crisis situation which demands a great deal of responsiveness in terms of decision-making Europeans have discovered with frustration the limits of the Union's governance and its "executive deficit".

Without changing the treaty, a simple measure would enable the creation of a clearer and more legitimate leadership. To do this the post of president of the Union would simply have to be created, the title-holder of which would be elected by the European Parliament after having led the campaign of the party which wins the European elections. The president of the Union would exercise the office of the present presidents of the Commission and the European Council. It is understandable that Herman van Rompuy and José Manuel Barroso, who are directly concerned by this measure, did not suggest it in their report. But this should be the focus of a debate during the European election in 2014.

A second proposal would be to redefine the composition of the European Commission. Several options are possible in view of breaking away from the present system in which

---

18. Speech on the State of the Union 2012 to the European Parliament, 12th September 2012.
19. Cf. Speech by J-C Trichet, then President of the European Central Bank on the occasion of the award of the Charlemagne Prize 2011 in Aachen on 2nd June 2011.
20. F. Hollande also said: "Political Union comes afterwards, it is the stage that will follow budgetary union, banking union and social union", interview given to *Le Monde* on 18th October 2012.
21. T. Chopin, J.-F. Jamet, F.-X. Priollaud, "A Political Union for Europe", *European Issue*, Robert Schuman Foundation, September 2012 - http://www.robert-schuman.eu/doc/questions_europe/qe-252-fr.pdf

the composition of the College of commissioners is based on the principle of the equal "representation" of the Member States. Indeed this system tends to reproduce the diplomatic balance within the College that prevails in the Council and also makes the appointment of the commissioners dependent on discussions between Member States. The president of the Commission – or the new president of the Union if the presidency of the Commission and that of the European Council were to merge together – should be able to choose the portfolio attributed to the commissioners (without this being a result of negotiations between States), which is possible without changing the treaties. Also he should be able to rank these portfolios with the creation of "delegate commissioners" and decide on the size of the College of commissioners himself, as is the case when a government is being formed. However this supposes a review of the treaties according to the ordinary procedure.

From an economic point of view a post of vice-president of the Commission and of the Council responsible for the euro and economic affairs might be created. The title-holder would jointly ensure the role of Economic and Monetary Affairs Commissioner and of President of the Eurogroup, which would lead to the creation of a European Finance Minister, requested by Jean-Claude Trichet and Wolfgang Schäuble. He would be responsible for communicating the decisions taken by the Eurogroup and of representing the Eurozone externally within the international financial institutions[22]. He would be responsible for explaining how the policies (budgetary, fiscal, wage, etc.) in the Eurozone Member States form a coherent policy mix with the ECB's monetary policy. Finally he would speak regularly about the Eurozone in the national parliaments. The remit of the Vice-President of the Commission and the Council responsible for the euro and economic affairs might be set out as part of the Protocol on the Eurogroup.

Apart from its executive deficit the European Union is also suffering from a deficit of legitimacy. The rising power of extremism and populism is a symptom of this. From Sweden to Hungary, including France, Belgium, Norway and Greece various general elections have confirmed the strength of the parties on the far right or far left and of populism which is asserting itself in public debate, the core of which comprises economic, cultural and identity protectionism. Moreover, anti-European extremism and populism traditionally denounce the power of the national and European elites. They exploit the challenge made to political and democratic legitimacy of the European institutions.

In terms of strengthening democratic legitimacy both the national and European parliaments have a decisive role to play. The realisation of article 13 in the Stability Treaty would lead to greater involvement by national parliaments in the decisions taken at European level in terms of budgetary control[23]. This might be achieved firstly on the basis of a meeting within a Eurozone Economic and Budgetary Committee comprising members of the European Parliament's Economic and Monetary Affairs Committee (except for those from Member States which have not ratified the Stability Treaty), as well as the President of the Finance Committees and Economic Affairs Committees from the Member States' parliaments. The Committee would be able to adopt initiative reports, issue opinions and resolutions. The means for the implementation of article 13 might be set as part of an inter-institutional agreement.

But the question of creating a specific assembly for the Eurozone has to be debated freely. The European Parliament obviously would prefer not to have to compete with

---

22. We should note that the report by the « Group of 4 » explicitly recommends that the Eurozone be provided with a common external representation. Unfortunately this point was not taken up by in the Conclusions of the European Council on 13th and 14th December 2012.

23. Article 13 of the treaty anticipates that, "the European Parliament and the national Parliaments of the Contracting Parties will together determine the organisation and promotion of a conference of representatives of the relevant committees of the national Parliaments and representatives of the relevant committees of the European Parliament in order to discuss budgetary policies and other issues covered by this Treaty."

this assembly and for it to be one of its sub-committees[24], as the Eurogroup is a sub-committee of the Ecofin Council and the Eurozone Summit is a sub-committee of the European Council. In this instance the Eurozone assembly would convene MEPs from the Eurozone Member States. Alternatively, this assembly might comprise the extension of the experiment enabled by the implementation of article 13. Its existence would however only be political and a modification of the treaties would be necessary for its decisions to be legally valid.

Whatever the solution chosen the legitimacy of the European Parliament should be strengthened. At present its composition is not in line with the principle of democratic equity[25]. The number of MEPs per inhabitant for example is more than twice as high in Finland than in France. But given the significant increase in the European Parliament's power as the treaties have been approved, strengthening the democratic legitimacy of this institution, which incidentally is the only one to be elected by direct universal suffrage, represents a real challenge. The jurisprudence of the German Constitutional Court reminds us of this regularly[26] since it considers, as matters stand, that the European Parliament does not enjoy adequate democratic legitimacy for it to adopt laws that impact significantly the German budget without the prior approval on the part of the Bundestag. A simple solution would comprise having an MEP for X (for example 1) million inhabitants with a minimum of one or two MEPs per Member State. However this would imply a revision of the treaties according to the ordinary procedure.

***

In just a few months and because of the euro crisis the issue of European Political Union has been transferred from the academic arena to the political agenda. But the leaders of Europe now have their backs to the wall because declared intentions are no longer enough. Real progress is possible, some without changing the treaties if the political will is real. Europe is facing an existential challenge and the present deepening of economic integration will be weak as long as the functioning of the European institutions suffers a lack of clarity, legitimacy and ability to take decisions.[27] If the markets do not call matters to order, the citizens might do so. And the awakening to this would be painful.

---

24. Not only is this idea defended by M. Schulz, President of the European Parliament but also by the European Commission; cf. A Blueprint for a Deep and Genuine EMU. Launching a European Debate, *op. cit.*

25. Cf. T. Chopin and J.-F. Jamet, "The distribution of MEPs seats at the European Parliament between Member States: a democratic and diplomatic issue", in *European Issues* –Robert Schuman Foundation's policy papers, n°71, 2007.

26. Decision of the German Constitutional Court in Karlsruhe on the Lisbon Treaty stresses that the democratic principle applied to a States makes the respect of certain conditions obligatory which the Union does not do – notably the fact that the European elections do not take place according to the principle "one man, one vote".

27. The political unification of the EU is also vital if it wants to exist in the world. P. Lamy said this clearly. "In the world as it now is I cannot see a future for Europe as a civilisation, for what it represents in terms of values, without greater integration. I see no place for what makes Europe specific a wise dose of security, social, market, efficiency – without political union," in a speech at the University College of Sciences Po, 31st August 2012. Beyond these values and also on the inevitable issue of interests we might refer to M. Foucher's article in this book "European Strategic Interests: choice or necessity?"

Franco-German co-operation: productive tension

Henrik UTERWEDDE

Since the start of the Eurozone crisis in 2010, the German and French governments have been in constant conflict when it has come to finding a political response. There have been many bones of contention: financial support for Greece, pooling of debt, the role of the ECB, the introduction of economic governance, criticism of the German export model, sanctions against lax countries, the fiscal pact and the introduction of a golden rule, to name just some. These disputes were amplified by the media and public debate, which both added their sometimes excessive share of polemic[1]. However, in the face of an unprecedented crisis, both governments have succeeded in overcoming their disagreements, reaching a necessary consensus. Does the usefulness of Franco-German cooperation lie in the intelligent management of these differences, which alone will lead to a convergence in their national positions and European progress?

From the time of confrontation...

All of the controversies have been marked by tension, polemic and mutual suspicion in public opinion both in France and Germany. In Germany, the excesses of Greek public finance led to a rejection of support for further loans to Greece, with the consequence that the Merkel government delayed necessary decisions, thereby making it the main culprit in the much criticised stance of giving "too little, too late" – a criticism which has often been levelled against Europe's response to the crisis. The rules included in the Stability and Growth Pact were discussed in depth, but have nevertheless proved ineffective against the crisis and the blame has been laid squarely on Greece. The German executive has found it hard to admit that the structure of the Maastricht Treaty, which largely matched the German vision of the EMU (independent ECB, stability as a priority, no bailout, stability pact with sanctions), was no longer adequate to deal with the problems encountered by the Eurozone, and that it was necessary to augment it. This

---

1. The most recent shots featured in the tabloid BILD which on 31st October 2012 questioned, whether "France was becoming the new Greece?" (http://www.bild.de/politik/ausland/euro-krise/wird-frankreich-das-neue-griechenland-26957242.bild.html); the front page of *Libération* (12th November 2012) with the title "Berlin à Paris : Achtung!".(Berlin in Paris: Achtung!)

was the reason behind the tension over existing rules, and the fear of opening the way to all types of potential excesses.

In France, criticism (which was necessary and often justified) of the German attitude rapidly became excessive. The German positions were misrepresented, their lack of solidarity attacked (although the Germans' concern was only to establish a link between the principles of solidarity and responsibility), or their wish to "punish" Greece (which was mainly a warning about the danger of the moral hazard linked to granting financial aid). The egoism of the "German export model" was criticised and blamed for the imbalances and the Eurozone crisis; the Merkel government was accused of wanting to "force" austerity on all of Europe (whereas it was merely a question of admitting the need for the re-balancing of public finances). Germany was also suspected of attempting to shun Europe, and towards the end of Nicolas Sarkozy's mandate, the absurd accusation of it wanting a "German Europe[2]" emerged. In an unhealthy climate like this, François Hollande's claim for a more balanced Franco-German relationship was inevitable, since he was dallying with new alliances in order to set a European agenda more in line with the French vision.

... to the quest for convergence

However, in spite of these confrontations, which have hampered the quest for solutions, both governments, together with the leaders of the other European countries have continuously addressed the issues and tried to find the necessary compromises for a common response. In the face of an unprecedented crisis, this mission has been inevitably prone to mistakes[3]. Nevertheless, after a great deal of trial and error, it seems that the main factors necessary to strengthen Monetary Union have now been agreed upon and are already the focus of European reform and agreements: more effective prevention, with the tightening of the rules of the stability and growth pact and the fiscal pact; greater macro-economic supervision; crisis mechanisms in the shape of conditional aid (ESM); better coordination of economic and budgetary policies, thereby improving growth potential and competitiveness (European Semester; Euro plus strategy, Europe 2020 strategy; national structural reforms; European growth agenda); a banking union that will enable direct aid to banks without involving public budgets. The question of debt pooling is still extremely difficult for the time being, and in all likelihood it will not be possible without progress being made on political integration, which would give the Union greater potential to impose national budgetary discipline.

Although a certain amount of controversy continues over priorities, the urgency and the concrete form of the measures, the roadmap towards the redrafting of the EMU (named "Maastricht 2.0" by the Council of five German economic experts[4]) now seems

---

2. Cf. Henrik Uterwedde, « L'Europe allemande, mythe ou réalité ? » *Allemagne d'aujourd'hui* (199), January to March 2012, pp. 51-60. For the denunciation of Germany-turning-its-back-on-Europe, a small sample : « L'Allemagne veut-elle encore de l'Europe ? », La Croix, 15th December 2010 ; Jean-Louis Bourlanges, « L'Allemagne ne croit plus à l'Europe fédérale », L'Expansion, 21st December 2010 ; « Pourquoi l'Allemagne n'est plus en phase avec l'Europe », www.latribune.fr, 18th December 2010 ; « L'Allemagne contre l'Europe ? », Le Nouvel Observateur, Nr. 2376, 20th May 2010 ; « Angela Merkel, la chancelière comptable de l'Europe », Le Monde, 1st April 2010 ; « L'incompréhensible stratégie de Mme Merkel, 'Madame Nein' », Le Monde, 26th March 2010 ; « Tentation solitaire », Libération, 26th March 2010.

March 2010 ; « Tentation solitaire », Libération, 26th March 2010.

3. Cf. Jean Pisani-Ferry, *Le réveil des démons*, Paris, Fayard, 2011.

4. Cf. The proposals put forward by the Council of Experts, available in English: German Council of Economic Experts, *After the eurozone Summit: Time to Implement Long-term Solutions*, Special Report, 30th July 2012 (http://www.sachverstaendigenrat-wirtschaft.de/fileadmin/dateiablage/download/publikationen/special_report_2012.pdf)

to be clearer. Both governments finally admitted that the concerns of their counterpart were legitimate, and that far from mutually excluding one another, the German and French approaches are often complementary: the tightening of rules and sanctions, dear to Germany, is not incompatible with the French desire for greater political coordination; concern over budgetary stability does not rule out action fostering growth; the quest for greater European solidarity does not exclude accountability on the part of the recipient countries, and so on.

This has resulted in an easing of tension on both sides of the Rhine. In Germany, words and actions have started to change, moving towards compromise. In 2011, the Federal government was still vehemently rejecting the accusation that its growth model was egoistic and was refusing requests to provide greater support for domestic demand, but its position has relaxed somewhat since. Salaries have risen since 2011, the coalition has taken some moderate measures to sustain domestic demand, and debate over the introduction of a minimum wage is being pursued with greater energy[5]. In May 2012, Finance minister Wolfgang Schäuble declared that a greater rise in German salaries than in neighbouring countries was justified and that this might help to reduce imbalances in Europe[6]. For its part, the Bundesbank seems to be admitting that the German inflation rate will be (slightly) above the European average of 2% defined as a goal by the ECB, which will facilitate the necessary adjustments in the countries in crisis. More recently, the federal government's budgetary policy also revealed that it aims to sustain German domestic demand[7].

Public debate over Greece, which was fed by the polemic of politicians in Angela Merkel's majority has died down. Merkel herself put an end to speculation over a possible Greek exit from the eurozone, travelling to Athens to support Antonis Samaras' government. Also, Wolfgang Schäuble has categorically ruled out Greece's exit from the eurozone[8]. Generally speaking, the Federal government has become more aware of the need to stimulate European growth. Following Draghi's speech to members of the Bundestag, the polemic aimed at the ECB president after he announced the unlimited purchase of sovereign debt if the need arose, has finally given way to a calmer debate.

In answer to these careful, pragmatic changes in attitude, the French also seem to be taking steps towards reconciliation with Germany on these issues. As a presidential candidate, François Hollande fuelled the polemic against the budgetary pact being promoted by Germany, which he wanted to renegotiate, and more generally against a German policy accused of wanting to impose austerity on all Europeans. His policy as President, however, is subtler. He has pushed through the ratification of the budgetary pact, which means the establishment of a golden budgetary rule in France and he has committed himself to bringing France's debt below the 3% mark. Likewise, the government has promised to address structural problems affecting the French economy

---

5. Cf. Henrik Uterwedde, « L'exception économique allemande », in : *L'État de la mondialisation 2013*, Alternatives internationales, special edition, January 2013.

6. « Schäuble : Die Löhne können kräftig steigen », www.faz.de, 05-05-2012 (http://www.faz.net/ak-tuell/wirtschaft/tarifverhandlungen-schaeuble-die-loehne-koennen-kraeftig-steigen-11740624.html). Cf. The comment made by the Financial Times Deutschland, which believes it perceived a certain turn in German policy : « Toll, dass Deutschland sich bewegt », www.ftd.de, 14th May 2012 (http://www.ftd.de/politik/deutschland/:wirtschaftspolitische-dogmen-toll-dass-sich-deutschland-bewegt/70036776.html).

7. Cf. « La coalition d'Angela Merkel adopte des mesures de relance, » www.lemonde.fr, 6th November 2012 (http://www.lemonde.fr/international/article/2012/11/06/la-coalition-d-angela-merkel-adopte-des-mesures-de-relance_1786363_3210.html); « Les patrons allemands furieux contre les mesures de relance de Merkel », lesechos.fr, 5th November 2012 (http://www.lesechos.fr/economie-politique/monde/actu/0202363960974-les-patrons-allemands-furieux-contre-les-mesures-de-relance-de-merkel-507152.php).

8. Schäuble schließt Euro-Austritt Griechenlands aus, handelsblatt.com, 14th October 2012 (www.handelsblatt.com/politik/international/eu-schuldenkrise-schaeuble-schliesst-euro-austritt-griechen-lands-aus/7252252.html).

(public debt, competitiveness). This promise, the implementation of which is still awaited, will reassure Germany, since it knows perfectly well that it needs a strong, dynamic partner. Of course, public debate in France still seems characterized by a certain obsession with "dominant Germany" which "conceals the fear of difficult reform and a certain amount of confusion as to the solutions to be implemented" as suggested by Jean-Dominique Giuliani[9]. However, there is reason to hope that these fantasies will give way to the more serious, realistic debate necessary for undertaking structural reform both in France and in Europe.

Making good use of differences

In the light of the 50th anniversary of the Elysée Treaty, it should be remembered that since 1963, Franco-German government cooperation has always experienced controversy, and even confrontation for one fundamental reason: since the beginning of European integration, both countries have pursued different approaches to economic policy and to economic and monetary Europe: the German ordo-liberal approach, which above all has promoted the opening of the markets and competition, as well as the single market; and a more pro-active French approach advocating European interventionism via common policies[10]. Hence both France and Germany opposed each other as early as the 1960s over the common trade policy and the building of a common agricultural policy; in the 1970s and 80s they challenged each other over a Monetary Europe, an industrial policy and macro-economic coordination, and from the 1990s they debated the structure of the Monetary Union and the trade-off between stability and growth. The history of European integration has been punctuated by Franco-German controversy. However, although these differences have illustrated how difficult European integration has been – comprising the convergence of structures, cultures, and extremely diverse national policies, they have not prevented the German and French governments from working together to formulate necessary compromises. In doing this, they have permitted the settlement of certain differences and enabled convergence on various positions. Thus there is now a common base to the broad direction of economic policy, too seldom mentioned: a common concern to defend an economic and social model typified by a regulated market economy and committed to social cohesion, as well as a common objective of adapting and renewing this model to guarantee its sustainability[11]. The differences that remain (and those which are emerging) are no longer so divisive, making compromises easier to find.

It could even be argued that Franco-German differences are a constituent part of the "driving" role that the two countries have played in taking Europe forward. Europe means diversity, it means compromise, it is a "grand coalition" that does not try to divide but to bring the various actors closer together. In this context, the German and French approaches have often been the poles which have structured European debate, as they represent the range of possible positions; the quest for a European compromise necessarily entails a Franco-German compromise.

Moreover, in a Europe which is now closely interdependent and where the decisions to be taken increasingly relate to "domestic policy", affecting taxpayers' money and

---

9. Jean-Dominique Giuliani, "France, a problem for Europe ?" Robert Schuman Foundation, *The Letter*, no. 555, 12th November 2012.

10. Cf. Henrik Uterwedde, « La politique économique : quelles(s) vision(s) franco-allemande(s) ? », *Allemagne d'aujourd'hui* (201), July-September 2012, pp. 102-111.

11. For these convergences cf the Franco-German report Commissariat général du Plan/Deutsch-Französisches Institut (dir.), *Compétitivité globale : une perspective franco-allemande*, Paris, La Documentation française, 2001.

national social models, debate and controversy are necessary. How can we accept a contradictory political debate when it comes to defining a national budgetary policy and reject it when it comes to European choices? Arbitration between the policies of supply and demand, between stability and growth, between European solidarity and national responsibility, between interventionism and the markets are political choices which call for Europe-wide debate. Franco-German controversy can be useful if it contributes to the European debate on society.

Furthermore, it is now too simplistic to argue solely in national terms, to oppose the "French position" or the "German position". In the recent quarrels over the Eurozone crisis, many voices (leftwing opposition, unions, certain economists, and some media) stood against Angela Merkel's position on budgetary rigour and pooling of debt, with arguments close to those of the French government. Likewise, Angela Merkel's position has found support in France, which deemed that the determination of the Federal Government to set conditions on financial aid was quite legitimate. There was support for her demand for balanced public finances. This is why it is necessary to broaden Franco-German governmental cooperation with regular and institutionalised debate between the two Parliaments, for example.

***

In conclusion, it is thus a case of "vive la différence" – on condition that we ensure that the argument is constructive. This calls for frankness in debate whilst respecting the culture and limits of the partner, without misrepresentation or manipulation of its political positions. It also calls for the will and ability to reach compromises as well as the courage to make European choices and to accept the consequences these entail. This is the direction in which leaders in both countries should be moving, in order to make the celebrations of the 50th anniversary of the Elysée Treaty meaningful.[12]

The author wishes to thank his colleague Joanna Ardizzone for critical reading and useful remarks.

Europe adrift: Illusions and Realities of the European Energy Policy

Joachim BITTERLICH

On 4th February 2011, the European Council, the solemn authority of the European Union, set a common goal on the proposal of the European Commissioner for Energy, Günther Oettinger: the completion of a common energy market by 2014. However in reality this seems to be a profound delusion: the Europeans are further than ever before from a true European market.

They are moving rather more towards the renationalisation of their energy policies in a bureaucratic system of technocratic planning which resembles Soviet style intervention than a European community system. There is one slight difference however: we do not need to nationalise companies – the system takes care of this thanks to regulation down to the finest detail and thanks to the toleration of vast subsidies whose compatibility with European law can barely be guaranteed!

Why does this paradox exist? We should not forget that the energy policy has only been included in the European Treaties since Lisbon. And even with Lisbon most Member States were reticent about including this policy into the Treaties. The result of this is that community competence in this area is relatively limited. Above all every Member State takes advantage of the fact that the definition of the energy mix has remained a national competence. In terms of energy policy each Member State can continue to do what it likes without bothering about Brussels and its partners.

Hence the Germans decided, in the wake of Fukushima, to give up nuclear power within the next ten years without even informing or consulting either the Commission or its partners. The somewhat arrogant, but probably founded German response to its neighbours' criticism was as follows: "we acted in line with the Treaties. Moreover the French did not consult or inform us about their nuclear or energy policy, so why should we do it, undoubtedly interpreted as a weakness on our part?"

The consequence of this choice is clear: Germany has opened the way to subsidies in support of renewable energies – windmills, solar, panels – even in regions which do not appear to be the primary target of these energies! The Germans, who are reputed specialists in the effective implementation of initial decisions, simply forgot or neglected the fact that to do this adequate electricity networks have to be planned and built. Of the 2,800 km of new cable necessary and of the 2,900 km cable that has to be strengthened, only one tenth has been built. As a result the existing system regularly reaches saturation and often produces too much renewable energy! Indeed for the last year Germany has been producing too much energy! They are exporting it to their neighbours. Given the subsidised price paid by the German taxpayer and the consumer, the Belgians and Dutch do not have much choice: they have to import this cheap energy – given the rock bottom prices offered by the Germans – and stop or reduce their gas fired powers stations. As a result national energy manufacturers are losing money and are calling on Brussels for help.

If we ask why they don't keep this green energy for themselves and stop using their coal and lignite fired power plants – which are terribly pollutant in terms of CO_2 – the Germans answer astoundingly *"we don't need to because with our windmills we are easily achieving our goals!"* At the same time the German government has not been able, to date, to rise to the enormous challenge represented by this change in system, nor has it been able to discuss the matter with the Länder. Specialists do not see just one German policy but seventeen, each of which is convinced of the wisdom of its ideas! Critics insist on the fact that the result of this first post-Fukushima period has led to the design of a system in which only one would pay: the private – but mostly the industrial, consumer – and because of this prices continue to rise regularly!

How strange Europe is! A secondary effect is that the Germans may very well destroy the comparative advantage they have created via social and labour market reforms. But the Germans are now aware that this policy is dangerous if not dead-end. For the last few months Ms Merkel has been working with one of her best MPs on the energy issue, in order to organise it smoothly, constantly talking with all of society's dynamic forces, even going as far as to include the opposition. We have to admit that Peter Altmaier, the new Environment Minister has made great progress in a short time, but unfortunately without achieving the results hoped for to date!

And where is France in all of this? In the post-Fukushima era the French at first deemed the stress-tests on nuclear power stations in Europe, ordered by the Commission as "crime of lèse-majesté". The results have highlighted however the need to step up security!

In this context the fact that France has placed all of its bets on one type of future reactor which will only prove itself in terms of daily practice by the end of the decade, is incomprehensible. For the time being it is being built in two countries – Finland, France with a constant accumulation of delays and price increases. It is a prototype, an example of European know-how at its best but which cannot provide a rapid response to either European or global energy requirements!

The French then decided to act as the Germans have done: they decided – alone, like "grown-ups" to change their energy mix without informing anyone. The aim is to reduce the use of nuclear power by 2030 which will still represent 50% of production and systematically to strengthen renewable energies. The specialists are talking of necessary investment of 400 billion €! And who will pay the bill of a State whose coffers are empty? It seems to me that there is one "cash cow", or perhaps two: the EDF and the consumer!

When will the European Commission, the guardian of the treaties, put its foot down, convene a European Council to make the Heads of State and government pay for their sins? Are the energy policy and its price not an integral part of the European Policy's competitiveness? The same applies to the external energy policy at a time when competition and the battle for raw materials have become much more difficult. When will it find the courage to make a legal assessment of the compatibility of national policy with European law and publish the results of this assessment?

Isn't a Member State, in line with European law, obliged to inform and even consult with the European Commission as well as with its partners if it makes in depth changes to its national energy mix since this cannot remain without effect on neighbouring systems?

When will the Commission – and its courageous Energy Commissioner Günther Oettinger being mostly on his own – prove to Europe that this change and modernisation of the European energy policy over to a true market, towards trans-European networks – the so-called "energy motorways" – towards a certain decentralisation of production, and the progressive use of renewable energies together with a common external policy, represents a marvellous way to revive the European economy and its policy for innovation and applied research?

Jacques Delors and his friends, including the author, made suggestions prior to and after Lisbon with the aim of creating a true European common energy market. In vain, rare is it for someone to be a prophet in his own land!

Six years ago I wrote in an article for the Robert Schuman Foundation entitled "In support of a European High Energy Authority" (26th June 2006)[1], that the design and implementation of a common energy policy *"represented one of the strategic challenges for Europeans in the 21st century."* This observation is still valid. Because other major nations have seen the same thing in the meantime and are trying to guarantee their future via different means, for example in the USA via the use of shale gas and oil with the aim of becoming independent on the international markets; China is doing the same via a national and international policy committed to guaranteeing the supply of necessary raw materials – we simply have to look at China's policy in Africa!

For Europe we simply have to add that the implementation of a common energy policy would be a vital tool for the revival of its economy!

It is not (or never) too late to correct things! Why don't France and Germany do the impossible? Why don't they accept that the national level is no longer the pertinent framework for the energy policy? Why, on the 50th anniversary of the Elysée Treaty – don't they take the initiative and draft together the vital factors of an historic compromise between two political approaches which on first sight are totally incompatible?

Not only would all of this show that their conscience is clear and assert their European determination, but it would also highlight that they see their policies in a complementary light, that they will work together in the future in all areas, in permanent, close contact with the European Commission or simply to stress that they have finally understood their common European responsibility!

---

1. http://www.robert-schuman.eu/question_europe.php?num=qe-33

Several Europes but which ones?
A proposal to rationalise European integration

Jean-François JAMET

2012 witnessed the return of 'variable geometry' to the centre of the debate about the future of European integration.

Firstly, it appeared in discourse. François Hollande spoke of it clearly: "my approach is of a Europe that advances at varying speeds, with different circles[1]". The French President in fact mainly distinguishes the eurozone, the first circle that is to comprise the "core of a political union[2]", from the European Union, which he sees as multi-faceted Europe. German Chancellor Angela Merkel follows a similar, pragmatic line of thought: "We cannot just stop because one or the other doesn't want to join in yet[3]." British Prime Minister David Cameron is not against this strategy either: he dreams of a Europe 'à la carte'[4] in which the UK would be free not to follow the supporters of greater integration.

As a matter of fact, the crisis has led to a strengthening of the Economic and Monetary Union (EMU) via new rules that have also been adopted by some States outside of the eurozone, including the Euro Plus Pact[5] and the Fiscal Compact[6]. In addition the first enhanced cooperation agreements have or are about to emerge pertaining to international divorce, the European unitary patent and the tax on financial transactions.

Geometrically variable Europe is becoming a reality out of necessity: it is the only solution to situations in which unanimity leads to stalemate[7]. But it is not the answer to everything because it also leads to an increasingly complex map of Europe. This complexity fosters "constructive ambiguity" which European diplomats so love – it allows

---

1. Interview with François Hollande published in Le *Monde* and *The Guardian*, 17 October 2012.

2. Jacques Delors uses the term *creuset*. See J. Delors and A. Vittorino, « La zone euro, creuset de l'Union politique », *Le Figaro*, 27 November 2012.

3. Gerrit Wiesmann, 'Merkel insists on two-speed Europe', *Financial Times*, 7 June 2012

4. See P. Schnapper, "What future for the UK in the European Union?", European Issues – *Policy papers by the Robert Schuman Foundation*, n°254, 8 October 2012.

5. European Council, "Conclusions of the European Council of 24 and 25 March 2011", EUCO 10/1/11 REV 1.

6. European Council, Treaty on the Stability, Coordination and Governance within the Economic and Monetary Union signed on 2 March 2012.

7. T. Chopin and J.-F. Jamet, "How to unblock the EU's unanimity stalemate", *Europe's World*, Autumn 2008.

every State to pretend that they have imposed their priorities in negotiations – but it may make the European project unclear and unstable. This has reached the point where there has been more or less founded speculation, for example about a possible exit by the UK from the EU or the exit of Greece from the eurozone.

Several Europes therefore, but which ones? Is it possible to rationalise the use of differentiation?

Two Europes: the EMU and the internal market

It is easy to see that at present there are two main levels of economic integration: participation in the internal market (first stage of integration) and participation in the Economic and Monetary Union. This situation in fact corresponds with one of the goals of differentiation: managing heterogeneity of the political preferences and economic situations of EU Member States.

Some Member States like the UK and the Czech Republic, as well as those Members States of the European Economic Area (EEA) that are not EU members (like Norway), believe that what Europe can bring them positively in economic terms is mainly limited to the internal market. They indeed believe that European integration is mainly about creating and benefiting from an area of free trade. Free trade does not necessarily involve the free movement of people however and the perimeter of the European Economic Area is thus different from that of the Schengen Area.

Other States have deemed it a good idea to share their currency and have adopted the euro. Their financial interdependence has led to greater integration of their economic policies. This integration needs to be articulated with the internal market and is creating more institutional complexity. For example the strengthening of the Economic and Monetary Union supposes the implementation of common tools for the prevention and management of banking crises. One of these is supranational banking supervision, which supposes the definition of common rules and the appointment of the institution responsible for their implementation. The definition of the rules is the responsibility of the European Banking Authority (EBA), a Union institution[8]. But supervision is to be granted to the ECB, whose prerogatives concern mainly the eurozone. Several States (UK, Czech Republic and Sweden) have refused the ECB's supervision of their banks. They also succeeded in setting a double majority requirement for the adoption of rules by the EBA (majority of the States covered by the ECB's supervision and the majority of the States having refused it).

The third category of Member States comprises the anti-chamber to the eurozone. Some of them (Latvia for example) want to join but must first fulfil the convergence criteria set for participation in the Economic and Monetary Union. The others are not sure of their choice: Denmark voted in June 1992 against participation in the euro but has not closed the door completely and has pegged its currency to the euro. These States, which are observers, are weighing up the pros and cons of participation in the single currency but take part in most of the mechanisms designed to strengthen the EMU like the Fiscal Compact and banking supervision.

Reforming the agreement on the European Economic Area to clarify the choice between the two Europes

Beyond the discourse on the advantages of a differentiated Europe the present situation satisfies none of the States involved in fact. Those States of the European Economic Area, which do not belong to the European Union, have to implement the rules of the

---

8. The EEA States which are not EU members have observer status within the EBA.

internal market but they do not take part in the votes to approve them (even if they give an opinion). Conversely a State like the UK wants to be part of the Union to take part in decisions affecting the internal market but is reluctant to finance the Common Agricultural Policy. The States which are planning to join the eurozone long term hope to have their say in the decision and in the implementation of the EMU rules in the knowledge that one day they may have to apply to them. Finally the eurozone Member States would like to be able to use the European institutions for the functioning of the Economic and Monetary Union but seek to avoid the interference of the States that do not belong to it.

With the aim of clarifying this situation an attempt must be made to realign the institutions with the various degrees of integration and with the various political choices made by the European States. To do this the simple solution would be to turn the European Economic Area into the pertinent institutional framework for the management of the internal market and ensure that the European Union corresponds to the countries that want to join the Economic and Monetary Union.

The agreement on the European Economic Area signed on 2nd May 1992 led to the enlargement of the Union's internal market to the Member States of the European Free Trade Agreement (EFTA), except for Switzerland, which did not ratify this agreement. It therefore includes the EU Member States plus Norway, Iceland and Liechtenstein. Whilst they do not belong to the Union these States enjoy the free movement of goods, people, services and capital. In exchange they have to apply the corresponding rules (the Community *acquis*) except for those which affect tax policy, agricultural policy and fisheries, as well as trade policy. They can also participate in some Union programmes in the area of research, education, environment and cohesion as long as they contribute towards the funding of these proportionally to their GDP[9].

A debate took place in the UK over the pertinence of the country leaving the Union[10] and yet remaining a member of the EEA, thereby achieving a similar status to Norway. However critics of this idea quite rightly stressed that the UK would then lose most of its power to influence the internal market rules since they would no longer be taking part in the vote to approve them.

The fact that the EEA States cannot take part in the vote affecting the internal market is in fact a democratic anomaly. This might be remedied by amending the seventh part of the EEA agreement devoted to institutional provisions. The EEA Council[11] would become the competent Council (instead of the Council of the European Union) in terms of co-decision on legislative proposals (directives and regulations) governing the internal market. Participation in co-decision might also be extended to the Union's programmes in which non-Union EEA States have chosen to participate (for example in the area of R&D). Likewise the mixed EEA Joint Parliamentary Committee might be transformed to include all of the Union's MEPs and a number of MPs elected by the non-Union EEA states. This "EEA Parliament" would meet within the European Parliament building in Brussels and would have the competence to participate in co-decision on an equal footing with the EEA Council.

Such modifications would be advantageous is several ways. The European States' choices would be clarified.

---

9. These contributions are additional to the EU budget and increase the resources of the latter.

10. The Lisbon Treaty introduced an exit clause from the European Union (article 50).

11. The EEA Council comprises the members of the EU Council, the relevant members of the governments of the EEA States that are not EU Members, as well as a representative from the European Commission. To adopt a similar functioning to that of the EU Council, only the ministers from the EEA Member States would hold seats and participate to votes of the EEA Council following the revision of the Agreement.

There would be clarification firstly for the States, which above all want to benefit from the internal market without participating in integration as a whole. It is likely that the UK would then decide to quit the Union whilst remaining in the EEA plus. This would enable it, for example, to end its funding of the Common Agricultural Policy and enjoy flexibility in terms of its participation in European programmes (including regarding foreign and defence policies in which it would likely prefer to remain involved). The UK would continue to participate in the internal market and be obliged to implement the corresponding rules, the definition of which it would continue to influence.

Then the other Member States would be able to use the Union's institutions for the management of the EMU, without having to resort to legal contortions. It would then become clear that all Union States should eventually join the EMU (as it is planned in the Maastricht Treaty). They would then have to take part in all of the EMU's economic governance rules in terms of supervision (macro-economic, banking and fiscal) but also the rules pertaining to the establishment of common fiscal instruments in the future to encourage structural reform and face asymmetrical shocks[12]. The European Union might then also be able to progress more easily towards political union[13] without necessarily having to create ad hoc structures for the eurozone.

Finally such a new structure could offer an intermediate solution for candidate countries since it would be possible to take part in the internal market and some European programmes without being Union members. This might facilitate the settlement of the case of Turkey. Indeed it would then be possible for it to take full part in the internal market without it being a Union member and if the EEA has been enhanced, this would be an acceptable alternative.

Via a simple modification to the EEA agreement it would therefore be possible to settle several of the European Union's present problems, and thereby provide a welcome clarification for both citizens, economic and financial players. Debate over the choice between the two Europes would be facilitated amongst national public opinion and some of the present disagreement within the Union (over the budget for example) might be settled more easily.

Differentiation as an instrument for convergence

On a number of issues it will still be necessary to have flexibility to facilitate convergence towards a common solution when this seems desirable, but some States are not immediately ready to implement it or have doubts.

The criteria conditioning entry into the eurozone are a first example of this differentiation. They aim to ensure adequate homogeneity in economic conditions within the EMU. Their main drawback is that their incentive loses effect as soon as the benefit associated to the respect of convergence criteria (entry into the eurozone) is acquired. The sanctions planned for in the event of the non-respect of these rules have illustrated their limits and the eurozone experienced far reaching internal divergence after it was launched. It is now necessary to find positive incentives for the convergence of the economies within the eurozone. The roadmap[14] put forward by the President of the European Council, Herman van Rompuy includes an intelligent proposal as far as this is concerned. It comprises making access to fiscal solidarity conditional to the respect of

---

12. See the recommendations in the Herman van Rompuy report written with Jose Manuel Barroso, Mario Draghi and Jean-Claude Juncker, *Towards a Genuine Economic and Monetary Union*, 5 December 2012.
13. see T. Chopin, J.-F. Jamet, F.-X. Priollaud, "A Political Union for Europe", *European Issue*, Robert Schuman Foundation, September 2012.
14. *Towards a Genuine Economic and Monetary Union, op. cit.*

the convergence rules. Solidarity would be provided as part of the newly created fiscal capacity which aims to encourage structural reform and to help eurozone Member States which are facing asymmetrical shocks. The same logic might be applied if common debt instruments were to be created. The emission of eurobills on the Member States' account might be conditioned by the respect of common economic, fiscal and financial standards.

The second kind of flexibility that it might be useful to continue implementing lies in enhanced cooperation agreements. Participation in such agreements might also be extended to those EEA Member States that are not EU members in the context of the revision of the EEA Agreement described above. Enhanced cooperation agreements allow for experimentation if some States have doubts about the benefits that they might gain from common legislation. Some States with greater conviction or which are ready to run the risk would then be able to pioneer the agreement. It is this mechanism that will enable the launch of the European unitary patent in 2014, whilst negotiations have been ongoing for many years without unanimity on the part of the Member States ever being achieved. Likewise the enhanced cooperation mechanism will allow the launch of a tax on financial transactions, which was initially rejected by several European States that doubt its effects on the competitiveness of their financial industries. Again some States, which are holding back for the time being (like the Netherlands), might choose to join the pioneers if the experiment proves successful.

The flexibility allowed by differentiation may prove useful in many fields such as energy, defence and the harmonisation of the corporate tax base[15]. On this last point divergence within the Union fosters tax optimisation by large companies and thereby their avoidance of corporate tax in several Member States[16]. Work is ongoing on a European level[17] but differentiation might accelerate developments or take harmonisation further. France and Germany have notably thought about this option[18].

***

The multiplication of the degrees of integration and institutional arrangements is making the European project increasingly difficult to interpret. By doing this it is reducing legal certainty, complicating democratic debate and limiting the effectiveness of European governance, which is frustrating for the Member States. We must now start rationalising, thereby re-aligning the institutions with the two main levels of integration: participation in the internal market and participation in the Economic and Monetary Union. Above all this work means modifying the Agreement on the European Economic Area, which will help re-align the EMU with the European Union, while at the same time offering an acceptable solution to the States which want to limit their participation in the internal market and some cooperation programmes. Many hurdles would thus be removed, and other forms of differentiation would allow the necessary degree of flexibility to enable convergence and experimentation.

---

15. Thierry Chopin and Jean-François Jamet, "Can differentiation help towards deepening Community integration ?" *European Issues -Policy papers by the Robert Schuman Foundation*, n°106 and 107, July 2008.

16. see "Amazon, Google et Starbucks payent-ils leurs impôts en Europe ?", *La Tribune*, 13 November 2012

17. Proposal for a Council directive on a Common Consolidated Corporate Tax Base (CCCTB) COM(2011) 121/4.

18. Nicolas Sarkozy et Angela Merkel, *Letter to the President of the European Council* 7 August 2011

Britain in Europe: neither in nor out

Hugh DYKES

Over the past twenty years, a dangerous experiment has been carried out in the United Kingdom. There has been a futile attempt to combine formal British membership of the European Union with detachment from its main policies, such as the single currency and the Schengen area. This has involved a grudging political acceptance by the British political classes of the rational need for Britain to be part of the Union, offset by ever deeper popular hostility to the Union and everything it stands for. The motives which led to this strange combination of attitudes were various. Lazy and cowardly politicians were able to emphasise, as it served their case, the pro-European or the anti-European side of the argument in their rhetoric and party programmes. A certain tenuous unity within the main political parties could apparently be maintained by this systematic split-personality approach. Some at least of those who acquiesced in it privately believed that when the ambiguities inherent in Britain's tortured relationship with the European Union were finally resolved, it would be to their advantage.

The new anti-european consensus

We now know that those from the Eurosceptic side of the argument who embraced the latter analysis have been proved right. Britain is teetering on the brink of resolving its incoherent European policies in favour of at best long-term semi-detachment, perhaps complete separation from the European Union. A heavy price is being paid for the insouciance with which those who have styled themselves as pro-Europeans in Britain over the past decades have always been ready to postpone indefinitely a principled defence and advocacy of a full role for the United Kingdom within the structures of the European Union. We now see the consequences of this emotional and political feebleness, which always stood in flagrant contrast to the emotional and political commitment of the anti-Europeans. The summer of 2011 has shown, a year after the Coalition government was formed, a crystallisation of British public and political opinion hostile to the European Union which must put Britain's continuing membership of the Union in serious doubt. The European Council of December 2011 was in retrospect a foreseeable culmination of this process.

In truth, the first year of the coalition government showed marked echoes of the wilful self-deceptions which have littered the British debate on Europe in recent British history. The unsavoury appeasement of the Eurosceptics in the Conservative party under the Major government,which allowed them to hijack the traditionally most pro-European leading party of British politics; the endless ambiguities of New Labour's policy, the damaging effects of which many pro-Europeans long refused to acknowledge; and the noticeable drift towards Euroscepticism in the Liberal Democrat party, a drift partly disguised by the rhetoric of some of its leaders – all these tawdry compromises have foreshadowed a qualitative change in the nature of Britain's membership of the European Union. The Coalition's European policy has been all the more insidiously threatening to Britain's position in the European Union because in the first months of the new Coalition, it was carried out discreetly. Initially, the Coalition did not seek confrontation for the sake of confrontation, but nevertheless worked remorselessly to shift the intellectual and political basis on which European debate is conducted in the United Kingdom.

Twenty years of anti-European propaganda in the British mass media, silence by British pro-European forces and the crisis of the Eurozone have interacted with the attitudes of the most Eurosceptic British government in a generation to create something very like a new anti-European consensus in this country. This consensus is reflected in the current British European debate, which takes for granted that Britain will not be in any foreseeable future a full member of the European Union. The current British debate revolves rather around the extent of British withdrawal from the European Union, whether it should be complete or merely partial. The role in government of the supposedly pro-European Liberal Democrat Party has been to provide some apparent political cover for this process. In private, its leading spokesmen have even claimed some credit for slowing down developments which would otherwise have been yet more destructive. Those who wish to be deceived will always find ways of deceiving themselves.

The sombre history of the passage of the European Union Bill through parliament last summer was a perfect example of this phenomenon. Liberal Democrat MPs were won over by Mr Cameron's propagandistic arm-twisting to support the Bill on all votes. All the amendments proposed by the Lords to mitigate some of the more absurd effects of a wholly destructive and appalling Bill were rejected by the Commons. As The Guardian put it on 7th December 2010, it was' a shameful moment to see ... the most pro-European party, and ....Tories such as Kenneth Clarke trooping in to the lobbies....in support of such a foolish and feckless and futile Bill.'

The disappearance of the Liberal Democrats as an even theoretically pro-European force should not be underestimated as a blow. Sadly, there is no politically organised current of British opinion today that aspires to join the single European currency at any stage in the future. There is no politically organized force that wishes to reverse the practical disadvantages of Britain's self-exclusion from the Schengen area; or that regards the range of British 'opt-outs' from the European treaties as damaging rather than helpful for our country's true national interests.

Eurosceptic mythology: between caricature and lies

On the contrary, a Eurosceptic mythology is becoming every day more powerful in the British political debate, a mythology founded on implausible but enthusiastically advocated claims about the imminent demise of the single European currency and the systematic reversal of the extraordinary achievements of European integration since the Treaty of Rome. The construction of this mythology is clearly being prepared to justify and to reinforce yet further psychological and political estrangement of the United Kingdom from the European Union. The very notion of pooling sovereignty, a concept at the very heart of the Union is routinely denounced and denigrated by even prestigious commentators and mainstream politicians in the United Kingdom.

The comment and reporting surrounding the European Council of June, 2011 may stand as one example for many of this terrible evolution. In the week of the Council, a string of articles appeared in the widest range of newspapers casting the deepest doubts on the future of the euro. Few if any attempts were made by journalists to recall the long-standing and considerable efforts devoted by the members of the Eurozone to confronting the consequences of the global financial crisis for the single European currency. Nor was any differentiation made between different possible outcomes and their implications for the Eurozone as a whole.

The assumption of all these articles was that the single European currency was doomed and that the refusal of European leaders to recognise this manifest certainty was simply another manifestation of their feckless stupidity. The British press is bizarrely proud of the now well-established tradition of regular devaluations to get the United Kingdom out of balance-of-payment and debt difficulties. It gives no heed to the obvious truth that a regime of competing national currencies in Europe after the financial crisis of 2008 would have led to economic crisis in our continent on a vast scale.

Self-deceptive and caricatural attitudes were also much in evidence in the media reporting about the Schengen arrangement, now a well-established pillar of European integration. Difficulties affecting a small minority of travellers in a small minority of countries were regularly presented by British commentators in the summer of 2011 as foretelling the universal reintroduction of national frontiers. One of the most prominent correspondents of the Financial Times, Philip Stephens, intoned in his column a funeral oration over the whole concept of European sovereignty-sharing. Interestingly, his more recent columns have shown an awareness of the at least premature nature of this obituary; and a recognition of the disastrous consequences of the disintegrative developments he seemed to be predicting.

Such a hysterical campaign of denigration bears little or no relation to the objective circumstances of the European Union. The difficulties posed by the interaction of the inadequate governance structures of the euro and the consequences of the global financial crisis have created real problems for the Union and the Eurozone. In times of economic difficulty, there are always siren voices claiming that short-sighted selfishness and national solutions are more likely to be successful than co-operative action. But any reasonable observer would have to recognise that, in these times of economic travails and popular uncertainty, it is striking how well the Union has held together rather than how much it has regressed from its ideals.

This is every bit as applicable to the Schengen arrangement as it is to the single European currency. Without the euro, the consequences for the economic life of Europe, including the United Kingdom, would have been catastrophic. The expectation that Europe's leaders will put at risk such an achievement is wholly far-fetched. In the same way, millions of Europeans daily benefit from the ease of travel and communication assured by the Schengen system. Marginal and transitional problems are extremely unlikely to reverse so obviously successful and rationally progressive a development. The loving care with which the problems of the Eurozone and the problems of the Schengen system are described at such length in the British media says much more about the view the British would like to take of the European Union than about the Union itself.

There is a long and discreditable tradition in the United Kingdom of underestimating the seriousness of the commitment of our continental neighbours to the process of European integration. There are remarkable echoes in today's European debate of the scepticism with which the British ruling classes greeted the aspirations of the Messina Conference and the Treaty of Rome. It is as if the intervening years, with all the progress made towards European unification despite British obstructionism, had never taken place. There is a persistent British resentment that the losing European powers of the Second World War in north western Europe found it so much easier than did the United Kingdom to put behind them the trauma of that period and evolve for themselves a fundamentally new set of relationships in Europe.

A favoured complaint of Eurosceptics is that European integration is proceeding undemocratically, with insufficient consultation of national voters. What is usually meant is that democratically elected governments in Europe do not always allow themselves to be browbeaten by sectional or demagogic currents of opinion to pursue the irrationality of short-term nationalistic policies. Those advocating such policies are eager to disguise their dubious motives in the cloak of democracy, or at least one version of democracy. It is no coincidence that the version of democracy most favoured by Eurosceptics throughout the European Union is that of the referendum. Notoriously, referendums are vulnerable to precisely the eddies and incoherence of public opinion which representative democracy is designed to avoid. The European Union is very definitely a product of representative democracy. Its creation does great credit to this form of democracy. It is indeed a conclusive demonstration of the superiority of representative government to the dangerous irrationality of demagoguery.

United Kingdom out of the EU ? The risk of self-fulfilling prophecy

Ironically, the fears of the Eurosceptic media may turn out to be correct, although certainly not in the way they think. There is a real danger that, without proper public discussion or consultation, Britain's position within the European Union is being increasingly eroded by the conscious decision of the majority party in the governing coalition, a decision accepted without protest, or even awareness, by the minority party in the Coalition. This study is a protest against the individual misconceptions about the European Union and its policies which have led to this dangerous position. It is also a warning that Britain is nearer to leaving the European Union than many observers believe.

If this disastrous outcome is to be avoided, it is urgently necessary for those who know that Britain has no acceptable future outside the Union to realise the gravity of the position in which we find ourselves. We must take lessons from our opponents about the need for organised, effective and determined campaigning action. Our opponents have never been willing to allow their anti-European case to be lost by default. Pro-Europeans have come perilously close in the past twenty years to allowing just that to happen to their cause. Complacency is a luxury that pro-Europeans in this country can emphatically no longer afford.

Nor need pro-Europeans give way to despair. The virus of Euroscepticism is one which primarily affects politicians and the press. The general public are far more intelligent and sophisticated than either of these self-regarding groups. The growing mobility, especially of younger UK citizens, around the other member states for a range of reasons ranging from mere backpacking to study, jobs and marriage, is slowly and unobtrusively creating a new generation of 'natural' rather than 'self-conscious' Europeans. These young people do not yet make the decisions which govern British responses to present and new EU initiatives. But opinion polls show greater support for the Union among the young than among their elders.

***

It would be a shabby inheritance of the older generation to deprive the new generation of their ability to participate fully in the political and economic future of Europe, their continent. An isolated, self-pitying, self-righteous and enfeebled (dis) United Kingdom is at the time of writing an entirely plausible legacy for our children. They do not want, need or deserve this legacy. Time is running out to offer them a better future.

This text is an excerpt from Hugh Dykes' book *On the Edge: Britain and Europe*, published with B. Donnelly, Forumpress, 2012.

II

Towards true European economic union

Eurozone: light at the end of the tunnel?

Jean-Marc DANIEL

Three years after the launch of battle against the euro due to the downgrading of Greece by a ratings agency, the question remains: is the euro crisis now being settled? Two options are still open. We might think that it is the case when we read the Treaty on Stability, Coordination and Governance (TSCG), the new treaty which completes the Stability and Growth Pact and adopts a public finance management rule focused on the mid-term via the rule of zero structural deficit; we might also consider that since the European Stability Mechanism (ESM) enables States in difficulty to refinance to a total of 1000 billion € without having to use the markets, this should guarantee a certain easing on the bonds markets; lastly we might think this in the light of the action taken by the European Central Bank whose balance sheet has continued to expand rising to more than 3000 billion € at the end of 2012, ie 30% of the zone's GDP, higher than the level of the American Federal Reserve (the ECB's balance sheet/GDP ratio lay at 15% in 2008).

But we might also continue to doubt European determination to maintain the eurozone as it is at present, notably within its geographic perimeter, when we see that Cyprus, which undertook the presidency of the Union during the second half of 2012, faced a deficit of 300 million €. And in spite of the fact that the amount was low, this country ended the year threatening to default, reviving warnings about real solidarity within the zone.

A glass half empty and a glass half full, the situation in the eurozone is still of concern, even though in practice we might say that no-one is expecting it to implode; of course we should still be aware of it, much to the dismay of some financial players, notably the Anglo-Saxons, for whom the famous Financial Times was the extremely active and militant mouthpiece.

In fact beyond the repeated rebounds in the crisis within the crisis, which has typified the eurozone's situation since the end of 2009, – rebounds which were maintained by communications on the part of the leaders who, in spite of increasing clarity and determination, are still too often imprecise and contradictory – the eurozone is suffering three ills which it will have to correct.

Lack of Growth

The first is the lack of growth. After the 2009 recession (-4.9%), 2010 was marked by a recovery (+1.8%), which also led to a slight revival of public accounts (from -6.5% of the GDP to -6.2%). Then doubt about the sustainability of the public debt in some countries, eloquently qualified by the Anglo-Saxon press as the PIGS (Portugal, Ireland, Greece, Spain) led to the introduction of heavy austerity policies, which contracted domestic demand all the more, since they were based on tax increases and not on spending reductions. In March 2012 the OECD was still expecting slight growth of 0.2% in the eurozone. In November the same institution was anticipating a contraction of 0.4%. For the "PIGS" the situation was even worse: in 2012 the contraction will have totalled 3.1% in Portugal, and 1.3% in Spain. Although Ireland's GDP continued to rise slightly (0.5%) the situation has taken a dramatic downturn in Greece: after a recession of 7.1% in 2011, it then suffered a further recession of -6.3% in 2012. In fact the entire Greek economy was disrupted, and it will take time before the country achieves a situation that we might qualify as normal. One of the indicators of the disruption in Greece has been the quantity of banknotes in circulation there. Whilst salaries have been declining, prices are maintained. This, together with a rapidly expanding circulation of currency has led to an increasing decline into a "black" economy, which has also been a predictable result of sharp tax increases. This particularly negative development in growth is inevitably leading to high unemployment rates (more than 20% in Spain, and Greece, 14% in Ireland, 13% in Portugal and 11% in the eurozone overall).

Of greater concern still for the zone is the fact that potential growth, i.e. apart from economic hazards linked to austerity policies amongst others, is collapsing. It is now below the 1% mark for two reasons: in the countries of the south, continuing underinvestment is withering away capital and is diminishing output growth; in the countries of the north demographic developments are reducing the labour force (Germany loses around 400,000 people per year from its active population and has a growth potential of barely 0.9%).

Given this ominous trend that is setting in, European leaders have two options. The first is to boost growth via public investment. This is the choice fostered by the new team that has entered office in France. However the more than disappointing results of revival techniques implemented during the 2009-2010 world recession both in the eurozone and in other countries like in the USA and the UK, which has increased the volume of its public investments by 22%, do not argue in favour of major action like this. This is what the players in Paris believe, forcing the adoption of a minimalist version of the growth and competitiveness pact so dear to François Hollande.

The second possibility, which is more in line with the reality of Europe's ageing economy and more particularly the eurozone, demands the release of major savings that can be placed in the emerging countries where growth is rapidly catching up and which therefore have high remunerative rates. Although the eurozone has an external surplus (therefore a savings surplus since we have the equation $(S-I) + (T-G) = X-M$, in which S is savings, I investment, T-G public deficit and X-M deficit/external surplus) of 1.4% of its GDP, this surplus is well below the requirements which future developments would demand.

Consolidating public finances for the recovery of savings

Redressing the savings situation clearly entails reducing the budgetary deficit in the eurozone countries rapidly. This reduction, which was launched under the constraints of the market and under the somewhat haphazard eye of the ratings agencies, was inevitable. The main problem is that it is occurring in a chaotic manner; above all it focuses on recurrent tax increases, whilst recent experience in reducing public deficits has shown that the least onerous solution for growth lies in a reduction of spending. Sweden, which is often held up as an example for its work to redress its budget in the 1990's, has reduced the social protection burden from 23% to 17% of its GDP. Moreover, it fully integrated the logic which distinguishes the economic deficit – acceptable, and even necessary, to cushion the effects of the economic cycle – from the structural deficit which has to be brought down to zero. But it has to be admitted that for the time being this logic, although it is the base for the new TSCG, only has marginal influence over the austerity policies undertaken by the PIGS or in France.

It is probably in Italy that the Monti government has most systematically organised its action according to this logic with, as the key element in its successful policy to redress accounts, a growth policy which focuses on competition and labour market flexibility. To make the restrictive policy as painless as possible Ricardian equivalence mechanisms should in fact be brought into play. A Ricardian equivalence implies the introduction of an adequately credible budgetary policy so that households can anticipate rationally and positively, thereby compensating for public demand via an increase in private demand. In the eurozone political uncertainty and hesitation over the last three years have prevented this positive element of budgetary correction policies from emerging; this has been extremely useful in terms of the Canadian and Swedish successes in this area. The result is that hopes of recovery are constantly delayed and in 2011, Ireland was the OECD country with the greatest budgetary deficit (11% of the GDP). Austerity policies are inevitable but they would be optimal if the eurozone countries reduced their public spending in a sustained, programmed manner.

Banking Union

Although the ECB finally went to the rescue of the struggling States, notably after the European Council in October 2011 on the cancellation of the Greek debt, the general atmosphere of mistrust succeeded in undermining the functioning of the interbank market and banks' activities long term. One of the reasons for the colossal increase in the ECB's balance sheet is that many banks, instead of lending to their counterparts, have preferred to demand their share of payment of the "central bank's monies" that were immediately replaced by savings with the latter. Hence of the 3000 billion in its balance sheet, the ECB had a liability of nearly 1000 billion in bank savings. The general, mutual mistrust between banks is due to undeniable weakness. In spite of repeated "stress tests" the situation has still not been settled. The rotten assets in the Spanish banking system, by far the most in difficulty, is said to have represented 18% of the country's GDP at the end of 2012. Before the European Council in October 2011 and its plan to restructure or cancel the Greek debt the German banks held the equivalent of 16% of the own funds invested in Greece and the French banks 27%! The recapitalisation of the banks is therefore necessary and this has to come from the shareholders, even if the States are called in to help as in Spain for example.

With growth down, public deficits that appear to be difficult to absorb, weakened banks – we must admit that we might legitimately have doubts about the future of the euro!

And yet...

Various factors however have helped to strengthen the credibility of the eurozone's sustainability. Firstly, even though the misfortune of some does not make others happy, developed countries exterior to the eurozone are also struggling, notably regarding growth. The recession hit the UK in 2012 (-0.1%), Hungary (-1.6%) and the Czech Republic (-0.9%), which is not doing as well as its Slovakian counterpart (growth of 2.6%). Then the adoption of the TSCG, which makes the Stability and Growth Pact more precise and complete, has made the eurozone's macro-economic policy logical and coherent – and it will now be clearer than it was in the past. Except for the "PIGS", increased clarity has helped to maintain long term interest rates extraordinarily low, notably in the two main eurozone economies – France and Germany. From a banking point of view, the European Council in December 2012 heralded real progress since the idea of defining a geographical zone of action for the ECB, likewise that of merchant banks using the euro has now been confirmed. The dynamics of an integrated eurozone in terms of banking was illustrated perfectly in a speech delivered by Christian Noyer, the Governor of the Bank of France at the beginning of December 2012, when he stated *"there is no reason why the most active financial centre for the euro should be situated "offshore"* (i.e. in London).

The eurozone, which has become the core of European integration, must become stronger and will do this thanks to the expression of greater internal coherence via banking union, to the detriment of those who, on principle, reject it. The federalism demanded by some as a condition *sine qua non* of effective solidarity in the face of the public debts is typified, for the time being at least, in the project of banking union. As is often the case with European issues, rather than introducing a measure that might be experienced by some as a fundamental attack against their political sovereignty, integration is occurring via the "Europeanisation" of private activities – in this instance, the bank, as in the past agriculture and competition – but increasingly via political impetus.

At the end of 2012 the apocalypse forecast a year ago about the end of the euro is no longer on the agenda. Everyone seems to agree that the exit of a country like Greece, with the specific aim of devaluation in mind, would not be timely from a political nor an economic point of view: the only real effect that devaluation would have on this country would be to revive inflation – the short term beneficial effects of which in terms of the debt would soon become a recessionary nightmare once the monetary policy is toughened in order to control excessive price rises.

The share of the euro in the world's currency reserves has started to rise again, comforting its position as the planet's second reserve currency. The central banks, like the Swiss National Bank, have adopted a fixed, although unofficial, exchange rate, with regard to the euro.

***

Although the emergency might have been settled, and although the most serious concern is behind us, we must now address deep running problems. This means, first and foremost reviving growth and Europe's capability of taking advantage of the growth revenues of the emerging countries; this then means the sustainable re-establishment of public finances and finally – after having avoided it a first time round thanks to banking union – of pooling our debts. This will return to the top of the priority list very soon. Although we might consider the ESM as the embryo of the euro bond, it remains that this still frightens German public opinion to death. It is therefore up to this country's partners to define a serious project in this direction since they know that as its growth prospects are amongst the lowest in the world because of its demography, its fate is increasingly dependent on its savings; the final goal for the "Eurobonds" being that no one will ever again believe that they can gain economically, politically and financially from conflict within the eurozone.

For a credible growth strategy for the eurozone: the obligation to produce results

Mathilde LEMOINE

Any growth strategy for the eurozone is doomed to failure if there is no improvement in the functioning of the Economic and Monetary Union (EMU). The incomplete nature of the euro's foundations became glaringly obvious during the most recent economic and financial crisis. However, thanks to the theory of optimal monetary zones developed by R Mundell in 1961 we know how to make the eurozone function satisfactorily. It comprises the development of alternative adjustment mechanisms to the exchange rate, such as the increased mobility of production factors. Then governments and the European authorities will be able to concentrate on freeing the traditional engines of growth, i.e. investment, innovation and training to improve the growth trend. But the real challenge lies in the definition of an integrated cooperative economic policy which prevents the market share gains of some being systematically made at the expense of those made by others as is the case at present. The rebalancing of the Member countries' current accounts, as it is being undertaken at present, cannot be considered a strategy for growth.

Reducing imbalances within the eurozone ...

Inadequate economic integration and a lack of European funds to face up to asymetric shocks, i.e. the crises that are affecting the eurozone Member States differently, have led governments to privilege the reduction of current account imbalances. This is a means of limiting mutual commitment and therefore of delaying the moment when the issue of co-sovereignty in terms of economic policy will have to be addressed. Hence the balance of current accounts has replaced the quest to improve the functioning of the EMU. But although the reduction in the current account deficit can be requested by the creditors when it becomes unsustainable, this cannot comprise an economic policy goal nor can it be considered a growth strategy.

Current account balance reflects the difference between the value of export and import of goods and services traded abroad. It also includes net revenues, i.e. interests and dividends, as well as transfers abroad. A current account deficit means that imports are higher than exports or that national investment is higher than national savings. A deficit might therefore be normal in the countries that are catching up, which only have low domestic savings rates, or in countries which import today to export tomorrow. Moreover the possibility of current account imbalance enables a reduction in the cyclicality of consumption and investment. In the event of a hurricane for example production stops but some consumption continues. Hence the deficit evens out the negative effects of the economic shock. Finally balance between national savings and investment can vary according to changes in the median age of the population.

As a result balancing eurozone Member States' current accounts at all costs can counter growth and can only be explained by the fact that the governments of Europe want to avoid an over coercive coordination of economic policy. Indeed, in the eurozone, since re-balancing via the exchange rate is no longer possible, the accumulation of commitments vis-à-vis European partners in the event of a current account deficit is only restricted by a country's ability to pay back its creditors. And so the problem is not as much the current account deficit but the country's real state of solvency. But it is not just determined by the development of public finances but also by that of private debt, which can also lead to a crisis in the balance of payments. Hence a coherent reduction of imbalances that targets growth calls for the coercive coordination of European economic policy and not the rebalancing of current accounts.

The crisis has reduced current imbalances in the Eurozone

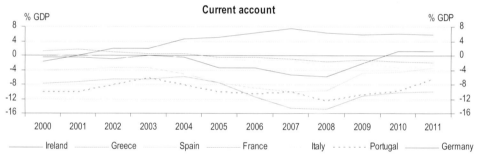

Sources: Eurostat, HSBC

.... will not lead to a correction of the faults in the design of Economic and Monetary Union

Not only can the quest for the balance of the current account not comprise a goal of economic policy but the optimal monetary theory developed by R Mundell shows that the priority lies elsewhere. Indeed the establishment of a monetary zone demands the mobility of the production factors in order for it to function if it is not optimal. But this goal is not being pursued at the moment. It would require the "defragmentation" of the eurozone's financial market, greater responsiveness of prices and wages to economic variations, and finally a harmonisation and simplification of the European regulatory framework. Moreover a compensation fund would have to be established to help the countries which bear crises unilaterally, with wage mobility remaining of marginal concern.

A monetary zone like that of the euro is only possible if the mobility of production factors compensates the disappearance of national exchange rates. Indeed the economies are too different in order to react in the same way to crisis. For example if the unemployment rate in one country rose sharply, the exchange rate would not decline because it would be an isolated case. However, according to R Mundell's theory, an adjustment to decreasing prices and wages would lead to a reduction in production costs, which would support exports. At the same time workers would be able to go and work in the countries which still had a dynamic labour market. Another possible solution would comprise the introduction of transfer mechanisms between countries in the zone such as compensation funds for example. Of course if the eurozone economies were integrated changes like this would not be necessary. But the deepening of integration cannot be seriously considered as an alternative to the mobility of production factors and the implementation of a European compensation fund. Firstly, the geographic particularity of one country may impede economic integration, as for example the size of a Member State. Small countries tend, for example to be importers of net capital, which means that they favour non-resident investments. They would be more attractive to capital intensive activities than the larger countries. Secondly, it is illusory to believe that wage convergence would strengthen economic integration. Indeed the alignment of costs increases concentration and specialisation phenomena in areas with greater output as we saw during the German reunification. Thirdly and lastly, European regionalisation has generated the diversion of trade between eurozone countries. But its effects are contradictory since the single market has fostered specialisation and major savings at the same time. But specialisation increases the asymmetrical nature of the shocks i.e. for example the fact that oil price increases do not affect the German economy as they do that of Spain.

Recent progress made in terms of coordination in Europe are not enough to correct the shortcomings in the design of the single currency, i.e. the introduction of economic policies to compensate for the disappearance of trade flexibility between the countries in the eurozone, nor to avoid an intra-zone marketshare war.

The development of adjusted productivity wage costs remains disparate

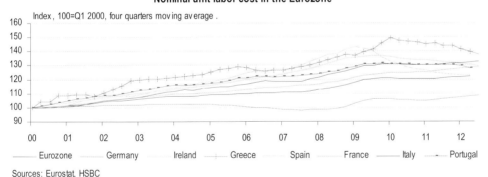

Nominal unit labor cost in the Eurozone

Sources: Eurostat, HSBC

The reduction of financing requirements of certain Member States does not exempt Europeans from coordinating their economic policies

The governments of Europe should initiate three types of action to reduce macroeconomic costs caused by the setting of exchange rates and the improvement of the running of the EMU, prior to releasing the traditional engines of growth.

The first comprises a strengthening of the link between GDP development and inflation across the entire eurozone. Greater wage coordination within the eurozone and greater

wage response to economic slowing would enable the European Central Bank to implement a more expansionist monetary policy and would limit unemployment increases, all
things being equal. But in France for example the rigidity of consumer prices leads to strong
resistance to wage stabilisation when GDP growth is slow or in times of recession. Indeed
whatever the GDP development, regulated service prices, i.e. on electricity, gas, postal services, estate agents, administrative documents for marriages and funerals continue to rise
sharply. And they represent a greater share in the French household budget than they do
in Germany or Italy for example. Hence it is not enough to "reassess wage setting measures
and if required, the degree of centralisation of the negotiation process" as put forward
in the Euro Plus Pact. An integrated economic policy framework is required that leads to
a harmonisation in price formation processes and not just wage adjustment. This means
that coordination will also have to focus on the development of regulated prices and
service competition. Then a reform of the wage formation process will have to be started.
It might take several shapes. The first would comprise centralised, collective negotiation
on a European scale. The second might comprise intra-European sectoral negotiations. At
the same time a European work contract might be drawn up including workers' rights.
Finally tax issues would no longer require unanimity, which would ultimately help to take
fiscal harmonisation forwards. The latter would do away with all types of market distor-
tion between businesses in the various countries but also between their markets without
challenging the redistributive principles in each country.

As a result mobility would be facilitated but it would remain limited due to linguistic
and cultural obstacles and would never be as strong as in the USA.

The geographical mobility remains weaker in Europe than in the US

% of residence-country population, 2005-06 average

* in % of working age population

Sources: European Commission April 2008,US Census Bureau, HSBC

Unblocking the traditional engines of growth

Simultaneous to the improvement in the functioning of the EMU the traditional engines
of growth will have to be unblocked. The 2020 Strategy is too similar to the Lisbon programme in order to comprise a credible growth strategy. On the one hand the quest for an
improved functioning of the EMU must also be part of the quest for growth. On the other
there are too many goals to be implemented rapidly. Finally there is no consensus on the
means to achieve them. Of course all of the goals included in the 2020 Strategy are important but we have to take the risk of ranking them according to their capacity to correct the
main weaknesses in Europe's principal economies and their expected impact on growth.

In view of these criteria four goals might be focused on: the improvement of employment rates, the rise in business investment in innovation, the increase in total factor
productivity and the transition over to a carbon free economy.

– The improvement of employment rates would lead to the support of growth; it would also facilitate the relay of innovation and therefore help speed up potential growth. Indeed the employment rate is particularly low in the eurozone even though national disparities are significant. This results in a lack of adapted vocational training, particularly in the countries of the South and in France. General training is rarely given in the latter, whilst it comprises a prior condition for worker mobility and an increase in employment rates. To achieve these goals, European businesses should offer vocational training that leads to certificates or diplomas according to a percentage of the workers which has to be defined.

– The increase in private investments in innovation would also lead to a strengthening in the eurozone's growth potential. Although business investments in innovation total 1.9% of the GDP in Germany in 2010, it only totalled 1.4% of the GDP in France, 0.7% in Italy, Spain and in Portugal. According to the OECD, business investment in innovation represented 2.5% of the GDP in Japan and 2% in the USA. Accelerated depreciation for this type of investment could be put forward to all businesses in the eurozone by the European Commission and financed by project bonds.

– Total factor productivity grew less between 2000 and 2010 in the eurozone countries than in the USA, Japan, South Korea and even in the UK. But according to our report for the Economic Analysis Council[1], greater flexibility on the goods and labour markets as well as more high school graduates would help to support growth. The means to achieve this would be the same as those implemented to improve the functioning of the Economic and Monetary Union. As for high school graduates a specific figure has to be estimated.

– Finally as far as the transition over to a carbon free economy is concerned the implementation of a carbon tax would increase the necessary investments for the renewal of equipment. If oil prices continue to rise, investments would become profitable with the reduction in energy intensity.

The eurozone's trend growth rate must be higher

The crisis has led to institutional progress which will improve the functioning of the Economic and Monetary Union. Banking Union will facilitate the transmission of the monetary policy undertaken by the European Central Bank, thereby reducing the differences in private players' borrowing rates between the eurozone countries. Budgetary integration and macro-economic supervision will enable a reduction in the financing requirements of States experiencing a balance of payments crisis. But budgetary recovery and the quest for current account balance cannot comprise a growth strategy. A strategy like this must comprise two parts. The first being the correction of design faults in the single currency which limit its positive effects on growth. The second suggests an unblocking of the four most exhausted growth engines in the eurozone and would set out the steps to follow to achieve this. This is how the eurozone would define a future for itself.

Bibliography:
Aghion P., G. Cette, E. Cohen et M. Lemoine, Crise et croissance : une stratégie pour la France, Rapport pour le Conseil d'Analyse Économique, la Documentation française, 2011
Boyer R., « Le gouvernement économique de la zone euro », Report by the Commissariat général au plan, 1999

---

1. Crise et croissance : une stratégie pour la France, la documentation française, 2011

Lemoine M., « *Une sortie de crise en zone euro passe par l'intégration et le partage de souve-raineté* », L'Hebdo Economie et Stratégie, HSBC Global Research 11-15 June 2012
Lemoine M, « *Zone euro, la souveraineté en question* », in L'Agefi Hebdo - 31st May to 6th June 2012

EU Banking Union: Sound in theory, difficult in practice

Josef ACKERMANN

In June 2012, the EU heads of state and government decided to pursue a so-called Banking Union as part of the effort to strengthen the cohesion of the European Union and to stabilise the eurozone. Banking Union is now part of the four frameworks – an integrated financial framework, an integrated budgetary framework, an integrated economic policy framework, and a framework for better democratic legitimacy and accountability – proposed by the President of the European Council, Herman van Rompuy, also in June, as the necessary elements for a genuine economic and monetary union.

The EU took a further step towards Banking Union in October 2012, following an agreement to establish a eurozone banking supervisor as part of "a Single Supervisory Mechanism [SSM], to prevent banking risks and cross-border contagion from emerging".

The rationale

The impetus for establishing a banking union is rooted in the sovereign-bank-nexus, i.e., the vicious circle between financial sector and budgetary instability. A banking crisis will worsen the budgetary situation if, as is likely, the crisis leads to a recession and even more so if public assistance is needed to make the banking sector healthy again. Likewise, a public debt crisis will create problems in the banking sector because banks tend to hold large volumes of public debt on their balance sheets (not least because they are encouraged or even required to by regulation) and also because banks' refinancing costs are closely correlated to those of the states in which they are headquartered.

Either can trigger a downward spiral, as we have seen in recent time. In the cases of Ireland and Spain, problems in the financial sector were the root-cause of a budget crisis in those countries which, prior to the financial crisis, had sound fiscal positions. In contrast, Italy is an example of a country where a basically sound banking sector has been hit by deterioration in the public debt position.

Conceptually, the idea of a banking union tries to break this vicious circle by weakening the connection between a national banking system and the public sector in its home jurisdiction.

• The link from public-sector instability to financial sector instability is broken if banks have a diversified asset and funding base. In this case, problems in the public sector will only have a muted effect on the asset quality and funding costs of the respective domestic banking system. This would require a fully integrated banking market, with cross-border institutions and no home-bias in banks' asset portfolios and funding structures.

• The link from financial sector to budgetary instability is broken if the costs of stabilizing a banking system no longer fall exclusively on the home jurisdiction of the banks in trouble, but are instead shared across jurisdictions – either directly via common public budgets (like the ESM) or indirectly via joint / interconnected resolution funds and deposit guarantee schemes.

But the rationale for a banking union goes deeper than breaking the bank-sovereign nexus. Market integration, financial stability, and banking supervision at the national level just do not go together. More broadly then, the push for a Banking Union stems from three inter-linked and, if pursued successfully, mutually reinforcing motives:

• Maintaining financial stability on the basis of effective supervision and crisis management,

• preserving the Single Market for financial services, and

• avoiding competitive distortions.

The objectives are (i) to enhance financial stability by overcoming market fragmentation and (ii) to preserve the Single Market in financial services. This becomes even more pertinent in the face of mounting evidence that the re-nationalisation of Europe's financial markets is becoming entrenched as a result of market forces and regulatory action in the wake of the financial crisis. A refragmentation like this not only reduces the efficiency and competitiveness of Europe's financial markets, it is also inimical to financial stability.

Conceptual elements

A comprehensive banking union would comprise, a minimum four elements:
• A single rule book, establishing materially uniform rules,
• pan-European banking supervision,
• a pan-European resolution regime including an EU bank resolution fund, and
• harmonised deposit guarantee schemes (DGS).

In September 2012, the European Commission presented its proposals for a Banking Union. While the four above-mentioned design elements are included in that proposal, the level of detail varies significantly. Whereas the Commission's proposals for a pan-European supervisory mechanism are fairly specific, the proposals on bank resolution and deposit guarantee schemes are less ambitious and essentially refer to proposals already in the EU's legislative process.

The different degrees of specification and detail on these four elements partly reflect the fact that progress has already been made on some of them – for example, successive versions of the Capital Requirements Directives, transposing the Basel capital requirements into EU law, constitute significant steps towards a single rule book. To a larger degree, however, the differences in specification reflect political opposition in Member States that stands in the way of bolder concepts. This is as deplorable as it is dangerous because the four elements form an integral system. Separating one, such as supervision, from crisis management will distort incentives for authorities as well as financial sector participants. This in turn could make the EU's financial system less resilient.

Design issues

There are a number of design issues with regard to the organisational and institutional set-up of a banking union that still need to be sorted out.

Authority for banking supervision: despite 2012 October-summit agreement to clear all remaining legal hurdles by the end of this year, there is still considerable debate over the ECB as the EU banking supervisor of choice and the scope of its powers. The June summit press release speaks only of a supervisory mechanism "involving the ECB". This was clearly motivated by the reputation the ECB enjoys and by the fact that the European Treaty (Art. 127.6) allows for the transfer of supervisory powers to the ECB, based on a unanimous vote by ECOFIN, which will make the legislative process easier.

However, there are a number of arguments against entrusting financial supervision to a central bank, most importantly potential conflicts of interest with the mandate of monetary policy as well as concerns over a concentration of power and question of how countries that are not members of the currency union should be represented in the decision making bodies of the supervisory mechanism.

The Commission's proposal would give the ECB sweeping powers and full control in all areas of prudential policies. This is sensible conceptually and rational from the point of view of the ECB as financial supervision is prone to grave reputational risks. National authorities however tend to preserve as much power as possible and to limit the powers of any pan-European supervisor.

Bifurcated vs. federal: a two-tier supervisory system that limits EU supervision to large, multi-jurisdictional institutions would create scope for competitive distortions and regulatory arbitrage. Worse, it would ignore the important lesson of the recent financial crisis that smaller, regional banks are at least as likely to cause systemic crises as large ones. Hence, the European supervisory system should be federal. For practical reasons, small and home-market oriented institutions would continue to be supervised by national authorities, but these would be subject to the final say of the EU-level authority, which would directly supervise systemically relevant financial institutions that operate on a pan-European basis.

Single Rule Book: arguably, the single rule book should be the most easily achievable element of banking union. Over the past few years, the EU has made considerable progress in establishing a harmonised framework for banking regulation and supervision. However, EU members have recently veered off that course and allowed for greater national discretion. Moreover, actual day-to-day supervisory practices have never been as closely aligned as the rule-books suggest. Clearly, both issues will need to be addressed to achieve a truly single rule book.

Resolution regime and fund: effective bank resolution regimes are needed to ensure that even the largest and most complex financial institutions can be wound down in an orderly way. A resolution fund to provide bridge financing, financed predominantly but not exclusively by contributions from the financial industry, would be a useful element of such a regime. While some EU Member States have set up such funds at a national level, a pan-European scheme has yet to be established as Member States cannot agree on a financing mechanism or resolution authority, both of which would inevitably infringe on national sovereignty.

Deposit Guarantee Schemes (DGS): DGS play an important part in maintaining depositors' trust in the stability of the banking system. Historically, DGS were developed in response to specific market structures and it is thus no surprise that the design of such schemes varies substantially across the EU. Given the complexity of bringing very different schemes together, and given the fact that DGS are of limited relevance in dealing with failures of large cross-border banks, it would probably be best that instead of aiming for a common supra-national scheme efforts be directed at ensuring that all national schemes are equally robust and equipped to meet potential demands. Beyond such minimum harmonisation (as is indeed sketched out in the current legislation), existing national DGS could remain in force and be complemented by a limited re-insurance scheme, which would kick in if national DGS were exhausted and the state in question was incapable of backing the system up.

The political process

The realisation of a full EU banking union will prove difficult. Some countries see banking unions as an integral part of the new institutional framework for a more stable European Monetary Union and a step towards closer economic union with tougher disciplines on economic and fiscal policies as well as towards closer fiscal and political union. They are therefore asking for a well-designed, comprehensive and consistent framework.

Other countries, however, see banking union in a narrower context, namely in the context of the debate about direct ESM assistance to individual banks, which necessitates taking banking supervision for those banks out of the hands of national authorities and transferring it to the EU.

The establishment of supra-national structures and institutions is evidently in conflict with national sovereignty. Financial supervision is inextricably linked to the exercise of sovereign power. More importantly, supervision creates a latent fiscal liability which may become real in the event of a systemic crisis. As the recent crisis has shown, in a systemic crisis fiscal resources may be required to restore confidence in the financial system. This is why, ultimately, the issue of how to organise financial supervision cannot be separated from fiscal liability. Supra-national supervision also threatens vested interests, in this case of national supervisory authorities bent on preserving their powers. Similarly, supra-national arrangements, especially those for supervision, would also disrupt the relationships between national authorities and banks in any given country, which are often marked by regulatory capture and, in times of crisis, a tendency for regulatory forbearance.

Cross-border burden sharing raises potential distribution conflicts. Those countries and institutions that expect to be net payers will be wary of committing their resources to preserve the stability of other country's financial systems. This is particularly true as long as it remains unclear whether the envisaged institutional arrangements for supervision will be strong enough to ensure effective discipline on risks accumulated in the financial systems of banking union members[1]. A banking union therefore pre-supposes elements of a political union.

In addition, the banking union plan puts the spotlight on a fundamental issue – that of how institutional arrangements for the eurozone can be reconciled with those for the EU-27 as a whole. Specifically, the question is whether it is more important to strengthen the stability of the eurozone or to safeguard and maintain the Single Market for financial services.

The relative importance of either objective has a bearing on the institutional design of a banking union. Stressing the latter objective favours a strong role for the EBA to ensure the consistency of rules and supervision in the EU-27, whereas emphasis on the former objective gives the ECB a prominent role and strives to integrate crisis management systems at the EU level.

---

1. As an added complication, the negotiating position of the German government is limited by the disproportionate political influence exerted by non-profit-oriented banks (savings banks and cooperative banks), which lobby massively against supra-national supervision for all EU banks as well as against supra-national crisis management arrangements.

***

Conclusion

As with so many other institutional arrangements in the EU, the design of the banking union – at least its *initial* design – will be the result of what is politically possible and not necessarily what is required to put Europe's financial system on a firmer footing. It is likely that instead of a consistent, integrated design, an incoherent system will be established that leaves out pan-European crisis management instruments – ignoring the fact that supervision and crisis management are inextricably linked. EU-level supervision will remain weak and dependent on the support of national supervisors which have little incentive to cooperate or to share problems in their banking sectors at an early stage.

If this were indeed the result, EU- leaders would have wasted an important opportunity to build a more unified and stronger Europe.

Towards a fiscal federation?

Alain LAMASSOURE

At last! The black hole in European debate that has been ongoing for the last two decades, the problem of the common budget, is back in the limelight and on the agenda of the European Council. The debt crisis has contributed to this immensely.

The last time the heads of State and government held a real debate on the budget dates back to … 1984, during the European Council of Fontainebleau! On that day François Mitterrand, Helmut Kohl and Margaret Thatcher decided on the main amounts and means of financing the budget of the "Single European Area", which could potentially rise up to 1.24% of the Community's GDP. Since then the European Council is supposed to update this mechanism every seven years by adopting a new annual general budgetary framework for the Union. But in the meantime an insidious phenomenon has occured – own resources which fed this budget have slowly dried up, whilst national contributions that were supposed to serve simply as top-ups, now fund nearly 80% of the revenues. Hence, for the last twenty years, whenever they have discussed the common budget the heads of State and government have left Europe out. Everyone has focused on the way to maximise the money his country can get from the Union and to minimise his own contribution to the family budget. A formidable gap has thus been created between the countries which receive more than they give, the net beneficiaries and the others, the net contributors, those who systematically have the last word "he who pays the piper, calls the tune". The result of this is that more than 25 years after Fontainebleau, in spite of the two-fold rise in the number of Member States the Community budget has remained frozen at 1% of the GDP, i.e. well below the level that even Mrs Thatcher found acceptable! It is globally twenty times less than the national budgets.

The next seven-year budgetary period covers 2014-2020. Might we hope that this time the crisis will help the main leaders to place the question on the level it deserves: what kind of European budget do we need for the rest of the decade? How big should it be? How should it be financed? What should it be devoted to?

To avoid frightening the net contributor countries, José Manuel Barroso simply put forward marginal adjustments: the budget would be brought up to 1.08% of the GDP by 2020, without even challenging the level of the agricultural appropriations, nor those of the cohesion policy – which alone take up 80% of the total. But even this symbolic increase was the cause of an immediate outcry – not only in London but also in Berlin, The Hague and all the Scandinavian countries, and, unfortunately, Paris believes that the right Europe is the one which spends less.

An approach revived by the crisis

Triggered off during the autumn of 2008 by the bankruptcy of Lehman Brothers, the thing we still call a "crisis", without being able to name it exactly, occurred mainly in Europe, then in the eurozone, then in two European countries, which were the most badly managed. Entering the 2009 world recession in debt already, some States are now the focus of banking suspensions. They can only recover with the help of their more fortunate European partners.

It has taken three years to shape how this help is to be provided. Steered by the European Council, the decision-making process proved to be particularly chaotic. But painfully and in spite of the contradictions, faux-pas and back-peddling, a true European model of solidarity has started to emerge. One might compare it to the treatment of a sick athlete.

The first stage of the operation comprised the ambulance service. The heart-attack victim was brought back to life at home with mouth-to-mouth resuscitation by the emergency service – this was the role of the ECB, which finally accepted to play the game.

The second stage involved the patient being taken to hospital. He was put under permanent monitoring and, if necessary, equipped with an intravenous drip. But he had to accept the diet imposed on him and also to take his medicine – this was the fiscal golden rule. Then the so-called European Stability Mechanism (ESM), which provided vital nutritional extras, entered into play. It could devote up to 700 billion € to it. One might note by the way that this amount is four and a half times more than the Community budget!

The stay in hospital might be long, but it is not supposed to go on forever. The third stage will be returning to normal life, once the patient has recovered and can start eating and living normally again.

But once this has been achieved – further work has to be undertaken. In an era of exacerbated world competition, Europe can be considered as an athlete who absolutely has to achieve maximum fitness if it is to compete, on an equal footing, in the merciless battle with its tremendous American, Chinese, India, Brazilian rivals, which have out-distanced it during its absence from the race. High-level training, muscle-building, a champion's diet – these are the goals of the future competitiveness and investment policies which are summarised in the "Europe 2020" programme.

And this is where the budget comes in, since rescue loans to reimburse old debts will not be enough. Financing research, new technologies, major continental networks, renewable energies cannot do without a real European-scale fiscal effort. In these areas efficiency demands a critical mass that can only be found on a continental level. Moreover the convalescent countries will not be able to provide themselves with an investment budget beyond the partial co-financing of the Community programmes for a long time. And so who will finance what and in which context?

The crux of the matter: who will be the tax payer of last resort?

Curiously enough for the last three years this purely fiscal dimension has systematically been left out of the projects meant to strengthen the EU and the eurozone. But it is constantly in the back of the minds of the leaders and public opinion of the countries in the North of Europe who are being called upon to help Southern Europe. Because lurking behind the experts' debates over the bank of last resort is the fundamental political question – if the loans granted to the indebted States are not paid back, who will be the tax payer of last resort? This is how we should now regard the question of European solidarity.

There are three possible answers to this question:

1 – First option – no one. There is no tax payer of last resort apart from the one in the struggling country. Hence, no default on the part of a debtor State towards the ESM

or any other creditor will be tolerated. This means that the beneficiaries are bound by exceptionally tough conditions. And this transfers all of the animosity over the consolidation policy over to Europe. This was the stance adopted for a long time vis-à-vis Greece. We have seen how unrealistic it is.

2 – The second option is that the tax payers in the countries of "ants", are the only ones, beyond all appearances, who can guarantee the Fund. This is the solution implicitly retained at present. But it is unacceptable to the electorates in the donor States, whilst the conditions set by the "ants" in exchange for their aid are also becoming intolerable for the public opinion in the "cicada" countries. With this option, a formidable infernal machine has been set in motion that might rekindle all of the worst nationalist resentment and prejudice in Europe. In the North it has made the electoral fortune of the populist, xenophobic parties, from Anvers, to Helsinki, Vienna to The Hague. Whilst in the South demonstrations of anger are rising during which effigies of German Chancellor Merkel are burned in the streets of Athens, Madrid, Barcelona and Lisbon. This is an unsustainable situation.

3 – Hence the third option, whereby the tax payer of last resort can only be the European tax payer. It is the only truly European solution. It is also the only one compatible with a democratic decision-making process and under parliamentary supervision worthy of the name. Therefore, we have to come up with new fiscal resources, levied across Europe in replacement of the national contributions and to have all European citizens assuming the commitments made in the Union directly. Whether this means guaranteeing loans made to struggling countries or especially financing future investments decided upon together.

This does not require a new treaty, but we simply have to adhere to the Lisbon Treaty to the letter: the principle is clearly set out that the Union's financial commitments must be financed by own resources affected to the Union. And this does not imply any transfer of fiscal sovereignty. The European Union must simply be considered as a territorial authority, which will be of a certain geographical size, bigger than each of the States which it comprises, but with fiscal resources delegated by the latter.

This is because the European Parliament has made it a specific condition in the negotiations over the next financial framework that the Commission has tabled, the proposals for which are now ongoing – the tax on financial transactions and a new VAT resource. One might naturally think of others, notably in the area of pollutant energies.

A false route: more budgets for less money

The autumn of 2012 witnessed a wealth of the most different ideas on how to complete monetary union thanks to financial solidarity that went beyond lending mechanisms merging all or in part with sovereign debts, a European Treasury issuing short term bonds, common redemption funds for banks in distress, a European guarantee fund for bank deposits, etc. The most spectacular was the proposal for a budget for the eurozone. Inspired by Berlin, it gave rise to eloquent one-upmanship on either side of the Rhine. On the right bank the idea was to help the struggling countries which were courageous enough to honour their roadmap by funding investments that they were no longer able to assume. On the left bank the idea was nothing less than "compensating asymmetric shocks" and pooling unemployment insurance schemes! They both wanted to take an additional step towards European integration. Which federalist would not support that?

But can you believe it? The players' basic logic has not changed – each one hopes to find the means to be generous ... with someone else's money! This is why the idea of providing the eurozone with its own budget has to be gauged against the answers given to four questions.

– Are we talking about a real budget or a new type of bank fund? Lending more to countries which are already in debt would be going over the top. Helping them to take advantage of a true budgetary transfer immediately points us towards the next question.

– Where would the money come from? Who is ready to pay and how much? The German leaders who support this idea endorse all of Ms Thatcher's arguments against any increase in the Union's budget. They are violently against the increase that was timidly put forward by the Commission of less than 1/1000 of the GDP by 2020! And they refuse to provide any new "own resource". 2013 is an electoral year in Germany and public opinion is extremely tired of the aid being given to our Southern partners. It is clear that the present European lyricism is not a bid to announce any additional facility but to compensate for its absence.

– Which type of spending would be covered? Aid to the poorest? Again Germany and its Northern neighbours have gone as far as referring to the Court of Justice to put an end to the only social spending financed by the Union, i.e. food aid to the most vulnerable. And what about vocational training aid to people who have been laid off? The Globalisation Adjustment Fund was created with this in mind and it is operating at full capacity – the means simply have to be increased. And what about competitiveness investments? This would mean re-inventing the structural funds and the framework research programme.

– And finally which countries would be involved? Only the eurozone members? This idea is now outmoded: a year ago, President Sarkozy, a firm defender of the organisation of an independent eurozone, had to accept including eight non-euro countries to the fiscal compact, since they absolutely wanted to remain at the core of Europe. This desire can but grow, because their national currencies already depend entirely on the euro, and their economies are totally linked to ours.

It made sense to imagine having an independent body in the euro countries fifteen years ago when we thought there would only be about half a dozen members. In 2013, the opposite problem has arisen. From now on "useful Europe" must not be seen as the "eurozone plus" but as the European Union "minus": minus our partners who do not want to go further, and who even want to go backwards. Article 50 of the Lisbon Treaty – the divorce clause – was designed for this. And the British Prime Minister has announced that he intends to submit the question of confidence to his fellow countrymen at the next general election in two years time.

Conclusion: the fiscal dimension of European solidarity will not emerge via new institutions, new treaties or new budgets but via the adjustment and adaptation of the good old Community budget.

In support of European budgetary solidarity

The crisis has provided an opportunity for audacious reform but unfortunately this does not entail public generosity beyond our national borders. On the contrary, the Flemish, the Scots, the Basques, the Catalans, the Lombards would even like to reduce the geographical framework by stepping away from national solidarity. Whether there are 17, 25 or 27 States, a budget that is worthy of being called "federal" remains out of reach. However a true qualitative leap might be achieved if the financial pillar of the solidarity model, which has been emerging over the last two years, is completed with a three-part budgetary pillar:

1 – The adaptation of the Community budget to the requirements demanded by the 21st century – from the point of view of resources: the financial transactions tax and/or the carbon tax to replace customs rights – and also from the point of view of spending – new technologies, the major continental networks, university exchanges, more excellence hubs, whilst intelligent decentralisation would transfer a share of traditional

policy, for which the European dimension is no longer pertinent, over to the national or regional levels.

2 – The creation of an investment fund that would complete the budget appropriations to finance long term projects with deferred profitability. Many solutions are possible to supply the fund – the pooling of future project bonds, the re-allocation of the loan repayments granted by the ESM or of its financial products, the pooling of national loans designed to finance future investments etc. A fund like this would aim to become the investment budget which the Union does not have right now. It would be a realistic translation of the idea that was clumsily launched under the name of the "eurozone budget".

3 – Finally, the introduction of fiscal coordination between the Member States that is not just limited to the respect of safeguards, but which focuses on the very content of economic and fiscal policy. If we make a musical comparison we would just have to check that each musician in the European orchestra does not play out of tune; the scores have to lead to a harmonious symphony, i.e. maximising healthy, sustainable growth for the entire Union. With the debt crisis we must not forget that the most serious problem in Europe is that of the pernicious anaemia of growth. Instead of constantly putting forward other treaties, other sanctions, other disciplines, it is time for the major leaders to discuss the content of their respective policies.

And so a new question arises then. If it seems that one Member State has a policy that is too selfish, we have to convince it to show greater cooperation towards its partners, who *will be the decision maker of last resort?* Shhhh! You'll find out in the next edition of the Schuman Report!

Europe's Sustainable Competitiveness Challenge

Stefaan De CORTE

Despite Europe's attention and initiatives to tackle the sovereign debt crisis, its low growth prospects and high unemployment levels, three 'super trends' that threaten the prosperity of future generations remain. The policy response should, however, primarily be found at Member State level. To tackle the impact of globalisation, population ageing and increasing costs and scarcity of primary resources, EU Member States, in close co-ordination with the European Institutions, should face their 'sustainable competitiveness challenge'.

Super trends threatening the prosperity of future generations

With growth forecasts for 2013 and 2014 revised downwards and the sovereign debt crisis in certain EU Member States not resolved, European policy makers, citizens and business face multiple short-term challenges. On top of this, slow, but steady changes in important parameters of long-term socio-economic development put an extra burden on future growth prospects.

The European economy in a global context

Despite consecutive enlargements, the total share of the European Union (EU) in world exports declined from 22.2% in 1986 to 16% in 2010. The main winners in this respect have been emerging economies like China (from 2% to 13.8%), Singapore and India, whilst the other main loser has been the United States (from 13.8% to 11.2%[1]).

On the one hand this has been a positive evolution, as the internationalisation of trade has allowed the emergence of global supply chains that increased productivity for European businesses and decreased prices for European consumers. This can be seen for example with many electronic devices and cars. On the other hand it has increased competition and challenged the European business community (e.g. Finnish mobile

---

1. Eurostat, External and intra-EU trade: A statistical yearbook Data 1958 – 2010 (Luxembourg, European Union, 2011) p. 14-15

phone device maker is being severely challenged by its American and South Korean competitors). However, the on-going difficulties (decline in exports) that European countries face in selling their own goods and services to third parties show that European economies are far from having found all the answers to the challenge.

Europe is an ageing society

The European Union's demographic structure is changing and becoming progressively older. By 2050, the projected number of people aged 65 and over compared to the projected number of people aged between 15 and 64, the so-called dependency ratio, is set to double from one to four to one to two. These figures represent a major shift and are indicative of where our societies are heading.

Great achievements in social policy such as unemployment support, old age pensions, health insurance and care provision are being severely tested by these demographic changes. In addition, ageing societies might see a decrease in their entrepreneurial spirit and risk-taking behaviour. An ageing population, therefore, represents an important challenge for any society and economy, with serious implications for public policies and budgets.

The cost of energy keeps rising

The downturn in the EU's primary production of hard coal, lignite, crude oil and natural gas in the last decades (in spite of new discoveries and exploration methods) has led to a situation where the EU is increasingly reliant on primary energy imports in order to satisfy demand. The shortfall between production and consumption increased the EU's energy imports from non-member countries from less than 40% of gross energy consumption in the 1980s to 54.8% by 2008[2]. All of this energy consumption is financed with European funds and, if this is not counter-balanced by the purchase of EU goods and services by non-EU countries, the EU's balance of trade deficit increases with the rest of the world.

Moreover, the overall increase in worldwide demand has raised the cost of energy significantly and this may become the new 'labour cost' for many highly productive[3], but energy intensive, industries (transportation, manufacturing etc). In addition, it negatively affects the purchasing power of households as more of their income is spent on heating or transport costs instead of other types of consumption.

The European Union and its Member States should face their sustainable competitiveness challenge

In the previous section we highlighted the short-term challenges of high levels of public debt, high unemployment and low growth in the European Union in general. In more detail, we described the long-term trends of an increase in global competition, a dramatic increase of the dependency ratio and increasing energy prices. The thesis of this contribution is that both the short and long-term challenges can and should be tackled with an improvement of the sustainable competitiveness of the different economies and sectors that make up the European economy.

---

2. Eurostat, Energy production and import, www.epp.eurostat.ec.europa.eu

3. Due to high labour costs many energy intensive industries invested capital to increase productivity of the, as a consequence, declining, workforce.

We deliberately use the phrase: 'different economies and sectors that make up the European economy', instead of the more commonly used notion of the 'European economy'. The main reason for this is that the economies that make up the European economy find themselves at different development stages. Therefore, there cannot be a one-size-fits-all strategy.

In addition to this and in agreement with Georg Zachmann's recent policy contribution[4], there is complementarity between the different factors that make up a competitive sector. Investing public resources in reducing manufacturing industry labour costs, while at the same time, not taking initiatives that could lower the energy costs is one example of this.

The total tax revenue to be redistributed by Member States of the European Union varies between 27.4% (Bulgaria) and 48.5% of GDP (Denmark). The European institutions themselves receive slightly more than 1% of the EU's GDP in funds to be invested at EU level. These numbers show that the biggest fiscal leverage for growth enhancing policies can be found at Member State level.

Given that there cannot be a one-size-fits-all strategy, given the complementarity between different levers of competitiveness and given that Member States have the main resources for policy action, our introductory remark to this section is an argument in favour of the subsidiarity principle.

However, this should not mean that Member States can decide on their own what policy would suit them best. It is an argument in favour of a strong European coordination of tailor-made policy strategies at Member State, regional and sectorial level.

In the following paragraphs we shall outline, which aspects we believe should appear in every economic reform strategy of a Member State in order to increase its competitiveness. However, some aspects will be more important than others for different Member States. We will first tackle cost competitiveness, dealing with labour costs, productivity and other costs. Next we will briefly analyse a series of other factors which we think are of major importance for Europe to maintain the prosperity of its future generations: creativity, good governance and infrastructure.

Cost competitiveness

The key indicator of the cost competitiveness of an economy is the evolution of the labour cost per unit produced (Unit Labour Cost or ULC). In order to improve their cost competitiveness, policy makers, employees and employers can therefore try to influence the cost per hour of labour, the number of hours worked and the productivity of each hour worked.

When we analyse the evolution of labour costs prior to the economic crisis in selected Eurozone Member States (2008 compared to 2004), we already notice great diversity amongst the European economies in terms of the development of this indicator. When we use Eurostat data, economies which are catching up, like Estonia or Slovakia, saw a wage increase of nearly 80% over four years. Belgium, France and Spain saw labour cost increases above 10%, whilst Ireland, Italy and the Netherlands experienced a more moderate increase of around 7 to 9%. The clear outlier in this indicator is Germany, with wage moderation via an increase of a modest 5.7% when comparing 2008 to 2004. Therefore, we could say that wage moderation contributed to increasing Germany's competitiveness vis-à-vis other Members of the Eurozone in the years prior to the crisis.

When we analyse the number of hours worked, we find that German workers (as an example for many EU countries) work, on average, 80% of their annual working hours in full employment as compared to workers in the United States. Although it is often said to be a societal choice, we think there is room to adjust regulatory burdens to offer more choice to employers and workers who prefer to increase the number of hours worked

---

4. Georg Zachmann, Smart Choices for Growth, Bruegel Policy contribution (November 2012)

(e.g. via fewer holidays) in return for a wage increase. This is particularly the case for the high number of women in part-time work. Moreover, extending working time without full wage compensation is a means to improve the unit labour cost and has been applied recently in different industrial sectors in the EU (aviation, car making, etc.).

The main drivers of productivity growth are both capital intensity and total factor productivity (TFP).

When we look to capital intensity[5] and use gross fixed capital formation as an indicator, we find that the countries of the Eurozone invested significantly more capital (19.2% of GDP) than the United States (15.2% GDP) in 2011[6]. However, studies show that the United States' capital productivity is higher than that of selected Members of the Eurozone[7], indicating that the United States' capital investments are made in more productive assets (e.g. information and communication technology assets).

Based on OECD data[8], total factor productivity[9] growth between 1995 and 2010 was significantly higher in the United States (1.3%) than in most members of the Eurozone: France (0.6%), Germany (0.8%), Spain (-0.1%), Italy (-0.2%) all experienced lower growth rates.

One might have hoped that the European economy would compensate for its more expensive and rigid labour market and lower capital productivity with a higher total factor productivity. However, the above numbers confirm this is not the case. Therefore, action is needed. The best long term policy action is, in our opinion, more investment in education and R&D. This might increase, e.g. the take-up of new information and communication technologies. As an example, a take-up of social technologies could increase the productivity of highly-skilled workers[10].

When we analyse the EU's R&D figures, the great disparity amongst EU Member States is evident. Investment in research and development ranges from 3-4% of Gross Domestic Product (GDP) in Scandinavian countries to 0-1% GDP in countries like Greece, Poland, Romania, and Bulgaria. A similar trend can be identified when analysing public investments in education.

It is worth highlighting one other increasingly important component of the cost competitiveness of the European Economy: its energy efficiency. The EU's final energy consumption increased by14% when we compare 2009 data with 1995 data. However, when we look at its Energy Intensity, which indicates the units of energy used per unit of GDP, we can see a decrease to 80% compared to its 1995 levels[11]. This encouraging trend can be found in all Member States and does not show the same diversity we have seen in other cost components.

Other factors

When reflecting on the competitiveness of economies and sectors, many other factors also play part in the equation. This contribution does not allow us to explore all of them

---

5. Is the term for the amount of fixed or real capital present in relation to other factors of production, especially labour.

6. Dataset: Gross fixed capital formation (investments) data extracted on 15 Dec 2012 13:10 UTC (GMT) from Eurostat

7. International comparisons of levels of capital input and Productivity, Paul Schreyer, OECD Statistics Directorate, 2005

8. Dataset: Multi-factor Productivity, data extracted on 15 Dec 2012 10:49 UTC (GMT) from OECD. Stat

9. Total Output of an Economy is a function of Labour input, Capital Intensity and Total Factor Productivity (TFP). TFP can be taken as a measure of an economy's long-term technological change.

10. McKinsey Global Institute, The social economy: unlocking value and productivity through social technologies, Mckinsey&Company, July 2012

11. EU Energy Figures, Statistical pocketbook 2012, European Commission, 2012

but in this section we will highlight those which we think are of particular importance for the European economies.

However cost competitive European economies become via lower labour costs, increasing productivity via capital investments and investments in education and R&D and increasing its energy efficiency, they will not be able to compete in the world market unless European policy makers and business invest further in their capacity to develop new sectors, new products and new services. When we analyse the number of patents (as an indication of the capacity to translate R&D investments into new products or services), we find, again, a rich diversity within the European economy.

Germany, Sweden, Finland, Austria are the best performers when it comes to the number of patents with over 200 patents per million inhabitants. Whereas Spain, Portugal, Greece, Poland and other central European countries are lagging behind with less than 50 patents per million inhabitants. In this respect we are satisfied with the recently decided unitary patent which will significantly decrease the cost of obtaining an EU-wide recognised patent. We can only hope that this lower cost will stimulate SMEs in economies which are catching up to embark on more innovative activities.

Foreign direct investors or entrepreneurs, to name just two examples, will feel more inclined to develop business and to invest in productivity-enhancing measures if they are reassured of the country's good governance. Although it is not often discussed in debates about competitiveness, we believe that high moral and social values are a key determinant in this equation. When we use World Bank indicators on control of corruption and government effectiveness (how well a government is able to deliver qualitative public goods), we find a clear link between countries that have a low level of control of corruption (Greece and Ukraine amongst others) and a low score on government effectiveness.

As a last element, we would like to mention that the European Union, as is the case with many other regions in the world, faces an on-going infrastructure deficit. In the EU's Multi Annual Financial Framework, the European institutions rightly point out the need to invest in energy, transport, water and ICT infrastructure as a basic condition for enhancing Europe's growth prospects and for allowing certain Member States to catch up with others.

***

In this contribution we have shown that the European Union (EU) faces not only short-term socio-economic challenges. If the EU wants to maintain its current prosperity, it should find answers to the increasing competition of non-EU economies, the ageing of its population and its rising energy dependency. Our thesis is that the EU can do so through an increase in its sustainable competitiveness. This contribution showed the great diversity in many of the components that make up that competitiveness: be it the cost of labour, the factor productivity, the capacity to develop new sectors or products, good governance or infrastructure. Therefore, the European institutions and the Member States should use the common strategic framework of the European Semester and the individual National Reform Programmes to agree on tailor-made and country/sector specific action plans. National and regional ownership of these reform programmes will be a key determinant for their success.

Europe and the Social Crisis: in support of a new European Social Contract

Ignacio Fernández TOXO
Javier DOZ

Social Europe faces the Crisis

Some analysts wonder whether "social Europe" or the "European social model" really exist, using the diversity of situation amongst the various countries in Europe as a base to their argument. Without denying that these differences exist they cannot bring into question the historic and political validity of the concept. The comparison of social and labour relations, as well as legal systems which guarantee rights in most European countries, with those in force in the rest of the world, notably in the emerging countries, is the greatest proof of this.

Whatever the various antecedents, social Europe, i.e. the European Welfare States were born of an implicit post-war social pact. To the backdrop of the Cold War, the victorious democratic powers sought to govern according to Keynesian economic ideas and to the primacy of public authority and general interest over policy. This was best part of what was left behind after one of the bloodiest wars in history. The post-war period, which ended in 1973 with the first oil crisis, was one that in Europe and also in the USA and other western countries, led to the highest level and the fairest distribution of wealth ever witnessed in the history of the world. Equality and social cohesion were values that political groups and dominant economic trends accepted out of conviction or because of a simple economic calculation. The intention was to distance workers and their organisations from the influence of communism and models that lay on the other side of the Iron Curtain.

Hence, thanks to progressive, satisfactory tax regimes, which enabled States to enjoy, by means of taxes and social contributions, the necessary resources for the redistribution of the wealth that was generated, western European nations built the most prosperous, fairest, most egalitarian and most democratic societies that Humanity has ever known. The State regulated the markets and intervened in both the economy and society to provide greater security and a maximum level of well-being to its citizens, from birth to death – thanks to a State benefit system (healthcare, insurance, unemployment, retirement pensions, social assistance etc ...) and a universal, free education regime that was open to all until the age of 16 at least. These benefits, acknowledged as subjective rights for everyone, were provided by public services of ever increasing quality. The most emblematic of these were the State education and national health systems.

In the economic and employment spheres, a modern European labour law (with national variations) was established with major progress being made in terms of workers' and union rights. The legal and political guarantee of collective negotiation and the autonomy of the actors involved were of particular importance. In Europe collective negotiation became the leading framework for the distribution of wealth, within the company, between capital and worker. This framework was less confrontational and much less violent than before, notably because the dominant Keynesian theory seemed to convince employers that well-paid workers were a key factor in domestic demand and growth and hence in their own profits. In some countries, as in Germany, Austria and various Nordic countries the model was complemented by the co-management of some major companies. Beyond the business and economic sectors, bipartite or tripartite social dialogue gradually became the norm as a means of participation on the part of organisations that represented workers and employers for the establishment of working and living conditions, as well as social rights. At the same time the nations of Europe – their governments, unions and employers' organisations – provided political support to the International Labour Organisation (ILO) and promoted the development and ratification of its conventions.

The political dimension of the European social pact was managed by democratic actors which lay both on the left and centre-right of the political scale. This also led to the creation of the foundations of European integration. Although the Union is a supranational structure which is pursuing a political goal, i.e. peace between European nations (notably between Germany and France via their mutual work together) it does so with pragmatism, which emerges in the relative weakness of political and social rules in comparison with those governing the economic domain. However we might say that the European social model exists due to the impetus provided by the post-war European social pact.

Even in the 1990's, when the offensive against the European social model and the Welfare State had already started in many countries, the political leaders of Europe again fought the tide and boosted the social model via the social protocol included in the Maastricht Treaty, i.e. the structural and cohesion fund and some social and professional standards which resulted from European social dialogue. Helmut Kohl came to an agreement with François Mitterrand and Jacques Delors to support social Europe and at the same time they created the single market and Monetary Union in exchange for what seemed extremely difficult at the time: the rapid unification of Germany.

In the 80's and 90's, whilst the erosion of the European social model was already underway in countries like the UK and Ireland, alongside similar developments in the USA, other countries in the south of Europe, like Spain, Portugal and Greece followed an opposite path building up their Welfare State – more limited in its services and social rights generally – at a time when they rediscovered democracy and joined the European Union.

But the political leaders of Europe also made some serious mistakes. The biggest one of these is preventing us from settling the present crisis. They created a single currency without forming a Common Treasury, nor a financial policy, nor European economic governance.

The oil crisis and the international monetary system of Bretton Woods together with the ensuing crises of the 1970's led to a sharp response against what was called the "excesses of the Welfare State" whose levels could apparently not be maintained because of the "State financial crisis". This was the concept advocated by those who made tax reductions their watchword. The Chicago School then started to dominate economic thinking. Milton Friedman was crowned; Hayek resuscitated and Keynes buried. The aim was to deregulate markets, particularly in finance and labour and to roll back the State, by reducing taxes on the wealthiest, inversing the progressive nature of the tax regimes, and by privatisation. The reduction of labour costs and the undermining of labour rights demanded the erosion of collective negotiation and the unions, together with the reduction of their influence and their ability to act within the company. In sum this demanded back-pedalling and the rejection of a major part of the progress achieved in the 20th century.

The second major globalisation of capitalism – the fruit of the IT and communications revolutions and the collapse of "real socialism" after the fall of the Berlin Wall served as a lever to the economic powers to strengthen their global offensive against the foundations of the Welfare State and the European social model. It was claimed that these were not fiscally viable in a globalised world which demanded competitiveness in terms of labour costs in the face of emerging countries, notably China. In reality it was about countering the fair distribution of wealth provided by the Welfare State. It was the era of the economic and financial hegemony of financial capital.

Other remarkable episodes and events over the last two decades of the 20th century also aimed to strengthen the power of capital, alongside an increase in inequality and a decline of some of the principles of the post-war social pact. There was a transition of State run economies over to those governed by the market – after the implosion of the Soviet Union and the collapse of the "popular democracies" – under the guidance of the "Chicago boys". The precepts of the Washington Consensus presided over the conditions that the IMF set on countries which had suffered financial crises in Latin America and Asia in the 80's and 90's.

The attacks of financial capitalism and the wealthiest have always employed a blunt tool: – money – which is required to corrupt, to purchase or influence politicians, intellectuals and journalists. With money even lies can become "scientific truths", including in open societies. This was notably the case with the supposed *"leap towards a growth society"* which deregulation, privatisation and tax reductions were supposed to create as of the 1980's. Any economist who consults the statistics can see that the peak of post-war growth until today, in both the USA and Europe, took place between 1945 and 1960. It was when taxes were the highest and regulation the strictest that more wealth was created and that full employment was achieved. Hence the European countries with a better developed social system are resisting best to the crisis.

During the more recent era of the "casino economy", it is easy to find striking examples of the collusion between the interests of financial capital and the public authorities, as for example the abolition of the Glass-Steagall law, by Robert Rubin, the Secretary to the Treasury under Bill Clinton, which since Roosevelt's time separated investment bank activities from those of the commercial banks. The most credible analysts believe this measure to have been the one which facilitated the Wall Street financial bubble the most, the collapse of which was the cause of the present crisis.

In spite of all of this social Europe managed to survive until 2008. This can be seen in the UK and in Ireland or more recently in Germany (Agenda 2010) which had to re-assess their social systems or with the entry of the countries of Central and Eastern Europe into the EU in 2004, - most of whom had labour and social norms well below those in the other Union States, but where the foundations of the Welfare State and the levels of social equality had been maintained in the main.

In support of a new European social contract

The deregulation of the markets, particularly those in the financial and real estate sectors, the predominance of the financial over the real economy, financial and real estate speculation together with the sharp increase in inequality in terms of income distribution are factors that have mainly been the cause of the crisis which has been fomenting over the last few decades.

After the default of Lehman Brothers the G20 responded quickly to save the financial system by injecting enormous quantities of public money. To boost domestic demand in a coordinated manner fiscal incentives were introduced (increase in public spending and tax reductions), but this was not enough and the programmes were not always best advised. Hence the in 2010-2011 recovery, which followed the severe recession of 2008-2009, was limited. Moreover, as of 9th May 2010 the EU relinquished all of its tepid attempts for a Keynesian revival by moving in the opposite direction with austerity policies and structural reforms, which are nothing more than grim cuts to salaries, social services and rights.

The consequences of this way of governing Europe are simple. On the one hand there has been recession and unemployment, with the non-respect of budgetary goals and the "rescued" or indebted States' unable to find financing on the markets at reasonable interest rates. On the other there is greater poverty and inequality, with a serious deterioration in social cohesion and of the Welfare State (public services, labour law; social dialogue and collective negotiation etc ...). Finally the worrying decline of political cohesion – both internal and between the Member States – as well as the loss of legitimacy of national and community political institutions are leading to the rise of national political and social movements, which are separatist, populist and extremist.

By repeating policies similar to those used to overcome the Great Depression of the 1930's the present leaders of Europe, who seem to have forgotten the lessons of history and maths, are reproducing a great number of the economic and political consequences experienced at that time. After having kept the sovereign debt crisis going for nearly three years in a totally irresponsible manner and of having led the European Union into a new recession, the European crisis has now become political. Originally it came about because of political leaders' inability and reticence to take the action required and because of the inadequacies of the mechanisms in the European decision making process. It is also political because of its effects: it is causing the failure of social and political cohesion, vital to the maintenance of a common project; this in turn is threatening the very existence of the latter as well as the European Union, undoubtedly the most important political edifice of the 20th century.

Europe is at an historic crossroads. To a large extent the European trade union movement is aware of this. After witnessing the destruction of the post-war European social pact, which held the well-being and social progress of the past 60 years and the European political project together, the trade unions of Europe are now organising within the European Trade Union Confederation (ETUC) and have not succumbed to the temptation of euroscepticism. In an article published in several European newspapers in December 2011 its leaders spoke in support of a '"new European social contract" which can only mean "more Europe", a more social and more democratic Europe.

On 14th November 2012, the ETUC called for a European day of action and solidarity. For the first time in history general strikes took place at the same time in four countries – Portugal, Spain, Italy and Greece – with mass action in many other Member States. This decision was taken under the political impetus and coordination of the most representative central trade unions in the Iberian Peninsula and the inestimable help of the major European unions. It was a moment chosen by European workers to express, in the most vigorous and unified manner that has ever been seen, their rejection of austerity measures and social cuts. In many countries this action received both political and social support. In Spain the Social Summit, the platform of more than 150 networks and social organisations, supported this action.

When the ETUC speaks of correcting unjust and/or flawed policies, it also suggests short term alternatives, coordinated European and national measures to stimulate growth and create jobs. These are vital for the mid-term settlement of deficit and debt issues, as well as resolution of the sovereign debt crisis via cooperation action in the shape of eurobonds, the ECB's intervention on the secondary debt markets etc. as well as rigorous financial regulation.

The main slogan on 14th November was "For a new European social contract". The ETUC's proposal has to be understood, beyond the real claims that it makes, as a political and social strategy, based on the autonomy of the union movement to save the European political project from the crisis. It is a proposal based on the protection and strengthening of social Europe.

The basis of the new European social contract is fiscal policy. The progressive nature of fiscal policies, undermined in many European countries by a process that began thirty years ago, has to be re-established. On the same basis, harmonised fiscal regime has to be established across the whole Union – which also provides adequate resources to greater European budgets. This would put an end to the present fiscal dumping. Furthermore in both its internal and external policies the European Union should give priority to the fight against fraud and fiscal evasion and the eradication of tax havens.

Another pillar of the new social contract must be the total respect of social dialogue, collective negotiation and of the results of this, – be they general agreements or collective conventions, which must be legally and politically guaranteed on a national and European level. Social partners' autonomy in collective negotiations must also be guaranteed. The third strategic axis should be the establishment of a set of basic European social standards which protect and standardize the main content of European labour law and vital services in the area of pensions, unemployment benefits, healthcare and education etc ....

Apart from what has been approved today by the leading structures of the ETUC, it has to be admitted that to achieve this goal an in-depth change of the key European treaties has to be undertaken. The changes to the treaties should focus on at least three main areas a) the construction of a pillar for the foundation of social Europe; b) economic governance of the eurozone and of the Union; c) the democratisation of the European Union (direct election of the political authorities, greater legislative capabilities and control of the European Parliament, social transparency).

***

Without more democracy, without social Europe, European economic government is unacceptable. Without more democracy and without social Europe, the European Union has no future. The European Union has to be recast if we are to overcome the crisis and the European trade union movement is prepared to help to do this constructively.

III

Europe in the world:
between values and interests

European strategic interests:
choice or necessity?

Michel FOUCHER

Building a centre of power and influence
– the third stage of the European project

The serious problems affecting Europe at present are not the result of a simple economic and financial crisis; they come from geo-economic change and a major world
geopolitical transition. The collective management of present weaknesses (sovereign
and private debt, public deficits and low growth) will lead to results but it is reducing
European action and discourse down to the economic dimension alone. It is a strategy
of necessity.

The time has come to move onto the third stage in the European project: establishing
a centre of power and influence in a polycentric world, which will be extremely interdependent not cooperative enough and which will face vital challenges. It will be a
strategy of choice.

This large scale change supposes that adaptation by the States of Europe to the risks
and opportunities of economic globalisation will not lead to excessive divergence in their
response to this, since this would weaken the internal cohesion of the European Union.
It is up to the European institutions to ensure this.

The completion of this project also implies the establishment of a short list of interests
that are objectively common and explicitly shared and which are not just limited to the
domain of the economy and trade. This action is a precondition to the definition of a
common external policy, which is other than an amicable "soft power". However the
rare texts which refer to the inclusion of the European project in the world highlight the
constant hesitation between the European Union's definition of itself as a community
of values and the assertion of its interests.

One of the cultural differences between the Americans and the Europeans lies in the
former's ability to demonstrate explicitly their collective preferences and interests long
term – which are extensive and will remain so[1]. The defence directive of 5th January 2012

---

1. «*The USA will in all likelihood remain « the first amongst the powerful » in 2030 thanks to heir pre-
eminence in many areas, a legacy of their role as leaders* » (Global Trends, National Intelligence Council,
Washington, 12/2012)

bears witness to this in its very title: *"Maintaining US global leadership"*. The speech by the re-elected President, delivered in Chicago in the night of 6th to 7th November 2012 was another illustration of this[2]. This is indeed a strategy of choice and anticipation.

In contrast with the two previous stages in European integration, nothing like this has yet occurred in Europe: the reconciliation of nations, followed by the successful extension of democratic *acquis* to the second third of the continent. In these two periods the Europeans shared and drove forward a motivating (geo)political project. This task is complete in the view of history and has enabled the extension of democratic values and the provision of the foundation economic growth in Central and Baltic Europe. Stability and security has been achieved at an unprecedented level including in support of our Russian neighbour. In contrast this double historic achievement which was European-centred undoubtedly explains the gap that has formed between the European elites and the way they have gauged the geostrategic changes ongoing in the world.

The final report on the future of Europe written by eleven foreign ministers[3] refers much more frequently to values than to interests. These are only mentioned twice in comparison with five references to the former. But the text stresses the dimension of the "global player" which has to rally its forces to build an integrated approach based on a series of themes (trade and economic affairs, development aid, enlargement and neighbourhood, migratory flows, climate negotiations and energy security). It also encourages the "quest" for a European defence policy. Crises and competition with other economies, other society models and other values are taken into account in this document, which calls on the Union to become a "real player" in the international arena, notably in terms of defence.

The conclusions of the European Council of December 2012 devote two pages and six paragraphs to the common security and defence policy, observing that the Union is already playing a regional (neighbourhood) and global role in the civil-military management of external crises: *"in a changing world, the European Union is called to assume greater responsibilities in peacekeeping and international security in order to guarantee the security of its citizens and for the promotion of its interests."* A mid-term assessment was made at the European Council in December 2013. The insistence on the development of its capabilities is in line with the demand made by the American allies addressed to the Europeans in its directive of 5th January 2012, inviting them to be "producers" of security rather more than "consumers" of it.

This approach rules out the rapid completion of a "white paper" on European defence which was planned for in the French white paper of 2008, whilst several European states like Poland are pleading for the revival of the European security strategy[4], arguing the USA's geostrategic re-orientation and the hardening of discourse on the part of the executive in Russia[5]. The prevailing analysis states that this kind of exercise is premature because of the pre-eminence of economic and financial issues and the extent of internal divergence.

---

2. « *You elected us to focus on your jobs, not ours. And in the coming weeks and months, I am looking forward to reaching out and working with leaders of both parties to meet the challenges we can only solve together. Reducing our deficit. Reforming our tax code. Fixing our immigration system. Freeing ourselves from foreign oil. This country has more wealth than any nation, but that's not what makes us rich. We have the most powerful military in history, but that's not what makes us strong. Our university, our culture are all the envy of the world, but that's not what keeps the world coming to our shores. What makes America exceptional are the bonds that hold together the most diverse nation on earth.* ».

3. Final Report of the Future of Europe Group of the Foreign Ministers of Austria, Belgium, Denmark, France, Italy, Germany, Luxembourg, the Netherlands, Poland, Portugal and Spain, 17th September 2012

4. Towards a new European Security Strategy, Food for thought, Buro Bezpieczenstwa Narodowego (BBN), Warsaw, October 2012

5. Described as *"growing assertiveness"*

A review of the 2003 strategy text recalls[6] nevertheless the pertinence of the analyses put forward a decade ago: the challenges of globalisation, terrorist threats, proliferation, continuing regional conflicts, failing States, organised crime and cyber-security and global warming. The text revealed a sense of anticipation as it added neighbourhood security challenges to distant threats: *"in the era of globalisation distant threats can be just as worrying as those immediately to hand such as North Korea, Southern Asia and proliferation"*. The settlement of the Israeli-Arab conflict was defined as a strategic priority for Europe and the quest for strategic partnerships with Japan, China, Canada and India were being planned. In terms of interests, continued commitment to the Mediterranean and the Arab world, the "good governance" of the countries lying on the Union's borders and the development of international institutions like the World Trade Organisation and the International Criminal Court were mentioned.

Interests which are rarely mentioned and never defined: some concrete proposals

Apart from these three exceptions the idea of European interests has never been clearly defined. The fear of divergence between hierarchies in State priorities, a kind of prevailing inhibition with regard to the USA which impose at best a strategic division of work, and finally the emphasis placed by political forces on a Union designed exclusively as a community of values thereby reducing its range of vision to its "soft power".

Some will regret that 2013 will pass without Mr Solana's document being reviewed beyond the mid-term assessment of 2008[7]. A first step would be to move forward in stages, establishing a short list of common or shared strategic interests. This would be a restricted but not an exclusive exercise and it would firstly be a part of the Franco-German partnership.

The 2003 document can only be a starting point: completing it would not be enough. We also have to review the Franco-German document written in view of the celebration of the 50th anniversary of the Elysée Treaty, the commitments made in the Franco-German Agenda 2020[8] and the various white papers and strategic reviews available in both States.

The main guidelines of this document would be as follows:

The starting point is the explanation or a reminder by each side of his own national interests as they stand, in a frank, lucid manner which then feed common interests. *"Every nation in a partnership has the right to its own interests; they have to be asserted peacefully."*[9] It is not a question of reducing them to the smallest denominator. Taking on board the "red lines" is realistic because they are legitimately different[10].

---

6. Une Europe sûre dans un monde meilleur. Stratégie européenne de sécurité, Brussels, 12th December 2003.

7. *Rapport sur la mise en œuvre de la stratégie européenne de sécurité – Assurer la sécurité dans un monde en mutation.* Brussels, 11/12/2008 (S407/08)

8. Adopted during the 12th Franco-German Council of Ministers, Paris, 4th February 2010

9. « *Histoire et l'avenir du partenariat franco-allemand en matière de sécurité* » Stéphane Bemelmans, Secretary of State at the Ministry of Defence of the Federal Republic of Germany, Institut des hautes études de défense nationale (IHEDN) 12th December 2012

10. France believes that it has the right to intervene in its former colonies except in North Africa (which shows that Libya cannot constitute a precedent), unlike Germany for whom the refusal of any type of intervention by the Bundeswehr in former colonies is a political axiom.

Once this premise has been accepted, because of changes in opinion in Germany,[11] which is drawing closer to the French analysis – talks must be held and the view of threats and strategic approaches have to be harmonised in order to develop a common strategic vision. This work should start with a common anticipation exercise in the face of the unpredictable, led for example by analysis and prospective structures in both States. Precedents already exist.[12]

The common strategic and geographic priorities should include:

– the upkeep of European strategic autonomy in terms of security (access to raw materials, security of maritime and land trade routes) and stock flows (vital networks and infrastructures);

– the draft of a long term plan for positive interaction with all neighbouring geo-political entities (enhanced and symmetrical cooperation with Maghreb, support to the transitions in the Mashriq, action that will promote European anchorage in Russia);

– commitment to joint action in crisis management in regions which are at a 3 to 6 hour flight from Paris, Brussels or Berlin;

– an integration strategy for middle-size emerging countries (China, Brazil and India apart) in the international system via strategic dialogue;

– a "third party" facilitating strategy in the half of the world extending to the east of Ormuz, in a part of Asia whose economic ascension is clearly visible and in which the EU has more than just trade interests; the Union cannot just content itself with an improbable duopoly between Washington and Beijing to co-manage future crises in regions which do not have any collective security structures and for whom neither the colonial period (Japan, China, Korea) nor the Second World War (Japan, Russia), nor the Cold War (Korean Peninsula) are over;

– the strengthening of multilateral organisations ensuring in particular the vigour of Romano-Germanic law;

– continued action in support of cooperation and development (11Bn€ in 2011). The Union is the first provider of development aid in the world: the aim is not primarily humanitarian but a contribution towards the long term stabilisation of neighbourhoods;

– the promotion and protection of trade interests. This falls within the domain of the community. Its scope is global. Given the asymmetry of the markets it is vital for it to emphasise the principle of reciprocity. The aim is also to protect and promote our industrial capabilities. As for the euro, its share in world reserves is rising (40% in the Central Bank of Russia, 26% in China, nearly 28% across the entire world), commensurate to the European Union's economic and trade weight, the leading partner in each of the major States.

The choice of geographic priorities, of political and diplomatic vision will be based on the distinction of degrees of interest which determines the means and the tools to deploy. It is clear that in terms of defence and the projection of forces whereby European States – which want to and can, act together as a regional player. But the European political model has a more global reach. Based on the rule of law and the joint exercise of sovereignty in some areas, it will increasingly become a reference in the eyes of other regional entities in quest of organisation (like ASEAN, where thought is being given to collective security framework for 2015, the African Union, whose support and external

---

11. Stances adopted by Wolfgang Ischinger (President of the Security Conference of Munich and Member for the French White Paper Committee on national defence and security 2012-3), Andreas Schockenhoff (Vice President of the CDU/CSU group and chairman of the Franco-German Friendship Group at the Bundestag) and Roderich Kiesewetter (Chair of the disarmament, arms control and non-proliferation sub-committee at the Bundestag) Strategic Franco-German Forum, IFRI and Konrad Adenauer Stiftung, Berlin, 29th November 2012

12. *L'Europe à trente et plus*, joint document by the Centre for Analysis and Planning and the Plannungstab, 1999; *L'Europe face aux défis de la mondialisation*, idem 2002

model are clearly European and South America, where the Union's experience is followed closely for domestic use).

The transition over to this third stage in the European project will suppose frank dialogue with the USA, outside of the NATO framework (which the present Secretary General would like to make the exclusive area for debate over affairs outside of the zone) and beyond simple task sharing. During the Cold War the continent's security was the reserve of our grand ally and economic power and prosperity that of the Europeans. Since 1991 and even since 2012 it seems that serious issues (Asia) have been managed by Washington (the famous pivot) and that Europeans have the task of emerging from the economic crisis (which affects American interests) and policing the region. Is this division of strategic tasks desirable? Our future depends on a choice: if the Union sees itself as a sub-section of the West and accepts this division of tasks, its added value is not worth much. If it believes that it is one of the centres in a multi-polar world and that it is taking on global interests, then it will enjoy real added value.

In this perspective of recasting the European project, progress in terms of European defence is a vital, necessary condition and an asset. Common action in this extremely sovereign area will bear witness to the confidence achieved between nations. Jean-Yves Le Drian, the French Defence Minister, sees in this a new means to cement European integration: *"I am convinced that it is European Defence that will be the final stone to be laid in peaceful Europe, because there cannot be any greater confidence between Member States than sharing, in the face of common challenges, the same ambition in terms of defence. This is our ambition."*[13]

---

13. Speech by Jean-Yves Le Drian at the Military School on 11th December 2012.

Europe and Globalisation:
the dangers and the assets

Nicole GNESOTTO

The euro crisis has been so strong that Europeans' have tended even more toward their traditional occupation of navel-gazing. But scrutiny of the Greek debt and the intricacies of the agreements made on banking supervision may indeed lead us to forget the main context i.e. globalisation to which the Union is trying to adjust. Of course globalisation significantly weakens what has been achieved, the comparative assets and the very model of European integration; this adds to the economic crisis a series of crises and challenges which are vital for the future of Europe. But globalization also brings to the fore the considerable assets held by the Union in the international arena, which political leaders have to acknowledge and make use of.

Globalisation presents three main dangers for the European Union

In many respects common sense is never wrong: the new world is full of extremely negative factors as far as the integration of Europe is concerned. The first of these dangers is the relative weakening of its influence in the international arena. Even though Europe is still the world's leading economic and trade power it is suffering the systematic erosion of its global importance. Shrinkage firstly concerns demography: in the 19th century, when it was at the height of its colonial expansion, Europe comprised 22% of the population. This is what China weighs now, whilst Europeans now only count for 7% of the world's population. This decline contributes towards the general shrinkage of the West in globalisation: in 2030, two inhabitants out of three in the world will be Asian. Globalisation is no longer and will no longer be fashioned mainly by the values, the power, the countries and the interests of the western block. For Europeans this demographic decline goes together with a net ageing of the population, unlike in the USA: in 2015 the number of deaths will be higher than the number of births in the Union[1], which runs alongside worrying prospects about innovation, of tensions on the labour market and the financing

---

1. Eurostat, 26th August 2008.

of retirement pensions. As for the weakening of the Union's economic power, the figures speak for themselves. The Union's share in world trade is declining to the benefit of the emerging countries and especially China. It decreased from 19% in 1999 to 16% in 2010[2]. The spectre of stagnation and even economic recession continues to haunt European performance, with growth prospects below 3% over the last five years and below 0.5% in 2013. As a comparison, the ascension of China is spectacular: in 2012 it represented 20% of the world's population, 30% of world growth, 10% of the world's wealth.[3] Finally in terms of energy the Union finds itself in a situation of alarming dependency: its economy is dependent to a total of 60% - in terms of oil and gas supplies – from three of the most unstable areas of the planet, Russia, the Middle East and Africa. And the Union's ability to influence these three regions politically is extremely limited.

The second danger which Europe faces is that of increasing political marginalisation, whether this implies international security management or the drafting of new world governance rules. On the one hand, the weakness of its political integration is preventing it from forming an effective hub of influence. As a Union it has no voice in the major international, economic or political institutions, except for within the WTO. But the Member States which take part in these bodies, whether this is the UN, the IMF or the G20, weigh relatively little in comparison with the USA or China. The Union sends no less than eight representatives to the G20, but this quantitative over-representation is paid for by notoriously low political influence. On the other hand the inexistence of a common foreign policy prevents the Union from influencing the development of its own environment. The Europeans were divided over the American intervention in Iraq in 2003, likewise they were unable to stand together in 2012 on acknowledging Palestine in the UN. France and the UK on the one side and Germany on the other, were divided over the military operation undertaken in Libya in March 2011. And when division is not clear, it is simply the lack of vision which prevails: the Israeli-Palestinian Peace Process, the development of Russia, the future of the Arab Revolutions, that of Afghanistan and Iraq after the American withdrawal, the future of nuclear Pakistan, are all major issues on which the Europeans prefer to be silent and to align with American decisions.[4] Indeed in many cases the Euro-American partnership embodied by NATO serves as an alibi to the Europeans for avoiding strategic responsibilities and delegating the permanent management of their regional security and planetary stability to the USA.

Together these dynamics add to the major crisis experienced by Europe at present. The crisis is primarily that of the European model as a whole: neither the citizens of Europe, nor the partners exterior to the Union now believe European integration to be an exemplary success. Impoverishment and the recession are now present in all Member States, feelings are emerging from the ashes of the past, solidarity is replaced by a new North/South split that could potentially cause the implosion of the eurozone (Greece), or cause political ill-feeling about the countries in difficulty (FRG), and even the withdrawal of one of the Member States (UK). The attractiveness of Europe, its famous "soft power" no longer bears the virtues of the past. In Europe itself citizens are also concerned about shortcomings in the European project, the effects of which the economic crisis accentuates. Primarily we might speak of an identity crisis: the trend towards enlargement since 2004 continues to confuse the frontiers of minimal solidarity, triumphantly lauded by Jacques Delors as "wanting to live together", which might define the Union's collective project. The border crisis in the East is supplemented by an identity crisis in the West, in that Europe no

---

2. Originally 19% of the world's exports in 1999, in 2010 is only counted for 16% of these exports (in comparison with 14 % for China, 11% for the United States). European Commission Report: The EU's Trade Policy, 2012 Toute l'Europe's website, 23rd February 2012.

3. Daniel Cohen, *Homo Economicus*, Albin Michel 2012, p. 113.

4. See the chapter by Nicole Gnesotto on the European Union in the collective work by Pierre Hassner, *Les relations internationales*, La Documentation française, coll. Les Notices, December 2012.

longer knows whether it should melt into a global West led by America or whether it can represent an identity axis with specific influence in the West. Then there is a crisis of efficacy. Europe, in the opinion of a growing number of citizens, no longer "delivers" the benefits which past generations have been accustomed to. Worse still it is often seen as an ultra-liberal player whose choices are held responsible for the economic and social impoverishment of the middle classes. Unemployment totals 10.7%[5] in the Union, where in 2012 there were nearly 17 million poor. The problem also lies in the functioning of the Union because the crisis has challenged the effectiveness and the pertinence of the Lisbon Treaty; once this was deemed to be the last major institutional effort to be made by the Union but it has been of marginal use in the management of the crisis, to the point that other treaties, Banking Union in 2012, Political Union tomorrow, have become necessary or are seen as such. It is finally a project crisis, in that there is no longer any agreement between the Europeans on the role and the finality of the Union in globalisation. Should it see itself as collective protection against the imbalances of globalisation? Or, conversely is it a springboard and a necessary stage to succeed within the world economy? Should the Union suffer the rules of the global game, at best protecting itself – at worst by avoiding them? Should it, on the contrary, aim to take part alongside other powers in drafting new rules for globalisation in the future? Originally, at the time of the Rome Treaties, the political project for European integration seemed clear: it was about Franco-German reconciliation and the return of prosperity to Western Europe. It was also legible when communism collapsed: it meant reconciliation between the two halves of Europe and helping towards the democratisation of the former communist countries. The project in the 21st century still lacks a major mobilising narrative.

Citizens are quite naturally the reflection of this profound crisis. Only 31% of them had a positive image of the Union in May 2012, whilst 50% believed the same in 2006[6]: this is the lowest rate recorded in five years. It is as if the feeling was spreading in Europe that the basic contract of the European adventure - that of political solidarity and shared economic growth, has been broken. The two major issues for the future of Europe are still without an answer: does the European project still make sense in the context of globalisation? Is growth still the pivot and the inevitable horizon for the economies in the West?

Real assets

However should we deduce from this that the European Union is doomed to disappear as an influential axis in globalisation? Obviously several factors force us to attenuate the darkness of these short and mid-term prospects. The first of these is of course the Union's economic power. Even in these times of major crisis Europe still weighs 19% in the world's GDP, which makes it the world's leading economic power. With nearly half a billion inhabitants it weighs much less than Asia demographically, but it represents a much bigger market than the USA or Japan. Since its enlargement to 27 it has become the biggest area of democratic stability on the planet, with revenue per capita of nearly $30,000. As for the eurozone, it alone ensures 20% of world trade[7] and if we include intra-community trade, the percentage rises to 42%.

The European Union's second asset is that its power of attraction is still considerable. From a monetary point of view the euro has become the world's second reserve currency, capitalising around 24% of the reserves in world trade in 2012 in comparison with 18%

---

5. Eurostat 30th November, quoted by www.touteleurope.eu

6. Conversely the percentage of negative opinions is increasing : it now lies at 28% against 17% in2006. Cf. Eurobarometer 77, published in July 2012, a survey undertaken in May 2012.

7. Thibault de Silguy, « Un peu de pédagogie sur l'euro », *Politique internationale*, n°128, Summer 2010.

when it was launched.[8] The Union's ability to produce standards, its legal know-how, also make it a player that is well adapted to the complexity of world economic competition. From a political point of view, the number of candidates for enlargement is constantly growing: in July 2013 Croatia will become the 28th Member State of the Union, whilst five other countries are on the candidate list (Iceland, Montenegro, Macedonia (FYROM), Serbia, Turkey). The eurozone crisis seems therefore to be one of public finances in some Member States and not a euro crisis or even of the attractiveness of the European project.

The third asset is that the European Union's mode of governance is striking because of the modernity of its principles: power sharing between all members, minimal redistribution of wealth between rich and poor, permanent negotiations in the quest for a legal order, these are the basic rules that have governed the functioning of Europe since 1950. And the driving principles of new world governance should be like this. In spite of their internal crisis Europeans have the keys to restructure the international system adapted to the complexity of globalisation, to the multiplication of the players involved, to the need for legitimate, effective institutions. If they were determined enough their power of influence in the debate over world governance might be considerable.

The fourth asset is the modernity of the principles of the European Union's action. First and foremost this is the case from an economic and financial point of view: a more moderate acceptance of the idea of the omnipotence of the markets, the need for a certain amount of political regulation in world trade and a minimal supervision of financial operators, together with a role for the State in support of a dose of protection and social cohesion – these are the factors of a European model for economic and social development which, with the crisis, have become more pertinent than the ultraliberal model put forward by the Anglo-Saxons. This is also true from a strategic point of view: the European vision of global security, proclaimed from 2003 on, in the European security strategy, continues to be confirmed by facts from across the world: that democracy cannot be forced upon a population, that military power is neither the only nor the leading instrument in crisis management, that dialogue with all and multilateral negotiation, are vital for the prevention of conflict, that poverty in the world is as destabilising as the violence of terrorism – this catalogue of common sense is indeed at the heart of the Union's strategic approach.

Above all the Union's major asset in globalisation involves its mass effect in terms of the nations. Not that these have become obsolete in terms of identification and political legitimacy – but in terms of collective, sustainable efficacy, their pretention to self-sufficiency is contradicted by the facts every day. Whether this entails climate change, future pandemics, the global issues that emerge with globalisation or solutions that can solve the economic crisis, or finally the response to major political strategic issues of the 21st century – the conditions for international security, support to the Arab revolutions, the fight to counter terrorism or nuclear proliferation – no solution is within the reach of one State alone – be it the most powerful on earth. Globalisation sacralises Nation-States as the legitimate players in international relations but it also shows their real inefficacy. Conversely, the European level, because of its coherence, size, its functioning structure, seems more promising in responding to the world challenges of globalisation, starting with the economic crisis itself.

Three conditions for recovery

How can we give value to these European assets? Beyond the economic situation and the necessary adjustment policies in the Member States, three conditions seem to govern the revival of a consensual, dynamic European project. The first supposes the clarification of the choice between a strategy of restoration and a strategy of renewal. Since 2008 the

---

8. Source IMF, quoted in *Le Figaro*, 29th June 2012.

leaders of Europe mainly seem to be attempting the restoration of the pre-crisis model: restoring the Maastricht Criteria and notably the rule of 3% thanks to the budgetary pact signed in 2012; restoring growth by the reform of public deficits and severe austerity measures. But nothing proves that growth and the purity of the Europe of Maastricht will be there at the end of the road. Hence the alternative advocated by others of a strategy to reshape European integration: whatever the flux of terms and intentions, the debate over Political Union renewal of the federal theme and proposals for greater Economic and Monetary Union, are all indicators of this strategy. France and Germany will play a decisive role in finding a more or less, harmonious solution to this dilemma.

The second condition entails rising above the historic split between the defence of national sovereignty and integration. The ascension of the European Council over the last two years bears witness to the enhancement of the national framework in comparison with the community institutions in terms of crisis management. The new budgetary pact is an intergovernmental treaty in the most traditional sense of the term, separate from the Treaties on the Union. France is the country where tension over State sovereignty is the most evident – in the realm of public rhetoric at least. But the reality of the situation is conversely proportional to policy making: in the world, as in Europe, nations have indeed lost the monopoly in terms of the efficacy and supervision of the major economic or political stakes. Both ordinary citizens and State players have proven impotent and disheartened before the world's upheavals. Indeed globalisation is a paradox in that it makes the national framework increasingly necessary and yet increasingly sterile, desirable and ineffective, politically vital and totally inadequate. Without challenging the nations' legitimacy the leaders of Europe ought to acknowledge that the European level has now become the true condition for their effectiveness.

The third condition entails collectively setting the question of democracy. Generally globalisation highlights this issue again: does the ongoing enrichment of the planet help towards democratising the world? Will democracy be an automatic outcome of China's growth? Is the finality of the revolutions that began in some Arab countries two years ago? Do new sustainable correlations exist on the other hand – which lie between a certain type of dictatorship and economic modernisation, in other words, a Chinese model that is able to compete with the universal model taken forward by western democracies? These unknowns raise the issue of world policy in a much more serious way than the American neo-conservatives pretended to do in the past with their theory of democratic dominoes set off by force if necessary. But the newest element involves the question being set within Europe itself –in other words one of the most democratic entities in the world. The populist parties, and even far right movements, are achieving high scores in many Member States: in Hungary, Romania, Bulgaria and Greece, where neo-Nazis made a remarkable breakthrough in June 2012 with 18 MPs and 7% of the vote, the Netherlands, Finland, Denmark, Austria and France. Whilst the democratization of the neighbouring countries is still the watchword in the Union's external policy, it is within its own fold, that paradoxically it is experiencing a sometimes violent challenge to the values and foundations of democracy itself. The ageing of the populations is linked to this, likewise the impoverishment of a share of the middle classes. The incomprehensible technification of the European debate, notably regarding budgetary or banking federalism together oppositely with the extremely real "effects" of the austerity policies also strengthens the aversion of many citizens to Brussels and the rise of ideologies advocating the return to the nation, the rejection of foreigners and the hatred of globalised economic liberalism. It is urgent for Europe to break the silence and its official torpor in the face of this groundswell.

***

Reviving growth, sharing sovereignty, defending democracy: it would be preferable that these principles feed the various technical roadmaps being drafted to emerge from the eurozone crisis. Indeed they might be fleshed out and provide virtue to the European governance model. And especially, they might be used as the base for the new political narrative which the citizens of Europe are expecting so that they can love Europe again in a globalised world.

Second Chance for Barack Obama:
A Sarajevo Moment

Simon SERFATY

Barack's Obama re-election in November 2012 was convincing. Yet, the ambivalence shown by many of his most loyal supporters – with less enthusiastic crowds, a smaller margin of victory, and a less serene tone than four years ago – points to the disappointment of a large part of American public opinion. Still, Obama learned a great deal over the past four years. And what he learned augurs well for his ability to assert his place in history with the audacity which he had initially claimed.[1]

It is in this non-partisan context that his triumph should be examined. At this particularly difficult time it will be good to count on the experience of an outgoing president, rather than be at the mercy of a newcomer whose untested ideas often depend on rigid advisors – a "new Bush administration," it was already said about a hypothetical Romney administration during the presidential campaign. Jimmy Carter in January 1977, Ronald Reagan in 1981, and Bill Clinton in 1993 all denied their predecessors a second term in office; but each also found it difficult to adapt to a world that was not consistent with their campaign rhetoric: Carter, the moralist, who promised to renew his country's moral superiority – as "a right of birth" – which the Soviet Union could not hope to match or challenge; Reagan, a realist who rebelled against the humiliation felt by middle America, and wanted to bring about the collapse of its adversary – the "empire of evil" – which he despised; and Clinton, the pragmatist, who hoped to return to the fundamentals – "the economy, stupid" – and believed he could somehow put the world aside.

The dynamics of change in U.S. foreign policy are not governed by the schedule of presidential elections: Jealous of its prerogatives, and always eager to surprise, History moves to its own clock. In the area of foreign affairs therefore, the most significant changes do not unfold from one American administration to the next but within the same administration. Thus, Dwight D. Eisenhower's foreign policy began to emerge

---

1. This essay was initially inspired by the remarks made at a conference on "the American Presidential elections" in Lille on 25th and 26th October 2012. See Julian Fernandez ed., *Élections américaines: Un bilan* (Paris: Editions Pedrone, 2013). A shorter version of this essay was published under the title "Une seconde chance pour Barack Obama" *Revue de Défense Nationale*, no. 756 (January 2013): 48-58. This is an adaptation of a French text published in L'État de l'Union. Rapport Schuman 2013 sur l'Europe, Lignes de Repères, 2013.

during the last two years of the Truman administration, after the Korean War had forced Truman to give his vision the global dimension which he had previously rejected. Similarly, Eisenhower's policies, too, were carried over into the Kennedy administration, whose agenda was overwhelmed by the legacy left by Kennedy's predecessor. Later, Reagan's abandonment of detente confirmed Carter's own adjustments late in his presidency in response to the hostage crisis in Iran and the Soviet intervention in Afghanistan. But Reagan's second presidential term soon became an era of détente and disarmament – with Reagan ending his presidency as a leading architect for a peaceful end to the Cold War, which was ultimately completed by George H.W. Bush.

More recently, the changes from Bush to Bush after the general elections of November 2004 were more significant than from Bush to Obama after the latter's election. Thus, the departure of the American forces at a date which only the Iraqi government could make certain was for the most part negotiated by President Bush in 2008, and a military pivot towards the war in Afghanistan, meant to ensure a "decent interval" before an American withdrawal promised for 2014, can also be attributed to an outgoing President Bush no less than an incoming President Obama. The same applies to the return of multilateralism, announced by George W. Bush when he turned to a 5+1 group (namely, the permanent members of the UN Security Council, plus Germany) to end the nuclear stalemate with Iran, and then confirmed by his endorsement of a G20 that was hastily convened in November 2008 as the result of a French initiative and while the financial crisis was at its worst.

In 2012, therefore, the consequences of Mitt Romney's victory on American foreign policy should have been played down. "Neither angel nor beast" – Pascal's expression applied to both candidates. In any case, at election time only one American voter in twenty made of foreign policy a priority issue. As the presidential campaign was drawing to a close, it was increasingly difficult to distinguish one candidate from the other: as Obama failed to assimilate his rival with "George W," he toughened up his own tone, on Iran for example; and as Romney, too, was unable to reduce the outgoing President to a caricature of Carter, he adopted many of his opponent's positions, including on the question of troops withdrawal from Afghanistan. One wonders what difference Romney's victory would have made, notwithstanding his immense unpopularity in Europe and elsewhere.

Re-elected, Barack Obama is starting a *mano a mano* with History: from now on, this is his only rival and his last ambition. This condition is not unusual: it is during their second mandate that American presidents have an opportunity to ensure their status as statesmen. Consider Truman and even Nixon – but not Eisenhower, whose reputation was already well established before his first election – and consider, too, Clinton's late efforts in the Middle East, where he hoped to find absolution for a presidency marred by his personal indiscretions. In comparison with his predecessors, who became what they did not want to be (harder in Carter's case, softer as far as Reagan is concerned) Obama's second mandate offers him a second chance to become what he had hoped to be, and thus justify, however belatedly, a prematurely granted Nobel Prize.

Teething Problems

That Barack Obama came to power in difficult conditions is well acknowledged. Suffice it to point to the totality of the crisis that awaited him from the moment he was elected and even before he entered office: America's declining confidence in its own government, and the world's in America. In 1933 Franklin D Roosevelt was able at least to choose between reviving the American economy and restoring a world order that appeared increasingly at risk after the election of Adolf Hitler in January of that year; his "New Deal" was a project to bring society out of the Great Depression of the 1930's while letting Europe succumb to its suicidal tendencies. In 1969 it was the opposite for Nixon: bogged down in the Vietnam War, which was going from bad to worse, and exposed to growing Soviet pressures that gained from widespread perceptions of a decline in American power, Nixon chose to make the world his priority, like his former rival, John Kennedy, had wanted to do in 1961.

Lacking the luxury of choice between the national and the international, Obama was welcomed in 2008 as the providential leader – the "great magician" who, having rid the country of the universally unpopular George W Bush, would put everything right by simply entering the stage. He would end wars, including religious wars, negotiate with adversaries, bridge inequalities, and save the environment – all of this and more. In short, he would help America dream again and restore his nation as the model it was meant to be to the world.

Unrealistic expectations guarantee widespread disappointments. Obama read like a fictional character. In France, he could have been assimilated initially to Dr Rieux, a character created by Albert Camus to put an end to "the plague," but he soon turned out to be more like Meursault, "the stranger" who kept his distance from those who, like France's Nicolas Sarkozy, wanted to be his "pal." In the United States, Obama was giving visibility to Ralph Ellison's "invisible man" – Ellison the noted black American author, successor to Richard Wright and the predecessor of James Baldwin: a man who remained "invisible" because he lacked the audacity to live out his "infinite potential." Surely, such resignation did not apply to Barack, who was given at birth the "baraka" that was to enable him to achieve his ambitions. Boasting "brothers, sisters, nieces, nephews, uncles and cousins of every race spread across three continents" Obama declared himself "a citizen of the world" – more, therefore, than just an American citizen which he was nonetheless proud to be in a world that had forgotten how to love the America that he intended to restore.[2]

Obama has been unique in that he was both the most thoughtful and the least prepared president in the country's modern history. Aware of his relative inexperience – he had hesitated before announcing his candidacy in 2007 – he acted with extreme prudence after his election rather than with the audacity which he continued to assert in his speeches. His first goal was to avoid an early error, like Kennedy in the Bay of Pigs in the spring of 1961 and even George W Bush after the events of 11th September 2001 – situations for which neither president was responsible but which were to define their respective presidencies: Kennedy's when the Cuban missile crisis threatened the country's survival in the fall 1962, and Bush's when a bad and worsening war in Iraq threatened to ruin it after March 2003. In September 2009 Barack Obama's inaction while demonstrations shook Teheran is one example, among others, of the wait-and-see approach he favoured during his first year in office. The "new beginning" he had promised might come later provided that there was no "false start" along the way of a "second chance" during another term in office.

To be sure, Obama restored his country's international image – a brand name that his predecessor had tarnished during the previous eight years. Abroad, Obama has been loved for who he is and represents, in spite of what he does or does not do: a "European President" in Europe where 75% of the citizens would have voted for him (and only 8% for Romney according to pre-election polls;[3] but also the "first world president" because of his African father and childhood in Asia. This is again a character born out of fiction – Henry de Montherlant's "universal man," an identity which would be confusing if it were not for the fact that a vote for Obama and the image he embodies proved to be a vote for America and the image it represents.

2. Simon Serfaty, « Obama peut-il réussir ? » *Politique Internationale*, no. 127 (Spring 2010): 287-299.

3. The German Marshall Fund, *Transatlantic Trends*, Key Findings, 2012, pp. 3 et and 28. In France the preference for Obama reached 89% (and 87% in Germany).

Even given this distinction, Obama's difficult apprenticeship since 2009 recalls that of Jimmy Carter. Hell is paved with good intentions – in this case, with a predilection for the desirable over the doable. In 2009, the newly elected President Obama said what he was going to do – in Strasbourg, in Cairo, in Prague, in New York, in Stockholm and elsewhere – but in the end he did not do much of what he had said – abolishing nuclear weapons, bringing peace to the Middle East, building a new partnership with Europe, a new start with Russia, reforming the multi-lateral institutions, and more. Killing Osama Ben Laden is not the sum of a grand foreign policy as Vice-President Joseph Biden pretended during the presidential campaign; nor is ending a war or two enough to put an end to all wars, as Obama has claimed as well.

On the whole, Obama, who had hoped to be a transformational president, may have been too timid. In the Middle East especially, after a visionary speech in Cairo in the Spring 2009, where he was received with unprecedented public enthusiasm, he remained surprisingly passive. During and since the "Arab Spring," past his eloquent words of approval he acted cautiously: "leading from behind," whether behind the French-initiated, UN-sponsored intervention in Libya in the spring 2011; or after Israel's military action in Gaza in the fall 2012, when the new regime in Egypt appeared to lead; or while awaiting a difficult end point in Syria, where Obama, mistrustful and hesitant, has preferred not to get involved. The same sense of some unfinished business follows Obama's anti-nuclear speech in Prague in the spring 2009, or repeated promises of a "re-set" in U.S. relations with Russia, or over relations such notable adversaries as Iran and North Korea, where offers of a renewed dialogue were not met. In short, beyond the two wars inherited from his predecessor Obama has been moved in "the world as it is" and become a realist in spite of himself, comforted by a good conscience that reminds him that the end justifies the means.[4]

The New Obama

"Yes I can," Obama pledged throughout the 2008 presidential campaign, with reference to his ability to be elected; "Yes, I must," a matured Obama now insists as reflective of his determination to act. Like Bill Clinton after his re-election in November 1996, when he preferred Madeleine Albright, the first woman to be appointed Secretary of State, over Richard Holbrooke, deemed too abrasive – but also like George W. Bush after his re-election in November 2004, who replaced Colin Powell with the loyal "Condi" Rice – Obama would have preferred his protégée Susan E Rice to Senator John Kerry in replacement of outgoing Secretary of State Hillary Clinton. The first presidential term made room for "a team of rivals" – but the second term calls for "a band of brothers." with whom the outgoing President can build a legacy History will be able to call his own.

During much of the year 2012, Governor Romney attacked his rival as a prophet of decline who did not respect his country's exceptional nature and character. In fact, of course, Obama represents the best of American exceptionalism: in 2009, his Nobel Prize should have been awarded to the American Union for overcoming its history of racism and electing Obama as its first African American president. In so doing, the United States gave the rest of the world a lesson in democracy. Rather than doubting or denigrating American power, Obama appreciates the facts of, and the need for an American superiority which he wants to preserve *in toto*, and which he views as vital to the emerging world order. But Obama also acknowledges the limits of the nation's power in a time of austerity, as well as an erosion of national will in a time of retrenchment. Even a nation

---

4. Simon Serfaty, "The Limits of Audacity", *The Washington Quarterly* (Autumn 2009); Ryan Lizza, "The Consequentialist", *The New Yorker*, May 2, 2011, p. 44-55.

without peers cannot act for long without allies: by instinct since his first inauguration, and out of experience since, Obama is all the more prepared to acknowledge a post-American order as he does not perceive anything that is fundamentally anti-American in any such order. Indeed, the reverse may well be true as it is rather America's partners that seem least prepared to adapt to a downgrading of American power – in Europe to serve as a counterpart to its own weaknesses, and in Asia to act as a counterweight to a surging China.

In a changing world, a multitude of states, institutions, and non-governmental organizations (NGOs) form a zero-polar structure in which even a preponderant power like the United States cannot act alone: allies and partners are required, but they have to be not only willing but also capable, not only capable but also relevant, and not only relevant but also compatible. By his own admission, Obama does not have for Europe "that special spark" which would help him feel at home there – since he grew up elsewhere and dreamt of other things, in Africa and Asia. With the European Union (EU) bogged down in institutional debates that Obama does not really understand, and with the states of Europe burdened by the relative mediocrity of its leaders with whom Obama does not spontaneously feel at ease, Europe does not look like a safe bet in comparison with other regions with which he can identify more easily and towards which he would rather turn. At least for the time being, however, a new strategy that would suggest a switch to Asia remains a long term speculation, relative to Europe which continues to pay high dividends on the strategic investments made by the United States after World War II and throughout the Cold War.

No less than his predecessors, Obama will continue to offer a right of first refusal to the states of Europe and their Union (in which Great Britain would hopefully remain, and which Turkey might possibly join): completing Europe is a requirement to reforming the Alliance. There is little new in the American preference for a united Europe as its privileged partner. This was John F. Kennedy's "Grand Design" in July 1962, when, barely five years after the signature of the Rome Treaties, Kennedy envisioned an "Atlantic Community" between his country and a united Europe; Henry Kissinger, too, spoke of this community when he launched the "Year of Europe" in April 1973 by inviting the members of the European Community, which had just completed its first enlargement to three new members (including Great Britain), to do their part in conjunction with their American partner; later, George H.W. Bush invited a newly-united Germany, firmly positioned within the EU established by the Maastricht Treaty, to assume the "co-leadership" of the new world order announced by the end of the Cold War. Finally, a similar commitment was also made by Barack Obama in April 2009, when he pleaded the cause of an enhanced partnership at the European Parliament, which hosted him in Strasbourg on his first official journey to Europe.

By fully accepting the end of the post-Cold War "unipolar moment" and by rejecting an "imperial temptation" to which George W. Bush succumbed at a high cost to him and the nation, Obama has relieved America from the burdens of unilateral action, assumed too readily by his predecessor in the wake of the dramatic events of 9/11. The wars waged since then having shown the difficulties of bypassing and acting without other powers, Obama's America is settling with and among them, beginning with the 33 other members of NATO and the EU, including the 21 European states, which are members of both institutions. Of course this transatlantic G2 faces sizeable competitors from the ascending rest of the world. But too much history (like the 1962 war between China and India) and too little geography (like hundreds of millions of Chinese on the doorstep of an immense, under-populated slice of Russian territory), or conversely too little history and too much geography (as is the case between these three states and Brazil), is impeding a sustainable strategic *entente* between the rising powers, which would all prefer closer relations with the United States and Europe than with each other.

Putting in place a better multilateral governance, through the United Nations or as part of the G20, for example, and forming coalitions with other states whose commitments reflect their interests and even values, is Obama's preference. Having attacked his predecessor's unilateralism, and not having fully experienced the post-war bipolar structure, the U.S. president can readily adapt to a multipolar world, whose flexibility suits him intellectually, even though he knows little of it historically.[5]

A Sarajevo Moment

The time is over when a small island could conquer and defy the whole world, like "Great" Britain or "Imperial" Japan; over, too, is the time when a state defined exclusively by its military power, like the Soviet Union, could hope to achieve a global hegemony without regard to its regional history; also over is the era when a government could blackmail its partners by denying them access to resources at affordable prices, or equal access to its markets; and surely gone is the time when two countries that knew little or nothing of each other, like the United States and the Soviet Union, could transform the history of those regions, in Eastern or Western Europe, which they occupied, either by invitation or by force. Finally, over, too, is the time when "cultivating one's garden" was a lucrative business and "gaining time" a profitable strategy. These situations seem to belong to a distant past – not only another century but another millennium.

Once again, then, History stands at a crossroads. Admittedly, these moments occur periodically, but the totality of the changes now underway is rare. Unlike 1815 there is no pre-revolutionary world to restore in a European Concert; unlike 1871 there is more than one rising power to manage and absorb; unlike 1919 there are no vanquished powers to punish; unlike 1945 there are no allies to save from each other; unlike 1991, there is no triumph to celebrate; unlike 2001 there is no "axis of evil" to annihilate; and unlike 2008 there does not seem to be a "providential" man to heal the world in want of history.

It is an "American moment" insists Hillary Clinton, and "we have to be everywhere."[6] And everywhere she went – a Secretary of State who wanted to lend an importance and seriousness to all the countries she visited, including the smallest, and to all the questions she addressed or which she negotiated, from the most traditional to the most innocuous. That was her vision of an integrated world, to be lived in real time and in all its dimensions. But by wanting to be everywhere even Hillary Clinton exhausted herself, gradually realising that her means did not match her energy, her energy did not match her will, and her will did not match her role after she had lost her presidential bid. Similarly, the time is also over for the image of an America which believed that it could be everything at once – policeman, midwife, foreman, banker, surgeon, priest, educator, and more.

Before asserting a post-American structure, extended to a greater number of countries with varying power and influence, there is, however, a region whose stabilisation cannot be left to lagging projects like the European Union or nuisance powers like China and Russia or struggling countries like Turkey. Obama's stated preferences "towards justice," which he asserted in Stockholm in December 2009, will have to wait after all, as will some elusive "pivot" towards Asia. In and beyond 2013, the "American moment" will be

---

5. See Simon Serfaty, "The Folly of Forgetting the West", *Policy Review*, no. 174 (August/September 2012): 35-48, and "The West in a World Recast", *Survival*, vol. 54, no. 6 (December 2012-January 2013): 29-40.

6. "A conversation with Hillary Clinton," "Council on Foreign Relations, Washington DC", September 8, 2010. Stephanie McCrummen, « The secretary of 1,000 things », *Washington Post*, November 26, 2012.

played out in the Middle East, and it is there that Obama will have to show his ability to guide the course of History: echoing the previous century when the centre of geopolitical gravity lay in the Balkans, where the long agony of the Habsburg Empire, started in 1815, was about to end in a suicidal war triggered by a relatively minor act of terror.

Making of the Middle East the central region of Barack Obama's second term is not a happy perspective. About to end the two wars directly linked to September 11, and after an "Arab Spring" which shaped a timid democratic opening for the countries involved, America is tired of this region: barely one American in two, for example, thinks that their country has an interest in arming rebels to bring down the Assad regime in Damascus.[7] After two enormously costly wars that went from bad to worse, the temptation to draw away from this region is understandable; but it now also seems conceivable as the United States seems about to emerge as the world's leading gas and oil producing country (by 2015 and 2017 respectively). Worse yet, here, in the Middle East, is a region where Obama appears to be the most handicapped, openly mistrusted by the Israeli government while paradoxically remaining compromised in the Arab world. From 1956 in Suez to 2006 in Iraq, it is there, too, that the United States has been most isolated, its leadership most controversial, and its results the most challenged. To an extent, the country's intimacy with the state of Israel has often been the reason for this condition, presented as the main obstacle to a sustainable structure for the region: 59% of Americans think well of Israel, as opposed to only 34% of the Europeans, and often less or much less elsewhere.

However urgent the Israeli-Palestinian conflict remains, it is not the most urgent priority in the region. Even more pressing and possibly more decisive is the crisis with Iran – a slow moving missile crisis that is drawing ever closer to its denouement. With an Israeli military strike increasingly feared in 2013 or soon afterwards, time is running out for bilateral negotiations that can satisfy an Israeli ally which the United States can neither abandon nor control. The stakes are too high to ignore the risks of any such conflict, from which no State would be spared, including the United States: for a clash with Iran would precipitate an oil crisis affecting already weakened economies and fragile institutions, political shocks that would worsen existing populist trends, and geopolitical alignments which might cause all kinds of "pivots" between large and smaller powers responding differently to the events in the Gulf. The echoes of earlier crises are amplified by the many new instabilities that have dominated the entire region since the Arab Spring: with nations in transition like Egypt, which might reappraise their treaties and alliances; rogue states like Syria, which might welcome a regional war as an unexpected rescue from its worsening civil conflict; failing states like Libya, which are sinking into chaos; and even, further away, states like Pakistan, whose nuclear weapons might be seized as security of last resort by Arab states like Saudi Arabia, which lack such capabilities and might seek new guarantees other than from the United States.

In sum, this is a Sarajevo moment: too many states, too many governments, too many groups, and quite simply too many people in the Middle East seem to have or perceive an interest in a conflict among their neighbours or between their rivals, with each conflict a possible catalyst for an explosion elsewhere. Disturbing echoes of the past: one hundred years ago, too, the inability of the heads of State and government to settle any of the "small" conflicts in the Balkans led to a "great" war which turned the first half of the 20th century into a bloodbath. This is also what makes of Obama's second chance the appointment with History which he had hoped for, and which he cannot postpone. It is in Europe's interest to help him in this task – for which he could surely use the experience and the capabilities of the European states and their Union – to avoid the threat of war which hangs over the entire region and, should it take place, manage and end the conflict before it runs out of control.

---

7. Bruce Stokes, "Americans on Middle East turmoil: Keep us out of it," Pew Global Attitudes Project, December 14, 2012.

Why the transatlantic economy still matters

Joseph QUINLAN

The post-crisis world of today remains challenging for the United States and Europe. Both parties are struggling to heal and recovery from the financial crisis of 2008 that has left deep scars on both sides of the Atlantic. Europe's sovereign debt crisis has crippled and divided the continent, and threatens to condemn Europe to a "lost decade" of low or stagnant growth. The outlook in the United States is not as dire although the aftershocks from the "Made in America" financial crisis have steered the U.S. economy into a slow-growth rut. The current U.S. economic recovery is one of the weakest on record.

Against this backdrop, many believe the U.S.-European economic alliance does not carry the same global heft and sway as in years past. This is understandable. When the feeble-growth, ageing and massively indebted nations of the transatlantic economy are juxtaposed against the vibrant, confidence and capital-rich developing nations, lead by China, it is easy (and logical) to jump to the conclusion that the future belongs to the "Rest" while the sun sets on the "West". Central to this narrative: that the transatlantic economy no longer matters, its global power and influence usurped and sapped by the uber-economies of China, India, South Africa and others.

Nothing could be further from the truth.

Yes, the global brand of the "West" has been devalued by financial crisis of 2008. True, growth prospects in the developing nations are brighter than those in the developed nations. And undeniably, the economic gravity of the world is shifting east to west. But all of that said, the transatlantic economy remains, and will remain, at the core of the global economy for some time.

Simply put, the global economy cannot grow or function properly without a strong transatlantic partnership. The health of the global economy is still largely dependent on the vital signs of the United States and Europe, a critical fact not lost on China, whose export-led economy has struggled over the past two years thanks to falling European and U.S. demand for Chinese goods. Weak demand in both the United States and Europe has rippled across the developing world, denting export growth, impairing job creation, reducing personal spending, and lowering budget revenues in variety nations in Asia, Latin America, central Europe, Africa and the Middle East.

The developing nations have failed to "de-couple" from the West due to the importance and primacy of the transatlantic economy. The global economy will continue to underperform as long as the transatlantic economy underperforms.

The primacy of the transatlantic economy

There is probably nothing more uninspiring in economics than to talk about the transatlantic economy. The latter is not in the vocabulary of Wall Street, is rarely mentioned in popular media outlets, and is on the radar screen of a very few in Washington. This negligence is understandable given the universal assumption that the future lies with the emerging markets.

But however unglamorous the transatlantic economy may appear to the mainstream, the economy that spans the Atlantic is the largest and most powerful economic entity in the world. The Atlantic commercial artery – valued at roughly $5 trillion in 2011 – is massive because no two economic entities in the world have been more melded together or economically fused that the United States and Europe over the past few decades.

It is foreign direct investment – the deepest form of global integration – that binds the transatlantic economy together, not trade. The latter, the cross-border movement of goods and services, is a shallow form of integration and often associated with the early phases or stages of bi-lateral commerce. In contrast, a relationship that rests on the foundation of foreign investment is one where both parties are extensively embedded and entrenched in each other's economies. This is a relationship that is more job-creating, income-producing and wealth-generating for both parties. The transatlantic economy epitomizes this type of economic integration, with the United States and Europe each other's largest foreign investors.

There is nothing as formidable as the combined economic strengths of the U.S. and Europe. To this point, the transatlantic economy accounts for nearly 40% of world GDP, is home to the largest and wealthiest consumer market in the world, is at the forefront of global foreign direct investment and M&A, and continues to set the pace when it comes to global competitiveness and technological change.

In terms of trade, it is the U.S. and the European Union that matters, with the former the largest single importer in the world, while the latter, the EU, represents collectively the largest import market anywhere. In 2011, the United States accounted for just over 12% of world imports, while the EU accounted for over 40% of the total. That compares with a share of 11-10% from China.

That the transatlantic economy drives and dictates global commerce is underpinned by the size and wealth of the U.S.-EU economic alliance.

Forgotten by many during Europe's financial crisis, the EU remains the largest economic entity in the world. What started out as a loosely configured market of six nations (Belgium, France, West Germany, Italy, Luxembourg, and the Netherlands) in the late 1950s is now an economic behemoth whose economic output accounted for 27.3% of world GDP based in nominal US dollars in 2011, while its share of world GDP based on a PPP basis was 21.2%. Both figures are larger than America's global share of world output.

What's more, five years from now, according to estimates from the International Monetary Fund, Europe's share of world output is still expected to be around 17% of the total. Hence, notwithstanding the rise of China and the emerging power of the BRICs, Europe will remain one of the largest economic entities in the world over the balance of this decade. Combined with the U.S., the transatlantic economy is still expected to account for nearly 35% of world GDP in 2017.

What's more, it's not just the size of the U.S. and Europe that sets them apart. Another key differentiator: the transatlantic consumer is among the wealthiest on earth, with the per capita incomes of both the U.S. and EU among the highest in the world. And wealth drives consumption; hence Europe accounts for roughly 30% of global personal consumption expenditures, a share slightly larger than the United States (27.7%). Combined, the transatlantic economy accounts for nearly 60% of personal consumption; the comparable share of the so-called BRICs (Brazil, Russia, India and China) is just 13.6%. The preponderance of global consumption in the West leaves the export-led developing nations dependent and exposed to economic trends in the U.S. and Europe.

Yet another strength of the transatlantic economy lies with the fact that many economies remain among the most competitive in the world. For instance, in the latest rankings of global competitiveness from the World Economic Forum, seven European countries were ranked among the top 10, and five more among the top twenty-five. Switzerland ranked first, Sweden ranked 3rd, Finland 4th, Germany 6th, the Netherlands 7th, Denmark 8th , the United Kingdom 10th, Belgium 15th, Norway 16th, France 18th, Austria 19th, and Luxembourg 23rd. The United States ranked 5th.

One specific strength of the transatlantic economy lies with the innovation and knowledge-based activities of such innovative leaders like the United States, and Switzerland, Denmark, Sweden, Finland and Germany in Europe, all ranked as innovation leaders in Europe according to the Innovation Union Scoreboard for 2011.

In that R&D expenditures are a key driver of value-added growth, it is interesting to note that Europe-based companies accounted for roughly 25% of total global R&D in 2010 and 2011. That lagged the share of the United States (32% in 2011) but was well ahead of the global share of R&D spending in Japan (11.4%), China (13.1%), and India (2.8%). In other words, when it comes to R&D spending, the transatlantic economy leads the way.

Innovation requires talent and on this basis, Europe is notably holding its own relative to other parts of the world. Europe leads the world in producing science and engineering graduates, with the EU, according to the latest data from the National Science Board, accounting for 18% of global natural science graduates in 2008, the latest available data. America's share was 10% of the total. The EU's share of global engineering degrees (17%) was even more impressive relative to America's – with the later accounting for just 4% of global engineering degree.

Yet another attribute of the transatlantic economy lies with the entity's ease of doing business. And on this basis both the U.S. and Europe rank highly, with 12 European economies recently ranked in the World Bank's top 25 most business-friendly nations. Denmark ranked 5th overall, followed by Norway (6th), the United Kingdom (7th), Iceland (9th), Ireland (10th), Finland (11th), Sweden (14th), Georgia (16th), Germany (19th), Latvia (21st), Macedonia (22nd), and Estonia (24th). Out of the top 50 rankings, European firms made up nearly half, with 24 nations placed in the top fifty. The U.S. ranked fourth, trailing only New Zealand, Hong Kong and Singapore.

China, meanwhile, ranked 91st in terms of ease of doing business, while Russia ranked 120th, Brazil and India were even further behind, ranked 126th and 132nd, respectively. The nations just mentioned are regularly hyped as among the most dynamic in the world, yet strong real GDP growth does not necessarily equate to a favorable environment for business. Neither does growth equate to competitiveness, technological innovation and internet-readiness, critical ingredients of prosperity both the U.S. and Europe score well on.

In the end, a large share of growth from the developing nations remains dependent on growth from the transatlantic economy. Think of the latter – the U.S. and the European Union – as the horse of the global economy, and the developing nations still the cart in many respects. Nations like China, South Africa and Russia will not emerge as global economic leaders until they shift their economies away from export – or investment – led growth towards more consumption – and service – led activities. This process is underway but is nevertheless a multi-year endeavor, meaning the primacy of the transatlantic economy will extend will into this decade.

A strong global economy needs a strong transatlantic economy

Given all of the above, no two economies are as important as the United States and Europe. Collectively, there is no greater economic force in the world that can affect change and steer the global economy.

Over the past sixty years, the transatlantic economy has been the anchor of the global economy and the prime example of the mutual benefits of deep cross border integration, or globalization via foreign direct investment. By standing together, by working towards common goals, by driver global growth and prosperity, and by not allowing specific issues from creating deep divisions within, the United States and Europe have succeeded in creating a global economic system that has lifted millions out of poverty and given millions more hope of a better tomorrow. The western-built system has benefited enormously the likes of China, India, Brazil and other developing nations, and hence their reluctance, despite countervailing rhetoric, for a radical overhaul of the post-crisis global economy. In the end, the developed and developing nations need each other to succeed.

Has the economic monopoly of the west over the global economy waned since the crisis? Answer: absolutely. But the argument that the transatlantic economy does not matter and that the United States and Europe have been relegated to secondary status among the global economic elite is false. Just ask the Chinese manufacturer whose exports to the EU have plummeted over the past few years; the Russian oil trader whose profits have dived on account of the EU recession; or the South African miner whose revenue has declined on weaker global demand owing to weak demand from the U.S. and the European Union. These parties would unequivocally agree that at the core of the global economy still lie the United States and Europe.

And the core of the global economy could become even stronger if the United States and Europe re-commit and redouble their efforts to deepen and strengthen the ties that bind the two parties together. Specifically, the U.S. and Europe should take the next step in solidifying transatlantic ties with a free trade agreement between the U.S. and the EU, a bi-lateral deal that has gained momentum on both sides of the Atlantic in the six months.

While average tariffs on trade in goods is already quite low between the U.S. and EU – less than 3%--a transatlantic free trade agreement that eliminates or reduces various tariffs and non-tariff barriers, and helps harmonize and standardize various industry rules and regulations between the two parties, would go a long way in further cementing the ties that bind the United States and Europe together. Such a deal would promote economic growth, and create jobs and income for workers of both parties. Importantly, such a deal would galvanize corporate leaders on both sides of the ocean and breathe fresh life into an economic relationship in need of a spark or catalyst to promote further economic integration. Finally, a deal would embellish the global economic competitiveness of both the United States and Europe relative to the rest of the world.

A transatlantic free trade agreement, in other words, would be a win-win deal for the United States and Europe, strengthen the transatlantic economy as the core of the world economy.

In the end, there may be a new world economic order taking shape but early in the 21st century, the global economy still rests squarely on the shoulders of the United States and Europe.

Europe and the Arab Revolution:
a missed opportunity?

Jean-Pierre FILIU

The Union for the Mediterranean (UPM) was, on the one hand, the result of a compromise between the desire to preserve the achievements of the Euro-Mediterranean process launched in Barcelona in 1995 and a three-fold calculation on the part of Nicolas Sarkozy on the other. For the French President this meant a project-based depoliticization of the Euro-Mediterranean process, thereby uncoupling the Euro-Israeli relationship from the Israeli-Arab Peace Process and offsetting Turkey, whose European integration has been delayed indefinitely.

This initiative led to the UPM's inaugural summit on 13th July 2008 with the participation, amongst others, of Bachar al-Assad, and the formalisation of the Sarkozy-Mubarak co-presidency. The "civil society" chapter in the Euro-Mediterranean process, which had already been undermined by the Arab governments and their GONGOs[1], were only of incantatory value. The French President was able to make successive declarations about the *"freedom progressing in Tunisia"*[2] or about *"excellent relations in all respects"* with Egypt[3], three months before elections that were marked by massive fraud and six months before the fall of Mubarak.

Libyan Division

The democratic uprising experienced by the Arab world since the winter of 2010-11 has flown in the face of all of these positions. There has indeed been an Arab revolution, not because every country has experienced revolutionary turmoil, but because of the dynamics behind the regional protest movements against all of the regimes in office. These regimes can choose the path to reform, which has to be far reaching and substantial. Or, as Libya and Syria have tragically proven, the despot can unleash

---

1. *Governmental NGOs*, an oxymoron meaning associations created artificially by the governments in question to quash the real representatives of civil society.
2. Tunis, 29th April 2008.
3. Palais de l'Elysée, 30th August 2010.

his repressive violence against initially peaceful protest, which has been forced to militarise.

After the overthrow of Presidents Ben Ali and Mubarak, Javier Solana said he was *"frustrated at the European Union's response."* The former chief of European diplomacy believed *"that we might not have done more, but we should have nurtured a better dialogue and a stronger empathy."*[4]. For his part President Sarkozy learnt his lesson and resolutely sided with the Libyan revolution, whose National Transition Council (NTC) was recognized by France as early as March 2011. Paris and London played a key role in the adoption of the UN Security Council resolution 1973, a prelude to NATO's intervention to save Benghazi from re-capture by the despot.

Beyond the fate of the Libyan revolution, the NATO operation helped prevent the destabilisation of post-Ben Ali Tunisia and post-Mubarak Egypt by Gaddafi, who would have been all the more vindictive had he been re-instated. But NATO's campaign, which ended in October 2011 with the death of the dictator, divided Europe instead of uniting it: Germany refused to join the Franco-British coalition, whilst in 2003 it was the joint opposition of Paris and Berlin against the American invasion of Iraq that antagonized London and the other "like-minded" capitals. This time it was Libya that separated Western, Southern and Northern Europe, committed albeit symbolically to NATO's operation, from a reticent and even hostile Central and Eastern Europe.

It was only in November 2011 that Catherine Ashton officially inaugurated the European Union's representation in the Libyan capital. Europe's commitment remained modest in a country which, admittedly, had always stood apart from the Euro-Mediterranean initiative. Apart from the 80 million € in humanitarian aid given during the conflict, 30 million € were affected to emergency programmes. The election of a "National Congress" in July 2012 that took over from the soon to be dissolved NTC was welcomed as a "significant turning point" for the "future democratic development of Libya"[5].

Renewed Partnerships

The formula "Arab Spring" ended up reducing an historical, long lasting groundswell, to a seasonal variation. Since the first free elections in the autumn of 2011 led to the victory of Ennahda in Tunisia, to that of the Muslim Brothers in Egypt, not much more is required for it to be declared an "Islamic Autumn". After a brief moment of self-criticism this has justified the implementation of past policies, with a relative change of contacts in relatively stable administrations in the Southern Mediterranean.

Of course Catherine Ashton and Stefan Füle announced in March 2011 the launch of a "Partnership for Democracy and Shared Prosperity in the Southern Mediterranean." The three pillars of this were *"the democratic transformation and strengthening of the institutions"*; *"enhanced partnership with the populations"*; *"sustainable, inclusive economic growth and development"*[6]. Aside the "democratic transformation", all of the terms employed here are part of a proven Euro-Mediterranean register. The idea of positive conditionality can be summarised by the bureaucratic expression "more for more" that is supposed to reward progress rather than sanction shortfalls.

The design of specific instruments to address this revolutionary situation has been ruled out. At best the idea of moving towards an "advanced status" as part of the

---

4. *El Pais*, 19th February 2011.
5. Conclusions of the Council on Libya, 23rd July 2012.
6. Joint Communication by the European and the High Representative, Brussels, 8th March 2011.

association agreements according to the status model already in application with Morocco and Jordan has been suggested. Therefore it is simply a question of adapting the European Neighbourhood Policy (ENP) to the new situation, without assimilating this group of Mediterranean countries with those in Eastern Europe. This was the goal of a European Commission Communication released in May 2011 on "a new strategy regarding a changing world."[7]

Contrary to this title the "new strategy" is hard to find in this document. At best we can read about the promotion of a commitment to "increased aid to partners who are trying to achieve *deep and sustainable democracy*":
– free, regular elections
– freedom of association, expression and assembly
– the rule of law and the independence of the judiciary
– the fight against corruption
– the democratic supervision of the armed and security forces.

The listing of these criteria indirectly highlights the extent of the active or passive blindness which marked cooperation in the past. The European Neighbourhood and Partnership Instrument (ENPI), which has been provided with 5.7 billion € for the period 2011-2013 is due to be supplemented with an additional 1.2 billion €. The ENPI involves 16 countries, including Israel and seven in Eastern Europe. Even though one third of this "supplement" is supposed to be allocated to the Arab countries[8], only 200 to 300 million additional € will be shared out amongst the eight partners in question. Within this group of countries, Tunisia, Egypt, Morocco and Jordan are privileged, unlike Algeria, Syria, Lebanon and the Palestinian Territories.

The fact that Morocco and Jordan are included alongside revolutionary Tunisia and Egypt is supposed to encourage the Arab leaders along the path of reform. But as much as the Constitution approved by referendum in Morocco in July 2011 is an undeniable yet incomplete step forward, Jordan is delaying the implementation of even limited reform. The European Union has not ruled out "a radical re-orientation" of the envelopes it has allocated to Egypt and Tunisia, but without making any significant increase. In all events there is nothing comparable, on the part of Europe, to the exceptional effort that was made after the fall of the Berlin Wall.

In July Bernardino Leon, the second in command in Spanish diplomacy, was appointed as "the European Union's Special Representative for the countries in the Southern Mediterranean". During the same month, in Cairo, Catherine Ashton announced the launch of the SPRING programme (*Support for Partnership, Reform and Inclusive Growth*), provided with 350 million €, of which 65 were given in 2011 and 285 in 2012. 40% of this allocation was granted to democratic reform and 60% to sustainable development.

It was not until September 2011 that the EU-Tunisia Task Force allocated 100 million additional euros to the young democracy (80 for the most impoverished regions and 20 for competitiveness assistance). The European Union was visible thanks to its electoral observation mission during the vote on 23rd October 2011 for the Constituent Assembly. Under the management of Michael Gahler, MEP (EPP, DE), ten experts and around 100 observers attended the first free elections in Tunisia.

---

7. Joint Communication by the European and the High Representative, Brussels, 25th May 2011.
8. Richard Youngs, "Funding Arab reform?", German Marshall Fund, Policy Brief, August 2012, p.2.

From one crisis to another

It is far from certain that Europe has learned all of the lessons from the mistakes it made in Tunisia and Egypt as far as relations with civil society are concerned. The GONGOs – the pseudo pro-regime NGOs continue to reap in a major share of the funds allocated to associations. There is a prevailing feeling that European leaders, both political and administrative, have upgraded their contacts to the level they should have reached before the democratic uprising, without taking into account the new union, cultural and revolutionary players.

European decision makers have reduced the problem of their political opening to that of their dialogue with the Islamists. Dialogue like this, which had been necessary for a long time, does not use up all of the opportunities made available by the opening of the partisan, militant camp in the Arab world. There is also a danger of going from one extreme to another and of behaving with the Islamist parties in government in the same way as with the presidential parties of the fallen regimes.

Arab societies are extremely diverse and lively. No overview, no dominating prism can perceive the complexity of this. It would be better to take one's time and provide oneself with the means to build a sustainable relationship with environments, regions, and sensitivities, which to date have remained beyond the reach of the European vision, because it is from there that future elites will emerge.

The need to cast off comfortable blinkers is particularly evident in Syria. The internal resistance which has maintained its civilian nature much longer than in Libya is frequently caricatured as being "Islamist", "radical" or "sectarian" whilst direct contacts with it are rare and haphazard. The European Union effectively leads in terms of its sanctions against Bachar al-Assad[9], but it has not taken the step which was decisive in the Libyan revolution, of fully recognizing the organised opposition. The acknowledgement of the Syrian National Council, just after it was formed in October 2011 would however have been the best obstacle to the centrifugal trend of an opposition marked by decades of exile and repression.

Finally although *"settling the Israeli-Arab conflict is a strategic priority for Europe"*[10], one has to admit that this "strategic priority" has led to very little practical effect. It would be wrong to pretend, as Brussels does that a process *"to build the Palestinian State"* is underway[11]: of the 460 million euros paid out in 2011, which by far makes the European Union the biggest creditor in the West Bank or on the Gaza Strip, only 35 million have gone to institutional aid and 22 to the development of infrastructures[12].

Most of this aid, which is significant, is affected to financing the UNRWA (the UN agency specialised in aid to the Palestinians) and the Palestinian Authority (whose agents in Gaza are banned from working for the local administration of the Hamas). This assistance helps towards perpetuating the status quo, notably the division between the West Bank and the Gaza Strip, rather than taking it towards a sustainable solution of two States living in peace.

---

9. Aside the embargo on weapons and oil together with economic and financial sanctions, 53 companies and administrations have had their assets frozen likewise 155 members of the regime (who are also banned from having a visa).

10. http://eeas.europa.eu/mepp/index_fr.htm

11. *Ibid.*

12. http://eeas.europa.eu/occupied_palestinian_territory/ec_assistance/eu_aid_to_palest_2011_en.pdf

***

It would be an understatement to say that the democratic uprising in the Southern Mediterranean has not been met with a response worthy of this historic upheaval. Europe, which is bogged down in its own financial crisis, has not succeeded in providing the means that would have enabled it to contribute concretely to this area of "shared democracy and prosperity" as it pretends to want in the Mediterranean. The precedent, which was enlightening however, of the transitions in Spain, Portugal and Greece was not considered seriously in this collective reflexion.

Beyond the budgetary constraints, it is the political vision which is at fault however. In regard to the Palestinian or Syrian issue, a more courageous position would undoubtedly use up less of the disputed payments. The weak consensus in dealing with crises in a "humanitarian" rather than "political" way which call rather more for strong policy, is not only costly in the short term, it also delays the settlement of problems that are worsened by this denial of responsibility.

It would have been good at least to have a European discourse that was worthy of the issue at stake. Only François Hollande has clearly spoken of *"political and social revolutions in the Arab world"*[13]. He has advocated a *"Mediterranean of Projects"* where *"concerns over security must always go together with the need for dignity"* and that it is up to France *"to encourage this movement boldly but vigilantly."* He has repeated that keeping Bachar al-Assad in power is not only *"unbearable for the world's conscience"* but *"unacceptable for the stability of the region."*[14]

The Arab Revolution has only just entered its third year. It is not too late for Europe and the Europeans to take the full measure of it.

---

13. Letter from François Hollande to Jean-Marie Guéhenno, 13th July 2012.
14. Speech by François Hollande at the Ambassadors Conference, 27th August 2012.

IV

Interview

José-Manuel BARROSO
President of the European Commission

1 – 2012 saw pressure ease on markets in the eurozone and its Member States, due to progress made in governance of the economic and monetary Union. Are you satisfied with the conditions under which this progress has been decided and implemented? In other words, how do you judge the spirit of cooperation within the Union?

The path taken by Europe to emerge from the crisis over the course of 2012 is highly significant. It's enough just to compare the conditions in place at the start of 2013 with those of last year. The risk of the fragmentation of the eurozone, ever present at the beginning of 2012, has been largely reduced.

This progress would not have been possible without the involvement of both European institutions and Member States. And yet, we cannot declare victory too soon, and let our guard down. The current situation, especially regarding the labour market, requires that we continue to act collectively to encourage growth and employment in Europe. This includes improving the health of public finances and supporting targeted investments, as well as ensuring the stability of the financial system. The 2013 workload is still very heavy and the spirit of cooperation to which you refer is still much needed.

2 – The European Commission has published its reform proposals with a view to establishing a real economic and monetary Union, suggesting a progressive roadmap that should result in a review of the treaties. Could you explain the spirit and priorities of this roadmap for us?

The roadmap is a central contribution made by the Commission to structure the debate. It encourages a joint understanding of the challenges that Europe has to collectively overcome to deepen the integration project and complete the economic and monetary Union in the short, medium and long term. First and foremost, the current crisis is a crisis of confidence and this roadmap clearly signals: we understand the challenges ahead and the means that will be required to meet them. It also offers a vision of the future economic and monetary union, one that is stronger, more resilient, more integrated and whose credibility results from the improved articulation between solidarity and responsibility.

3 – How do you see the Union in 10 years time? Will it have maintained its place in international exchanges? Will it have increased its role on the world scene?

Contrary to the pessimists and declinists who foresee the end of the European project, I'm certain that in 10 years time the Union will be stronger and more integrated. Firstly, the Union's place in the world is much stronger than assumed. For example, if I take trade flows, the Union is by far the world's leading player and continues to capture a major share, with 28% of the benefits derived from world manufacturing production (note that the United States has only 18% and China 16%). Despite the crisis, the Union continues to be very attractive as a result of its currency (the world's second most valuable), its universities, its culture, its wealth, its democratic model and its values. In a world of giants, size matters. The European project, even as it undergoes difficulties, remains an absolute reference in terms of cooperation between states and shared sovereignty. That was what was signalled by awarding the EU the Nobel Peace Prize. Europe will be even stronger in 10 years' time because the current crisis forces us to implement difficult reforms regarding competitiveness and public spending.

4 – In your opinion, have the Europeans who have been asked to make efforts in terms of rigour, in some cases very big efforts, understood the importance of the necessary recovery in public accounts, and will they have the patience and courage needed to carry through with these reforms?

I would firstly like to say that I am impressed by the determination shown by Europeans facing this economic storm and I am aware of the difficulties they are going through and the courage they show. My daily priority is to ensure that the Union resolves the problem of high unemployment, which is currently affecting a historic 11.8% of young people in the eurozone. The situation must improve and that is what I work towards every day. In particular, I believe that the citizens of Europe have understood two things. Firstly, that out of control public debt is a burden that holds back economic and social development. Secondly, that our economic and social model will have to adapt to the new conditions of globalisation, in which the Union has its part to play. It is not a matter of giving up on the European economic and social model, rather it is adapting to it, because, in the end, those who are doing best in Europe are those who are combining social protection and economic efficiency.

5 - Do you believe that 2014 will be the year in which the European Union returns to growth?

In general, yes. But that of course will depend on our ability to continue to reform. External players will also have a key role, notably, the United States' recovery and growth in emerging countries; many of which are also having to face up to major political, economic and social challenges.

6 - What is your judgement on the implementation of the Lisbon Treaty, notably the institutional reforms it contains? Has it complicated or facilitated the role of the European Commission? What needs improvement in the way in which the Union operates?

Overall and given the current economic situation, I would say that the Lisbon Treaty has considerably strengthened the community method and has provided the Union a much more robust, efficient and legitimate framework within which to deal with the crisis. To date, almost all regulations are adopted according to the process of co-decision. The qualified majority vote has been widely extended, most notably in the areas of "justice and internal affairs". The Commission itself has seen its competencies reinforced, and even extended, particularly in terms of the economic and monetary union and in regards to external relations. External representation of the Union is also clearer and more coherent, relying on an external affairs service that is entirely dedicated to representing the Union's interests in the world and to formulating the elements of a joint foreign policy.

We are a long way from reaching the Treaty's limits on our road towards increased integration, as indicated in the roadmap towards a deep and genuine monetary union. And that's why, if there is something to be improved in the short term with regards to how the Union operates, it's the "team spirit". This "team spirit" must inspire all, from the Union's institutions to its Member States. All too often national reflexes dominate and act as obstacles to identifying common analyses and action.

Finally, in the long term, it is clear that achieving European integration and a complete economic and monetary union will call for an evolution of the Union, which is impossible without reviewing the Treaties. As I said in my State of the Union speech in September 2012, the Commission will present its outline of this future European Union between now and the next European elections in 2014. I will present concrete ideas on how to modify the treaties, within a time frame that will allow for the organisation of a real debate.

We are currently in a position in which the States no longer have the capability to address all the challenges of the 21st century, and Europe does not yet have all the instruments needed to do so efficiently. It is this gap, this vacuum that we must fill, including from an institutional point of view.

V

Summary of political and legal Europe

2012, a Swing Year?

Corinne DELOY

Six countries in the European Union renewed their parliament in 2012, four of which did so early, notably due to domestic political crisis. The left – and it is a first in six years – was the winner in these general elections. Indeed three Member States swung from right to left: Slovakia, France and Lithuania; in Romania the left/right coalition that has governed the country since May 2012 won the ballot. In Romania, the left/right coalition – in power since May 2012 – won the election on December 9th. In the Netherlands, the Liberals formed a coalition government with the Labour Party (PvdA). Lastly, in Greece, the government formed by the right (ND which won the elections on June 17th), the PASOK chose four of its ministers even though it decided not to take directly in government.

However the right remains predominant in the European Union. It governs in 18 Member States (in coalition with the left in Finland, Ireland, Luxembourg, and in the Netherlands) whilst the left governs in seven (in coalition with the right in Austria and Romania)[1]. Socio-economic issues (debt and eurozone crises, public deficit reductions, revival of growth, the future of the industrial policy, etc.) featured at the heart of the electoral debate in each of these countries where an election was held this year.

Finally in 2012 the Irish also voted on Europe: on 31st May they ratified the treaty on Stability, Coordination and Governance – otherwise known as the European Budgetary Pact.

---

1. Italy and Belgium – led by governments of national union – were not included in this typology.

The government majorities within the European Union on 31st December 2012

Countries governed by a left majority	Countries governed by a right majority
Austria (left/right coalition)	Germany
Cyprus	Bulgaria
Denmark	Spain
France	Estonia
Lithuania	Finland (right/left coalition)
Romania (left/right coalition)	Greece (right/left coalition)
Slovakia	Hungary
	Ireland (right/left coalition)
	Latvia
	Luxembourg (right/left coalition)
	Malta
	The Netherlands (right/left coalition)
	Poland
	Portugal
	Czech Republic
	United Kingdom
	Slovenia
	Sweden

1. A clear swing to the left

Slovakia: the return of Robert Fico

Direction-Social Democracy (SMER-SD), led by former Prime Minister (2006-2010), Robert Fico, easily won in the early general elections in Slovakia on 10th March. The party won 44.4% of the vote and 83 of the 150 seats in parliament, i.e. the absolute majority, a first since the country's independence in 1993. The early elections followed the fall on 11th October 2011 of Iveta Radicova's government which comprised the Democratic and Christian Union-Democratic Party (SDKU-DS), Most-Hid, Freedom and Solidarity (SaS) and the Christian Democratic Movement (KDH). The Prime Minister chose to associate the adoption of the European Financial Stability Facility (EFSF) by parliament with a confidence vote on her government. MPs chose to say "no" to the government in office to the detriment of the EFSF. Some months later the Democratic and Christian Union-Democratic Party collapsed winning 6% of the vote and 11 seats (-17) just like its government partner, Freedom and Solidarity which won 5.8% of the vote and 11 seats (-11). Turnout totalled 59.1%

The election undoubtedly bears less witness to the triumph of the left than to the collapse of the right. Already weakened, it also suffered due to the Gorilla scandal, the name given to the politico-financial affair that came to light after the recordings of internet conversations at the end of 2011 were put on line revealing bribery and money laundering that had taken place during the privatisations of 2005-2006, a period when the right was in office. The scandal also benefited the Party of Ordinary People and Independent Personalities (OL'aNO) led by Igor Matovic which made its entry into parliament.

In spite of the extremely social announcements made by Fico ("*We are against privatisation, support a better protection of the workers and greater public investment*") the results of the first government he led (2006-2010) plead for the continuity of the policy undertaken by the right. During his time as head of State the leader of Direction did indeed succeed in protecting the heritage of the liberal right whilst increasing State social spending, notably to attenuate the effects of the international economic crisis.

The French give a majority to a leftwing President

One month after the presidential election the Socialist Party and its allies won the majority in the National Assembly, the lower chamber of the French parliament, during the general elections on 10th and 17th June. The leftwing forces together won a total of 346 seats (+119).

With 215 seats the UMP faced an acceptable defeat. The dilemma was Cornelian for the voters of the right who were fighting for the victory of their camp and yet were opposed to cohabitation.

The National Front remained isolated in the political arena but asserted itself as the country's third political force. It won two seats whilst none of its candidates had succeeded in entering parliament since 1988.

Turnout was the lowest ever recorded in general elections in France: 57.2% in the first round and 55.4% in the second. The election, which since 2002, follows immediately after the appointment of the head of State, generates little interest and mobilises few, since voters are convinced that the match has already been won before it has even been played.

Jean-Marc Ayrault (PS) was appointed Prime Minister and formed a government including socialists and ecologists. One thing is certain however: with François Hollande in the Elysée and the majority in the National Assembly, in the Senate and in most of the regions (24 out of 26), departments and major cities, the French left – which holds an hegemonic position – can afford to make no mistakes.

Right-Left Alternation in Lithuania

The leftwing won the general elections on 14th and 28th October in Lithuania. The Social Democratic (LSP) Party led by Algirdas Butkevicius became the country's main political force with a total of 38 seats in the Seimas, the only chamber of parliament. It came out ahead of the Homeland Union-Conservatives (TS-LK) led by outgoing Prime Minister Andrius Kubilius which won 33 seats. The latter, the first head of government to have completed a mandate since Lithuania won back its independence in 1991, and this in spite of an extremely difficult economic context, paid the price of the austerity policy which he had introduced to counter the economic crisis which sorely affected Lithuania (the GDP contracted by 15% in 2009). Although the country had recovered growth, wages and retirement, pensions decreased dramatically and unemployment rose to 13%.

The Labour Party (DP) led by billionaire Viktor Uspaskich came third with 30 MPs and the populist movement, For Order and Justice (TT) led by former President of the Republic Rolandas Paksas, won 11 seats. Together the Social Democrats and Labour won 78 of the 141 seats in Parliament. Turnout totalled 52.9%.

The Labour Party and the Social Democratic Party formed a government, joining forces with For Order and Justice and Electoral Action of the Poles of Lithuania (LLRA), a party representing the country's Polish minority.

2. The Netherlands and Romania: repeated political crises

The Liberals re-elected in the Netherlands

The People's Party for Freedom and Democracy (VVD) led by outgoing Prime Minister Mark Rutte came out ahead in the general elections on 12th September in the Netherlands. It won 26.5% of the vote, i.e. the highest score in its history, taking 41 seats (+10 than in the election in 2010). The Liberals drew slightly ahead of the Labour Party (PvdA) led by Diederik Samsom, who won 24.7% of the vote and 39 seats (+9). Together the two parties formed a government after the election.

The electoral campaign focused on the European crisis (eurozone and debt crisis) and for a long time benefited the opposition forces which were more radical and hostile to the European Union (Socialist Party, SP, and the Freedom Party PVV) before the pro-European parties won back some ground. The Liberals, who were forced to take on board the rising hostility of the population to the reforms asked of the country by the European Union, took a firm stance against the States in the South of Europe.

The populists suffered a resounding defeat. On the right the Freedom Party won 10.1% of the vote and 15 seats (-9); on the left the Socialist Party won 9.6% of the vote and 15 seats (=), i.e. well below the results that the polls were forecasting. The Christian Democratic Appeal (CDA) was the other loser in this election It recorded the lowest result in its history: 8.5% of the vote and 13 seats (-8). Turnout totalled 74.3%

The VVD did not suffer therefore from its cohabitation with the Freedom Party (PVV) led by Geert Wilders nor did it suffer from the crisis which had led to the withdrawal of the PVV's support that had forced the government to resign. On 12th September the Dutch clearly said "yes" to Europe, which they visibly deem to be the only organisation to guarantee their future.

Easy victory for the outgoing left/right coalition in Romania

Since May 7th 2012 Romania has been governed by a motley left/right coalition. In February 2011 the Social Democratic Party (PSD) led by Prime Minister Victor Ponta and the National Liberal Party (PNL) formed the Social Liberal Union (USL) with the aim of bringing down the President of the Republic Traian Basescu (PD-L), who was appreciated by his fellow countrymen for a long time, but whose popularity collapsed after he imposed austerity measures on the country in a bid to counter the serious economic crisis affecting it.

The Romanian parliament approved the destitution of the Head of State on 6th July but the operation failed: the referendum organised by the government on 29th July on the issue was invalidated because turnout was not high enough (46.1%).

Four months later the Social Liberal Union won the parliamentary elections organised on 9th December. The coalition won 58.6% of the vote in the general election (and 60.1% in the senatorial election), i.e. the highest score ever achieved by a coalition since the collapse of communism.

The Alliance of the Romanian Right (ARD) led by former Prime Minister (February 2012-May 2012), Mihai Razvan Ungureanu, who rallied the main opposition forces (the Democratic Liberal Party (PD-L), the National Party of Christian Democratic Farmers (NP-CDP), the New Republic Party (NRP), the Christian Democratic Foundation (FCD) and the Civic Force Party (PFC)) won 16.7% of the vote in the Chamber of Deputies and 16.7% in the Senate. The People's Party (PP-DD) led by Dan Diaconescu came third with 13.8% of the vote in the legislative elections and 14.7% in the senatorial vote. Only four Romanians in ten turned out to vote (41.6%).

The only true issue at stake in these elections was the extent of the Social Liberal victory. Victor Ponta was appointed Prime Minister on 21st December.

3. Greece on the edge of collapse

The general elections on 6th May constituted a political earthquake in Greece which was in the midst of an extremely serious financial and socio-economic crisis. The electorate voted massively against austerity and the European Memorandum, the name given to the agreement signed by Athens with the International Monetary Fund (IMF), the European Union and the Central European Bank. The two "major" government parties – the Pan-Hellenic Socialist Movement (PASOK) and New Democracy (ND) – collapsed, winning 32% of the vote only (18.8% and 108 seats + 17 for the rightwing party in comparison with the 2009 elections and 13.2% of the vote, 41 seats, - 119 for the leftwing party). Both were punished for having accepted the drastic austerity conditions that went with the two rescue plans for Greece (May 2010 and October 2011) in exchange for which the government had committed to implement major austerity measures.

With 16.7% of the vote (52 seats, + 39), the Radical Left Coalition (SYRIZA) was the true winner in the election on 6th May. The break through by the neo-Nazi party, Chryssi Avghi (CA, Golden Dawn), which won 6.9% of the vote (21 seats), was the other major event in the election, in which 65.1% of the Greeks took part.

Since the results made the formation of a government impossible another election was organised on 17th June. New Democracy then came out ahead with 29.6% of the vote and 129 seats (21 more than in May). The Radical Left Coalition scored even better: it won 26.8% of the vote and 71 MPs (+ 19). PASOK won 12.2% of the vote and 33 seats (- 8). Chryssi Avghi won 6.9% of the vote and 18 MPs (- 3). Turnout rose to 62.5%.

Although the vote on 6th May was an expression of anger, that on 17th June was one of fear – of what the future of the country might be outside of Europe and the fear of seeing Athens leave the eurozone. The Greeks voted in support of their country keeping the single currency and for the continuation of budgetary spending control, with the hope however of being able to modify the aid plan.

Antonis Samaras, the New Democracy leader was able to widen the electoral base of his party in both elections by embracing four leaders from the far right Orthodox Alarm (LAOS) and above all by re-integrating into his party the Democratic Alliance, founded by Dora Bakoyannis. After the election he formed a government in which the left chose not to take part but PASOK and the Democratic Left (DIMOK) did choose four of the 25 Ministers in the new team.

The 2012 elections fragmented the country's bipolarisation that had been in force since Greece's return to democracy in 1974; with political divisions giving way to the split opposing the pro- and anti-Europeans.

The leftwing has asserted itself in the European ballot boxes in four of the six countries which renewed their parliament. Has the supremacy of the right started to wane and was 2012 the start of a swing to the left by the European electorate? Political alternation, which is almost natural in politics, can also be explained by the difficulty experienced by the teams in office (mainly rightwing in Europe), as they were forced to undertake austerity policies and face the electorate's discontent. Some managed however to stave off the electoral verdict and were re-elected, as in the Netherlands.

The elections in 2013 will show us how this electoral trend towards the left is developing. Six Member States will be renewing their parliament including Germany, governed by the right since 2005; Italy, led by the right since 2008, and above all Austria, governed by a left/right coalition but where the far right has become the leading force, if we are to believe the polls.

Five new heads of State in Europe

Five new presidents of the Republic were elected in 2012 in the European Union; three were appointed by universal suffrage and two others were elected by their parliament

On 5th February, Sauli Niinistö (Conservative Assembly, KOK) won the Finnish Presidential election with 62.6% of the vote (37% in the 1st round). He came out ahead of ecologist Pekka Haavisto who won 37.4% of the vote (18.7% in the first round). Sauli Niinistö, who belongs to Prime Minister Jyrki Katainen's party had the support of five of the six candidates who took part in the first round. The presidential election focused more on the personality of the candidate, both pro-European, rather than on their programmes. The lack of any real left/right opposition enabled Sauli Niinistö to rally the vote well beyond his own party. He put an end to thirty years of Social Democratic reign and became the first centre-right Head of State in Finland since Juho Kusti Paasikivi (1946-1956).

Joachim Gauck, with no political label and supported by five of the political parties represented in parliament, except for the Left Party (L), was elected on 18th March as President of the Federal Republic of Germany in the first round of voting, 991 in support out of the 1,232 votes cast in the German Federal Assembly (*Bundesversammlung*), the body responsible for appointing the head of State. This presidential election followed the resignation on 17th February of Christian Wulff, suspected of having benefited from his position as Minister-President of the Land of Lower Saxony (2003-2010) to gain various financial advantages and of then having tried to cover up the scandal.

A pastor, Joachim Gauck defines himself as "a social democratic conservative with liberal leanings". Well loved by his fellow countrymen he is a symbol of the work of remembrance undertaken on the communist dictatorship (he chaired the committee responsible for the dissolution of the State Security Ministry (STASI) after the fall of the Berlin Wall in 1989). After this election Germany now has at its helm two Protestant personalities, who originally came from the former German Democratic Republic.

On 2nd May, Janos Ader (Democratic Youth Alliance, FIDESZ) was elected President of Hungary by Parliament (262 votes in support, 40 against). He was the only candidate running in this election, which followed the resignation of Pal Schmitt on 2nd April, the latter being accused of plagiarism in his doctoral thesis devoted to the Olympic Games of 1992. Janos Ader is the author of two extremely controversial laws; the new electoral law that favours the "major" parties and the reform of the judiciary.

He owes his election to his loyalty to the government majority and to his extremely close relations with Prime Minister Viktor Orban (FIDESZ).

On 6th May with 51.6% of the vote François Hollande (Socialist Party PS) became the second French President of the 5th Republic to come from the left. He drew ahead of outgoing President Nicolas Sarkozy (Union for a Popular Movement, UMP), who won 48.3% of the vote. The French punished the party in office. The election emerged as a referendum on the personality and style of government of the outgoing President. The victory of the Socialist candidate can be explained in part by the rejection of Nicolas Sarkozy as a person. He was elected as Head of State in 2007 thanks to a programme focused on three main ideas (economic flexibility, increased growth and the consolidation of the public finances) before the international economic crisis obliged him to modify his policy.

In 2012 the outgoing President undertook a campaign on the right which caused tension within his own party. Between rounds he vainly tried to rally Marine Le Pen's voters (National Front, FN) and those of François Bayrou (Democratic Movement, MoDem) to his name.

With 18.1% of the vote in the first round Marine Le Pen succeeded in positioning her party as an inevitable political force. She easily drew ahead of Jean-Luc Mélenchon (Left Front FG) who won 11.1% of the vote, as he articulated his campaign around French concern over globalisation, and by using a communist political culture, which is firmly set on the left, and very much alive in France. François Bayrou did not succeed in rising beyond the 10% mark (9.1% of the vote.). Turnout was high and totalled 80.4% in the first round and 79.3% in the second.

Borut Pahor (Social Democratic Party, SD) was the source of surprise as he won the presidential election on 2nd December in Slovenia. The former Prime Minister (2008-2011) won 67.4% of the vote coming out ahead of outgoing head of State Danilo Türk who won 32.5% of the vote. Turnout was drastically down: 41.9%, i.e. 16.5 points less than in the second round of the election in 2007.

Borut Pahor, who gave his support to the austerity reforms undertaken by Janez Jansa's government (Democratic Party, SDS), has set the goal of "rallying the majority on the right and the left opposition to put Slovenia back on the path of growth." The country, which is experiencing a serious economic crisis, should benefit from the combined work of the head of State and the Prime Minister.

A resounding YES by the Irish to the European Budgetary Pact

On 31st May the Irish approved the Treaty on Stability, Coordination and Governance otherwise known as the European Budgetary Pact. More than six voters in ten (60.3%) voted YES whilst 39.7% opposed the ratification of the European text. Turnout was low (50.6%). Ireland was the only Member State to organise a referendum on this text.

This vote was unique and contrary to past events regarding the adoption of the two most recent European texts – the Nice (2002) and Lisbon Treaties (2009). Dublin had no right to veto the European treaty since this one had to enter into force once at least 12 countries had ratified it.

Fine Gael (FG), of Prime Minister Enda Kenny, the Labour Party (Lab), a government coalition member and Fianna Fail (FF) the main opposition party supported the ratification.

Three parties represented in the Irish Parliament – Sinn Fein (SF), the far left nationalist party; the Socialist Party (SP) and the People's Movement before Profit (PBP) – were against it. In the "no" camp there were also several independent MPs, including the founder of the organisation Libertas, Declan Ganley.

In a country that is still recovering and aware that they would not be given another chance to vote, the Irish were not convinced that rejecting the treaty would improve their daily lot.

Summary of the Legislative Election Results in 2012
in the European Union in %[2,3,4,5,6]

Country	Turnout	Far Left	Left of government	Right of government	Far Right	Others
Slovakia	59.1		44.4	29.4	4.6	21.6
France[2]	57.2	0,9	46.7	34	13.7	4.7
Greece[3]	62.5	31.4	18.6	37.2	6.9	5.9
The Netherlands	74.3	9.6	27	35	10.1	18.3
Lithuania[4]	52.9		38.2	33		28.8
Romania[5]	41.7		58.9[6]	16.5	15.2	9.4

Electoral Shifts in Europe in 2012

	Previous Elections	2012 Election
Slovakia	Right	Left
France	Right	Left
Greece	Right	Right (coalition right -left)
The Netherlands	Right	Right (coalition right -left)
Lithuania	Right	Left
Romania	Right	Left (coalition left – right)

2013 Elections in the European Union

11th -12th and 25th -26th January: Czech Republic – Presidential election
17th -24th February Cyprus – Presidential election
24th – 25th February: Italy – Parliamentary elections
9th March: Malta – Legislative elections
May: Italy – Presidential election
7th July: Bulgaria – Legislative elections
22nd September: Germany – Legislative elections
September: Austria – Legislative elections

---

2. Results of the first round of voting on 10th June 2012.
3. Results of the vote on 17th June 2012 (it is obligatory to vote in Greece).
4. Results of the proportional vote only.
5. Results of the elections of the lower chamber of parliament.
6. The Social Liberal Union (USL) won 58.6% of the vote but this is a motley coalition (left/right) led by outgoing Prime Minister Victor Ponta, rallying amongst others the Social-Democratic Party (PSD) which lies on the left of the political scale and the National Liberal Party (PNL) which lies on the right. The result given here is that of the coalition as a whole.

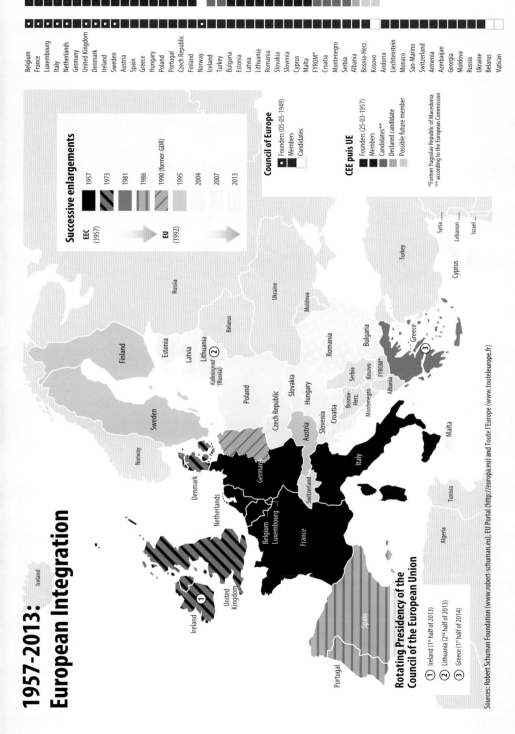

1957-2013:
European Integration

Successive enlargements

EEC (1957) → **EU (1992)**

- 1957
- 1973
- 1981
- 1986
- 1990 (former-GDR)
- 1995
- 2004
- 2007
- 2013

Council of Europe

- Founders (05-05-1949)
- Members
- Candidates

CEE puis UE

- Founders (25-03-1957)
- Members
- Candidates**
- Declared candidate
- Possible future member

*Former Yugoslav Republic of Macedonia
** according to the European Commission

Rotating Presidency of the Council of the European Union

1 Ireland (1st half of 2013)
2 Lithuania (2nd half of 2013)
3 Greece (1st half of 2014)

Countries listed:
Belgium, France, Luxembourg, Italy, Netherlands, Germany, United Kingdom, Denmark, Ireland, Sweden, Austria, Spain, Greece, Hungary, Poland, Portugal, Czech Republic, Finland, Norway, Iceland, Turkey, Bulgaria, Estonia, Latvia, Lithuania, Romania, Slovakia, Slovenia, Cyprus, Malta, FYROM*, Croatia, Montenegro, Serbia, Albania, Bosnia-Herz., Kosovo, Andorra, Liechtenstein, Monaco, San-Marino, Switzerland, Armenia, Azerbaijan, Georgia, Moldova, Russia, Ukraine, Belarus, Vatican

Pascal Orcier for the Robert Schuman Foundation, January 2013, © FRS.

Sources: Robert Schuman Foundation (www.robert-schuman.eu), EU Portal (http://europa.eu) and Toute l'Europe (www.touteleurope.fr)

Territories of Europe

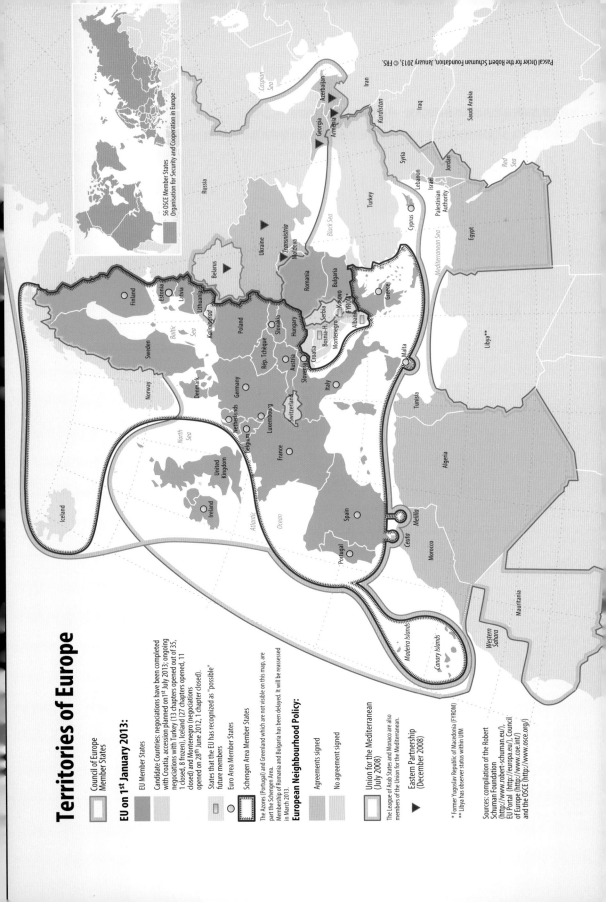

Council of Europe Member States

EU on 1st January 2013:

EU Member States

Candidate Countries: negociations have been completed with Croatia, accession planned on 1st July 2013; ongoing negociations with Turkey (13 chapters opened out of 35, 1 closed, 8 frozen), Iceland (27 chapters opened, 11 closed) and Montenegro (negociations opened on 28th June 2012, 1 chapter closed).

States that the EU has recognized as "possible" future members

Euro Area Member States

Schengen Area Member States

The Azores (Portugal) and Greenland which are not visible on this map, are part the Schengen Area.
Membership of Romania and Bulgaria has been delayed. It will be reassessed in March 2013.

European Neighbourhood Policy:

Agreements signed

No agreement signed

Union for the Mediterranean (July 2008)

The League of Arab States and Monaco are also members of the Union for the Mediterranean.

► Eastern Partnership (December 2008)

* Former Yugoslav Republic of Macedonia (FYROM)
** Libya has observer status within UfM

Sources: compilation of the Robert Schuman Foundation (http://www.robert-schuman.eu/), EU Portal (http://europa.eu/), Council of Europe (http://www.coe.int/) and the OSCE (http://www.osce.org/)

56 OSCE Member States
Organisation for Security and Cooperation in Europe

Pascal Orcier for the Robert Schuman Foundation, January 2013, © FRS.

Population of the EU Member States (2012)

Population of the EU Member States

EU States demographic dynamics

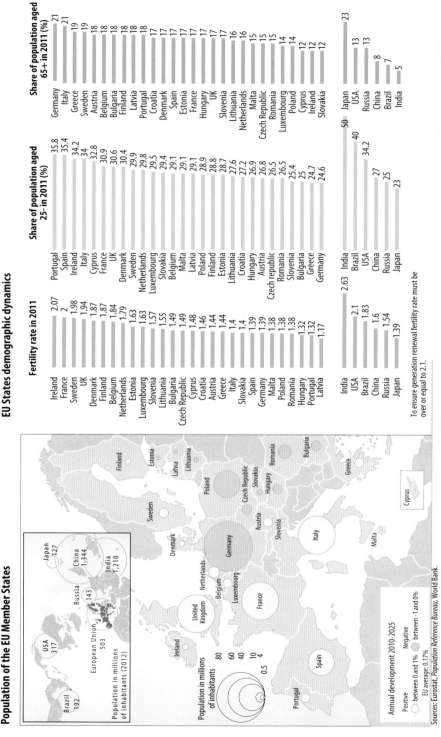

Fertility rate in 2011

Ireland	2.07
France	2
Sweden	1.98
UK	1.94
Denmark	1.87
Finland	1.87
Belgium	1.84
Netherlands	1.79
Estonia	1.63
Luxembourg	1.63
Slovenia	1.57
Lithuania	1.55
Bulgaria	1.49
Czech Republic	1.49
Cyprus	1.48
Croatia	1.46
Austria	1.44
Greece	1.44
Italy	1.4
Slovakia	1.4
Spain	1.39
Germany	1.39
Malta	1.38
Poland	1.38
Romania	1.38
Hungary	1.32
Portugal	1.32
Latvia	1.17
India	2.63
USA	2.1
Brazil	1.83
China	1.6
Russia	1.54
Japan	1.39

To ensure generation renewal fertility rate must be over or equal to 2.1.

Share of population aged 25- in 2011 (%)

Portugal	35.8
Spain	35.4
Ireland	34.2
Italy	34
Cyprus	32.8
France	30.9
UK	30.6
Denmark	30.4
Sweden	29.9
Netherlands	29.8
Luxembourg	29.5
Slovakia	29.4
Belgium	29.1
Malta	29.1
Latvia	29.1
Poland	28.9
Finland	28.8
Estonia	28.7
Lithuania	27.6
Croatia	27.2
Hungary	26.9
Austria	26.8
Czech republic	26.5
Romania	26.5
Slovenia	25.4
Bulgaria	25
Greece	24.7
Germany	24.6
India	50
Brazil	40
USA	34.2
China	27
Russia	25
Japan	23

Share of population aged 65+ in 2011 (%)

Germany	21
Italy	21
Greece	19
Sweden	19
Austria	18
Belgium	18
Bulgaria	18
Finland	18
Latvia	18
Portugal	18
Croatia	17
Denmark	17
Spain	17
Estonia	17
France	17
Hungary	17
UK	17
Slovenia	17
Lithuania	16
Netherlands	16
Malta	15
Czech Republic	15
Romania	15
Luxembourg	14
Poland	14
Cyprus	12
Ireland	12
Slovakia	12
Japan	23
USA	13
Russia	13
China	8
Brazil	7
India	5

Population in millions of inhabitants (2012)

Brazil 192
USA 317
Russia 143
Japan 127
China 1.344
India 1.210
European Union 503

Population in millions of inhabitants
80
60
40
10
4
0.5

Annual development 2010-2025

Positive — between 0 and 1% — EU average: 0.17%
Negative — between -1 and 0%

Sources: Eurostat, *Population Reference Bureau*, World Bank.

Pascal Order for the Robert Schuman Foundation, January 2013, © FRS.

Internal migrations

Policies of Openness to Internal Migrations
(situation on 1st December 2012) :

→ Major internal migrations*
⇢ Return after the economic crisis and expulsions

⬛ EU Member States that have opened their labour market to workers from all EU Member States

⬜ EU Member States that have opened their labour market to workers from all EU Member States with the exception of Romania and Bulgaria (gradual opening of the labour market through until 2014)

Share of migratory balance in the population increase (1999-2009)

⬛ 5 - 12%
⬛ 0 - 5%

negative
⬛ 0 - 5%
⬛ 5 - 6.6%

EU average: 2.3%

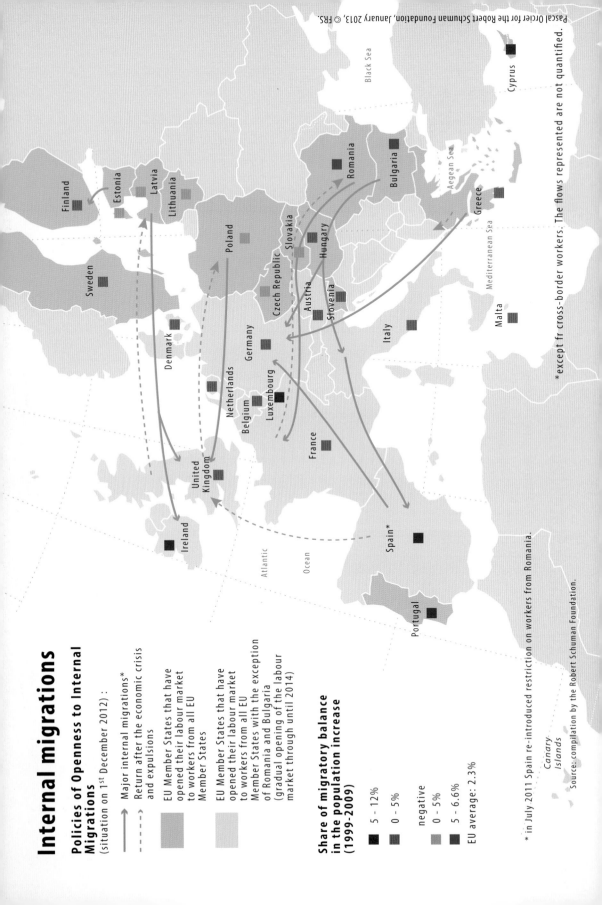

Black Sea
Cyprus
Finland
Estonia
Latvia
Lithuania
Poland
Slovakia
Hungary
Romania
Bulgaria
Sweden
Czech Republic
Austria
Slovenia
Greece
Aegean Sea
Denmark
Germany
Italy
Mediterranean Sea
Netherlands
Belgium
Luxembourg
France
Malta
United Kingdom
Ireland
Spain*
Portugal
Atlantic
Ocean
Canary Islands

* in July 2011 Spain re-introduced restriction on workers from Romania.

Source: compilation by the Robert Schuman Foundation.

*except fr cross-border workers. The flows represented are not quantified.

Pascal Orcier for the Robert Schuman Foundation, January 2013, © FRS.

External migrations

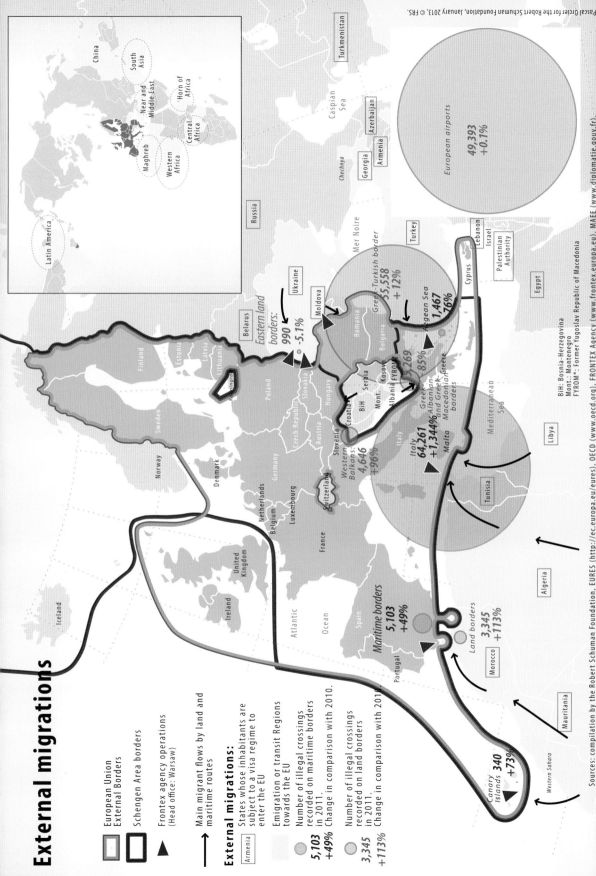

European Union
External Borders

Schengen Area borders

Frontex agency operations
(Head office: Warsaw)

Main migrant flows by land and
maritime routes

External migrations:

Armenia States whose inhabitants are
subject to a visa regime to
enter the EU

Emigration or transit Regions
towards the EU

5,103 Number of illegal crossings
+49% recorded on maritime borders
in 2011.
Change in comparison with 2010.

3,345 Number of illegal crossings
+113% recorded on land borders
in 2011.
Change in comparison with 2010.

Map labels

European airports
49,393
+0.1%

Eastern land borders:
990
-5.1%

Greek-Turkish border
55,558
+12%

Aegean Sea
1,467
-76%

85%

5,269

Greek-Albanian
and Greek-
Macedonian
borders

Western Balkans:
4,646
+96%

Italy
64,261
+1,344%

Maritime borders
5,103
+49%

Land borders
3,345
+113%

Canary Islands
340
+73%

Countries/regions
Turkmenistan, China, South Asia, Near and Middle East, Horn of Africa, Central Africa, Western Africa, Maghreb, Latin America

Caspian Sea, Azerbaijan, Armenia, Georgia, Chechnya, Russia, Mer Noire

Turkey, Lebanon, Israel, Cyprus, Palestinian Authority, Egypt, Libya, Algeria, Tunisia, Mauritania, Western Sahara, Morocco

Mediterranean Sea, Malta, Italy, Greece, FYROM, Albania, Kosovo, Mont., Serbia, BiH, Bulgaria, Romania, Moldova, Ukraine, Belarus, Hungary, Austria, Slovenia, Croatia, Slovakia, Czech Republic, Poland, Lithuania, Latvia, Estonia, Finland, Sweden, Norway, Denmark, Germany, Luxembourg, Belgium, Netherlands, France, Switzerland, United Kingdom, Ireland, Iceland, Spain, Portugal, Kaliningrad

Atlantic Ocean

BiH: Bosnia-Herzegovina
Mont.: Montenegro
FYROM*: Former Yugoslav Republic of Macedonia

Sources: compilation by the Robert Schuman Foundation, EURES (http://ec.europa.eu/eures), OECD (www.oecd.org), FRONTEX Agency (www.frontex.europa.eu), MAEE (www.diplomatie.gouv.fr).

Pascal Orcier for the Robert Schuman Foundation, January 2013, © FRS.

The EU and Asylum Requests

Total EU: 277,370

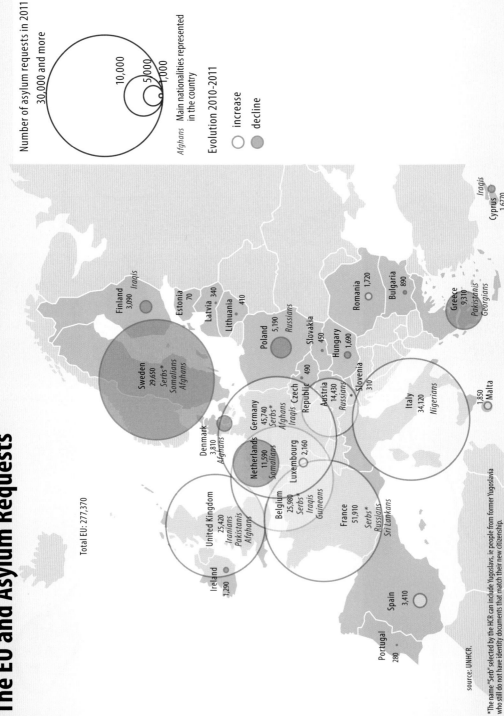

Number of asylum requests in 2011

30,000 and more

10,000

5,000

1,000

Afghans Main nationalities represented in the country

Evolution 2010-2011

○ increase

● decline

Finland
3,090 *Iraqis*

Estonia
70

Latvia 340

Lithuania
410

Sweden
29,650
Serbs*
Somalians
Afghans

Poland
5,190
Russians

Slovakia
450

Hungary
1,690

Denmark
3,810
Afghans

Germany
45,740
Serbs*
Afghans
Iraqis

Czech
Republic
490

Austria
14,430
Russians

Slovenia
310

Netherlands
11,590
Somalians

Luxembourg
2,160

Belgium
25,980
Serbs*
Iraqis
Guineans

United Kingdom
25,420
Iranians
Pakistanis
Afghans

France
51,910
Serbs*
Russians
Sri Lankans

Ireland
1,290

Portugal
280

Spain
3,410

Romania
1,720

Bulgaria
890

Greece
9,310
Pakistanis
Georgians

Italy
34,120
Nigerians

Malta
1,850

Cyprus
1,6770
Iraqis

source: UNHCR.

*The name "Serb" selected by the HCR can include Yugoslavs, ie people from former Yugoslavia who still do not have identity documents that match their new citizenship.

Pascal Orcier for the Robert Schuman Foundation, January 2013. © FRS.

Political Europe in 2013

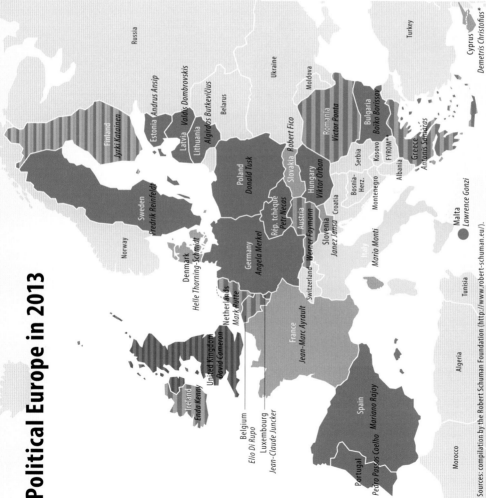

Political Colour of Governments

▨ Left	▨ Left/Right coalition
▨ Right	▨ Left/Right/Green coalition
▨ National union government	▨ Liberal/Conservative coalition

Andrus Ansip   Head of Government

Elections planned in 2013:

11th-12th & 25th-26th January: Czech Republic, *presidential*
17th-24th February: Chypre, *presidential*
24th-25th February: Italy, *parlementarian*
9th March: Malta, *legislative*
April: Montenegro, *presidential*
27th April: Iceland, *legislative*
May: Italy, *presidential (by the Parlement)*
23rd June: Albania, *legislative*
7th July: Bulgaria, *legislative*
September: Austria, *legislative*
22nd September: Germany, *legislative*

2014

March: Macedonia (FYROM), *presidential*
April: Malta, *presidential*
April: Hungary, *legislative*
May: Lithuania, *presidential*
June: European Union, *parlementarian*
July: Belgium, *federal and regional*
September: Sweden, *legislative*
Autumn: United Kingdom, *referendum on Self-Determination in Scotland*

* posts of both President and Prime Minister.
**Former Yugoslav Republic of Macedonia

Pascal Orcier for the Robert Schuman Foundation, January 2013. © FRS.

Sources: compilation by the Robert Schuman Foundation (http://www.robert-schuman.eu/).

Populism in Europe

Results obtained by populist parties in the latest general election*

Source: compiled by the Robert Schuman Foundation   *in France and Hungary only the first round of the election was considered.

Pascal Orcier for the Robert Schuman Foundation, January 2013, © FRS.

⬛	> 20 %
⬛	12 - 20 %
⬛	5 - 12 %
⬜	0.1 - 5 %
⬜	0 %

Populists' Results in the last presidential election (1st round)

France (2012):	30.8%
Romania (2009):	22.2%
Finland (2012):	14.9%
Portugal (2011):	7.14%
Slovakia (2009):	1.1%
Austria (2010):	15.6%
Poland (2010):	1.5%
Lithuania (2009):	9.7%
Bulgaria (2011):	3.64%

To make this map the far right parties and far left parties were selected. Examples : the National Front (FN) in France, the Slovakian National Party (SNS), the Dutch Socialist Party, (SP), the true Finns (PS) or the Radical Left Coalition (SYRIZA) in Greece. Also on this map feature both the right and leftwing populist parties. Qualified as populist are the parties which have in part given up an extremist discourse but which all or party share the following positions: criticism of the elites; challenge made to representation; value given to the national (or regional) dimension; total opposition to immigration; rejection of Islam and rejection of a multi-ethnic society. Examples: Ataka (A) in Bulgaria, the Northern League (LN) in Italy, the New Flemish Alliance (NV-A) or the People's Party (PP-DD) in Romania.

The Confidence Deficit of Citizens in the European Institutions

Citizens' Confidence in the European Union

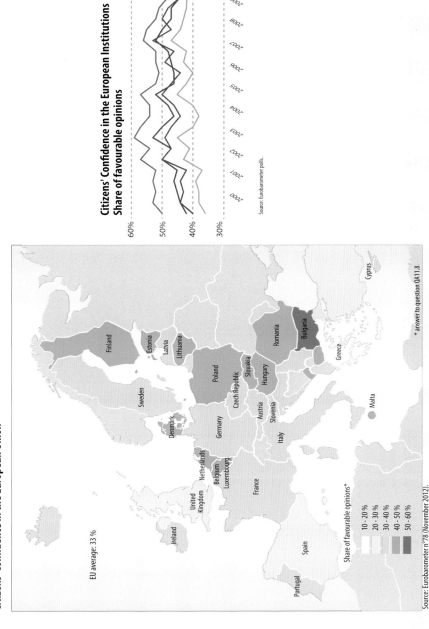

Citizens' Confidence in the European Institutions
Share of favourable opinions

European Parliament
Commission
Central Bank
Council

Source: Eurobarometer polls.

EU average: 33 %

Share of favourable opinions*

10 - 20 %
20 - 30 %
30 - 40 %
40 - 50 %
50 - 60 %

* answer to question QA11.8

Source: Eurobarometer n°78 (November 2012).

Portugal, Spain, Ireland, United Kingdom, France, Luxembourg, Belgium, Netherlands, Germany, Denmark, Sweden, Finland, Estonia, Latvia, Lithuania, Poland, Czech Republic, Slovakia, Hungary, Austria, Slovenia, Italy, Romania, Bulgaria, Greece, Cyprus, Malta

France - Germany, 2012

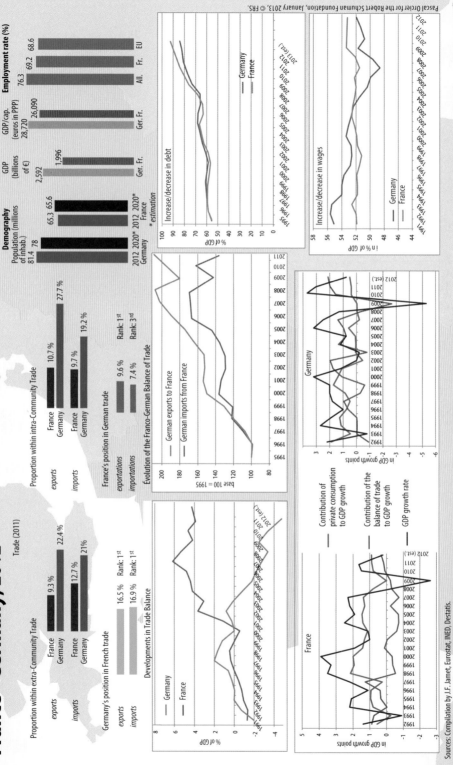

Trade (2011)

Proportion within extra-Community Trade

exports	France	9.3 %
	Germany	22.4 %
imports	France	12.7 %
	Germany	21%

Germany's position in French trade

| exports | 16.5 % | Rank: 1st |
| imports | 16.9 % | Rank: 1st |

Developments in Trade Balance

— Germany
— France

% of GDP

Proportion within intra-Community Trade

exports	France	10.7 %
	Germany	27.7 %
imports	France	9.7 %
	Germany	19.2 %

France's position in German trade

| exportations | 9.6 % | Rank: 1st |
| importations | 7.4 % | Rank: 3rd |

Evolution of the Franco-German Balance of Trade

— German exports to France
— German imports from France

base 100 = 1995

Demography
Population (millions of Inhab.)

	2012	2020*
France	65.3	65.6
Germany	81.4	78

2012 2020*
France
Germany
*estimation

GDP (billions of €)
Ger. Fr.
2,592 1,996

GDP/cap. (euros in PPP)
Ger. Fr.
28,720 26,090

Employment rate (%)
All. 76.3
Fr. 69.2
EU 68.6

Increase/decrease in debt
% of GDP
— Germany
— France

Increase/decrease in wages
in % of GDP
— Germany
— France

France
in GDP growth points

Germany
in GDP growth points

— Contribution of private consumption to GDP growth
— Contribution of the balance of trade to GDP growth
— GDP growth rate

Pascal Orcier for the Robert Schuman Foundation, January 2013. © FRS.

Sources: Compilation by J.F. Jamet, Eurostat, INED, Destatis.

A Differentiated European Union

Europe as an area of free trade and the circulation of people

Economic and Monetary Union

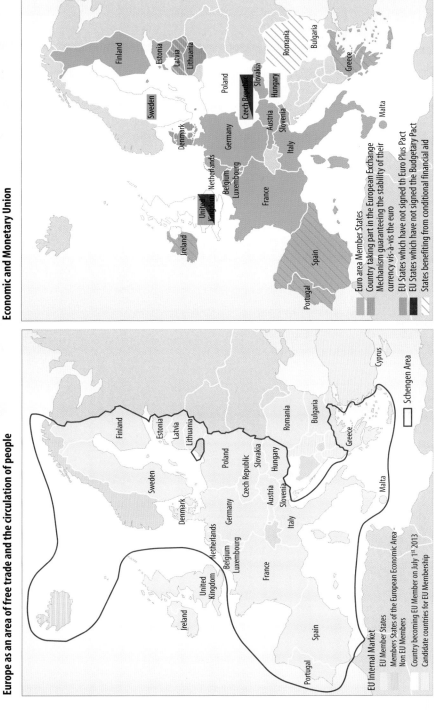

EU Internal Market
- EU Member States
- Members States of the European Economic Area – Non EU Members
- Country becoming EU Member on July 1st 2013
- Candidate countries for EU Membership

Schengen Area

Euro area Member States
Country taking part in the European Exchange Mechanism guaranteeing the stability of their currency vis-à-vis the euro
EU States which have not signed th Euro Plus Pact
EU States which have not signed the Budgetary Pact
States benefiting from conditional financial aid

Pascal Orcier for the Robert Schuman Foundation, January 2013, © FRS.

Enhanced Cooperation Agreements

Status:	Enhanced Cooperation Agreements		
	Divorce	EU Unitary Patent	Tax on Financial Transactions
	In force since 2010	Adoption on-going – implementation planned for 2014	Procedure on-going (request lodged on 28th September 2012)
	Participating States		
Austria	■	■	■
Belgium	■	■	■
Bulgaria	■	■	
Cyprus		■	
Czech Republic		■	
Denmark		■	
Estonia		■	■
Finland		■	
France	■	■	■
Germany	■	■	■
Greece		■	■
Hungary	■	■	
Ireland		■	
Italy	■		■
Latvia	■	■	
Lithuania		■	
Luxembourg	■	■	
Malta	■	■	
Netherlands		■	
Poland		■	
Portugal	■	■	■
Romania	■	■	
Slovakia		■	■
Slovenia	■	■	■
Spain	■		■
Sweden		■	
United Kingdom		■	
Number of participants	15	25	11

European Economic Area (EEA)

The European Economic Area extends the EU's internal market to the Member States of the European Free Trade Agreement except for Switzerland. These States enjoy the free movement of goods, people, services and capital and have to implement the matching rules (except for those which affect the political sphere, agricultural policy and fisheries, likewise their trade policy towards third countries). They also take part in certain EU programmes in the area of research, education, environment and cohesion.

Schengen Area

The Schengen Area includes the States applying the principle of the free movement of people in virtue of which any individual who has entered one of the participating States can cross the borders of the other countries without being controlled. A State cannot re-introduce border controls unless there is a breach of public order or national security and after consultation with the other States in the Schengen Area.

European Exchange Rate Mechanism (ERM)

The European Exchange Rate Mechanism pegs the euro to the currencies in certain EU countries thereby controlling fluctuations in the exchange rates. Entry into the euro zone is conditioned by participation in this mechanism for at least two years and by the respect of a limited fluctuation margin of 2.25% more or less.

Euro Pact Plus

The signatories of the Euro Plus Pact have committed to adopting real measures that aim to increase competitiveness and foster economic convergence.

Budgetary Compact

The Treaty on Stability, Coordination and Governance within the European Economic and Monetary Union (often called the "Budgetary Compact") controls the structural deficit of the Signatory States - once the public deficit has been corrected, economic variations and the deduction of one-off, temporary measures do not have to exceed 0.5% of the GDP, except in exceptional circumstances, for example during a serious economic recession.

The UK in Europe, the UK and Europe (1)

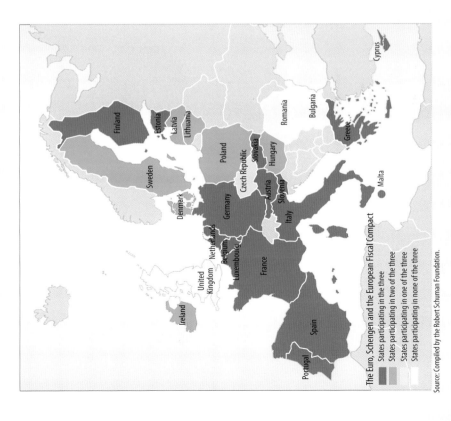

The Euro, Schengen and the European Fiscal Compact

- States participating in the three
- States participating in two of the three
- States participating in one of the three
- States participating in none of the three

Source: Compiled by the Robert Schuman Foundation.

Composition of the House of Commons (elected in 2010) in 2012

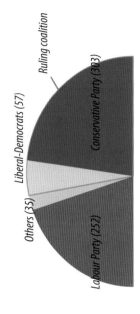

Ruling coalition

Conservative Party (303)

Liberal-Democrats (57)

Others (35)

Labour Party (252)

UK MEPs in the European Parliament

73 MEPs (3ʳᵈ rank)

751 MEPs

0 / 269 EPP (European People's Party)
13 / 190 S&D (Progressive Alliance of Socialists and Democrats in the European Parliament)
12 / 85 ALDE (Alliance of Liberals and Democrats for Europe)
5 / 59 Green-EFA (The Greens/European Free Alliance)
26 / 53 ECR (European Conservatives and Reformists) *(Conservative Deputies who left the EEP)*
10 / 34 EFD (Europe of Freedom and Democracy) *includes 10 UKIP MEPs* ⎤
1 / 34 GUE-NGL (European United Left-Nordic Green Left)   ⎥ eurosceptics
6 / 29 NA (non-attached members) *includes 2 BNP MEPs*   ⎦

UKIP: *United Kingdom Independence Party, demanding the withdrawal of the UK from the EU*
BNP: *British National Party, nationalist party*

* also the Chart of Fundamental Rights for UK in 2007

Pascal Orcier for the Robert Schuman Foundation, January 2013, © FRS.

The UK in Europe, the UK and Europe (2)

The Weight of the UK in the EU

Share of population

12.5%

Share of GDP

13.8%

Contribution to EU budget

12.6%

Share of the EU in the UK trade

Imports

51.3%

Exports

53.4%

The UK contribution to the EU budget (2011)

received from the EU: €6,570 millions

Payed to the EU: €13,825 millions*

Net operational budgetary balance: -€5,565 millions
↑ *The UK is a net contributor*

The "rebate" or "UK Cheque"
received by the UK, since 1985

€3.5 billion per year, of whose
1 billion supported by France,
700 million by Italy,
500 million by Spain,
200 million by Germany,
182 million by Poland...

Source: Compiled by the Robert Schuman Foundation.

The City, first European financial centre

40% of transactions in euro in the exchange market, ie more than in the euro area

Breakdown of exchanges made, by currency

2011
€ 48.7%
£ 45.9%

2012
€ 32%
£ 55.4%
others

* taking account of the "rebate".

British Mobility in Europe

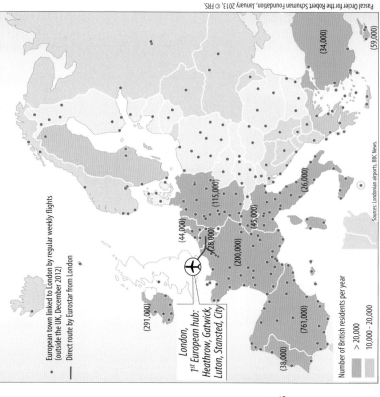

London,
1st European hub:
Heathrow, Gatwick, Luton, Stansted, City

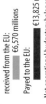

● European town linked to London by regular weekly flights (outside the UK, December 2012)
— Direct route by Eurostar from London

(291,000)
(44,000)
(28,000)
(115,000)
(200,000)
(45,000)
(26,000)
(34,000)
(59,000)
(761,000)
(38,000)

Number of British residents per year

▮ > 20,000
▯ 10,000 - 20,000

Sources: Londonian airports, BBC News.

Pascal Orcier for the Robert Schuman Foundation, January 2013. © FRS.

Women's Europe on 1ˢᵗ January 2013

Share of Women in Governments*

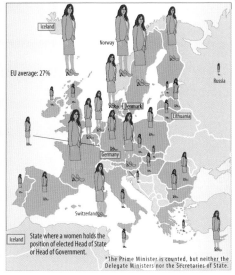

EU average: 27%

| Iceland | State where a women holds the position of elected Head of State or Head of Government. |

*The Prime Minister is counted, but neither the Delegate Ministers nor the Secretaries of State.

Share of Women in National Parliaments (Single or Lower Chamber)

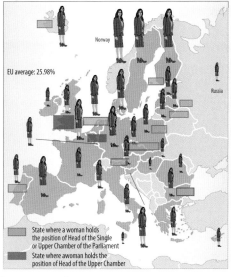

EU average: 25.98%

State where a woman holds the position of Head of the Single or Upper Chamber of the Parliament

State where a woman holds the position of Head of the Upper Chamber

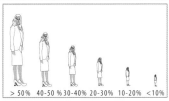

> 50%   40-50 %   30-40%   20-30%   10-20%   <10%

South Africa

Canada   Brazil   China   Japan

USA   Australia   India

Non-EU States average:
Women in Governments: 25.49%
Women in Parliaments: 23.47%
Women involved in decision making in the biggest companies: 8.97%

Share of Women amongst MEPs

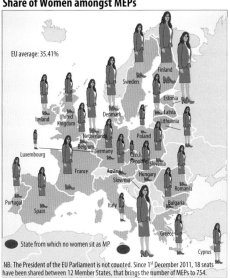

EU average: 35.41%

State from which no women sit as MP

NB: The President of the EU Parliament is not counted. Since 1ˢᵗ December 2011, 18 seats have been shared between 12 Member States, that brings the number of MEPs to 754.

Share of Women involved in decision making in the biggest companies (floated in the stock exchange)

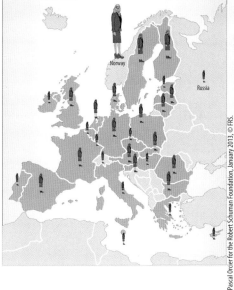

Source: Compiled by the Robert Schuman Fondation.

Pascal Orcier for the Robert Schuman Foundation, January 2013, © FRS.

Peripheral Nationalism in Europe

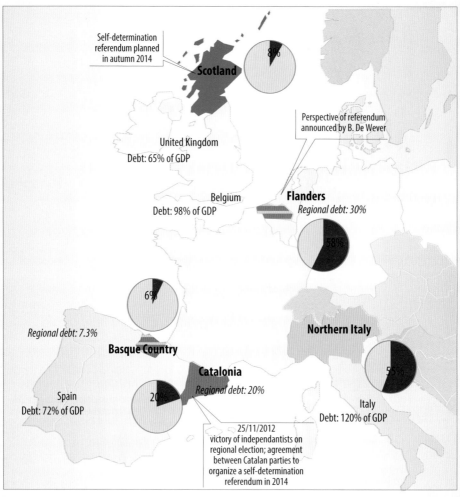

Self-determination
referendum planned
in autumn 2014

Scotland

Perspective of referendum
announced by B. De Wever

United Kingdom
Debt: 65% of GDP

Belgium
Debt: 98% of GDP

Flanders
Regional debt: 30%

58%

Regional debt: 7.3%

Basque Country

Northern Italy

Catalonia
Regional debt: 20%

Spain
Debt: 72% of GDP

55%

Italy
Debt: 120% of GDP

25/11/2012
victory of independantists on
regional election; agreement
between Catalan parties to
organize a self-determination
referendum in 2014

Eldorados ?
Share of the region in the National GDP

Identity revendications based on:

Linguistic particularism

Religious and territorial particularism

Claim of ethnic particularism

This map does not pretend to cover the entire issue of regionalism in Europe. It is a close up of cases mentioned specifically by Magali Balent in her article on the European Union and the challenges of national populism.

Pascal Orcier for the Robert Schuman Foundation, January 2013, © FRS.

European Public Opinion and the Crisis

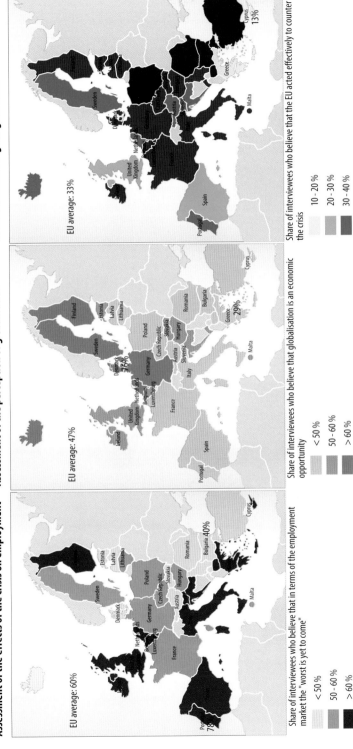

Assessment of the effects of the crisis on employment

EU average: 60%

Share of interviewees who believe that in terms of the employment market the "worst is yet to come"

- < 50 %
- 50 - 60 %
- > 60 %

Assessment of the perception of globalisation

EU average: 47%

Share of interviewees who believe that globalisation is an economic opportunity

- < 50 %
- 50 - 60 %
- > 60 %

EU effectiveness in fighting the crisis

EU average: 33%

Share of interviewees who believe that the EU acted effectively to counter the crisis

- 10 - 20 %
- 20 - 30 %
- 30 - 40 %
- 40 - 50 %
- 50 - 60 %

Pascal Orcier for the Robert Schuman Foundation, January 2013. © FRS.

Sources: Eurobarometer Polls n° 76 and 77, Autumn 2011 and Spring 2012.

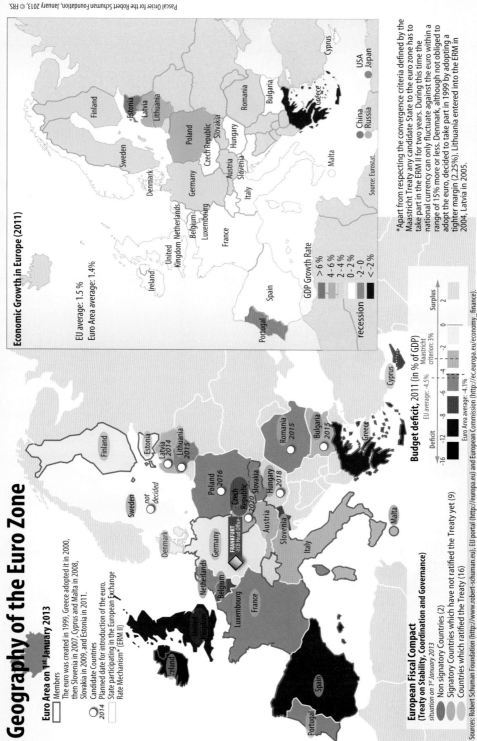

Geography of the Euro Zone

Sources: Robert Schuman Foundation (http://www.robert-schuman.eu), EU portal (http://europa.eu) and European Commission (http://ec.europa.eu/economy_finance).

Public Debt

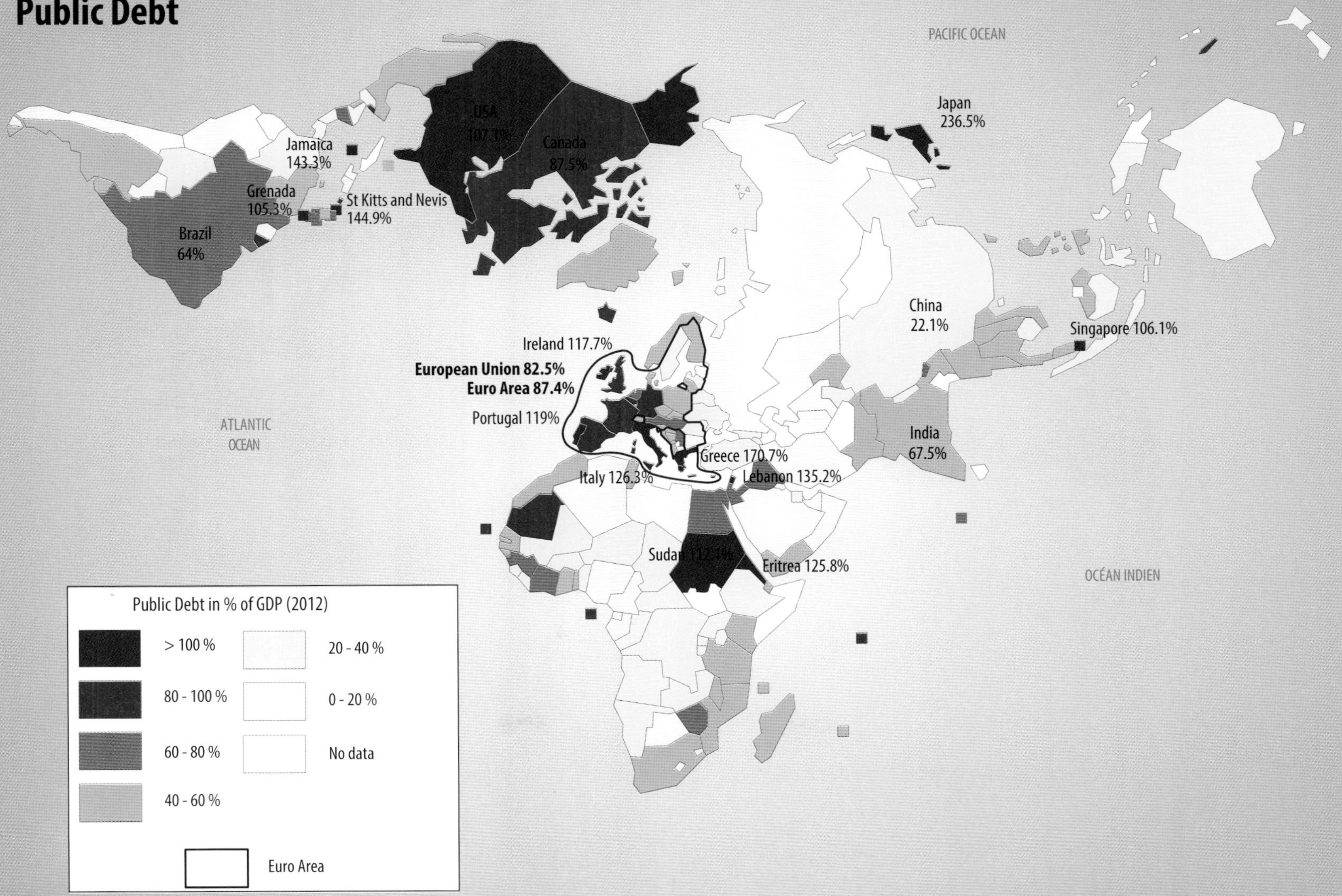

Singapore 106.1%

Japan 236.5%

China 22.1%

India 67.5%

Lebanon 135.2%

Eritrea 125.8%

Greece 170.7%

Suda 112.1%

Italy 126.3%

Ireland 117.7%

European Union 82.5%
Euro Area 87.4%

Portugal 119%

Canada 87.5%

USA 107.3%

St Kitts and Nevis 144.9%

Jamaica 143.3%

Grenada 105.3%

Brazil 64%

PACIFIC OCEAN

OCÉAN INDIEN

ATLANTIC OCEAN

Public Debt in % of GDP (2012)

> 100 %	20 - 40 %
80 - 100 %	0 - 20 %
60 - 80 %	No data
40 - 60 %	

Euro Area

Pascal Orcier for the Robert Schuman Foundation, January 2013 © FRS.

Source: International Monetary Fund, World Economic Outlook Database, October 2012.

EU Budget, 2012

Member States' Contribution to Community Budget, 2011 (in %)

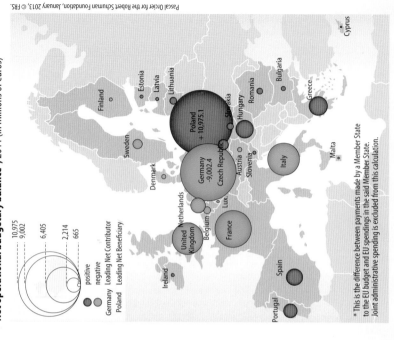

Statistical model:
nested averages

19.5
9.75
3.70
1
0.05

Source: EU portal (http://europa.eu/).

Net operational budgetary balance*, 2011 (in millions of euros)

Total Commitments Payments

2007-2013:
€975.7 billion

2010: €140.9 billion

2011: €142.2 billion

2012: €148 billion

2013: €152.5 billion

positive
negative

Germany Leading Net Contributor
Poland Leading Net Beneficiary

10,975
9,002
6,405
2,214
665

* This is the difference between payments made by a Member State
to the EU budget and EU spendings in the said Member State.
Joint adminstrative spending is excluded from this calculation.

Pascal Orcier for the Robert Schuman Foundation, January 2013, © FRS.

Unemployment and Activity in the EU Member States

Unemployment Rate (2012)

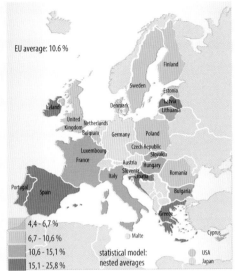

EU average: 10.6 %

4,4 - 6,7 %
6,7 - 10,6 %
10,6 - 15,1 %
15,1 - 25,8 %

statistical model:
nested averages

USA
Japan

Unemployment rate of the 15-24 year olds (2011)

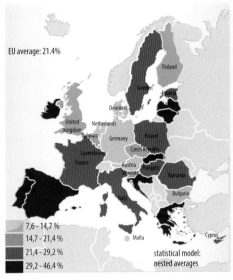

EU average: 21.4%

7,6 - 14,7 %
14,7 - 21,4 %
21,4 - 29,2 %
29,2 - 46,4 %

statistical model:
nested averages

Employment of the 55-64 year olds (2011)

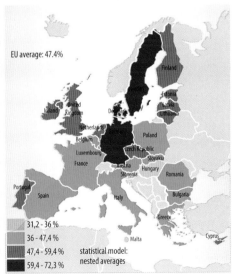

EU average: 47.4%

31,2 - 36 %
36 - 47,4 %
47,4 - 59,4 %
59,4 - 72,3 %

statistical model:
nested averages

Women's Employment Rate (2011)

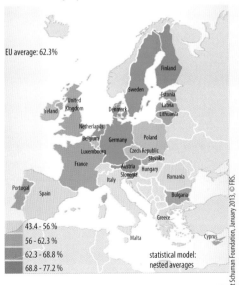

EU average: 62.3%

43.4 - 56 %
56 - 62.3 %
62.3 - 68.8 %
68.8 - 77.2 %

statistical model:
nested averages

Source : Eurostat.

Pascal Orcier for the Robert Schuman Foundation, January 2013, © FRS.

Industry in the EU Member States

Share of industry in the GDP (2012)

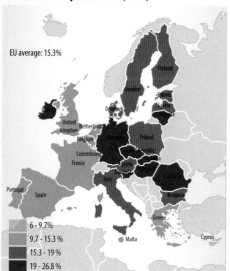

EU average: 15.3%

- 6 - 9.7 %
- 9.7 - 15.3 %
- 15.3 - 19 %
- 19 - 26.8 %

Share of industry in the GDP Development 1995 - 2012

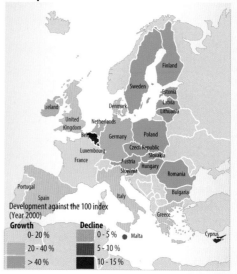

Development against the 100 index (Year 2000)

Growth	Decline
0 - 20 %	0 - 5 %
20 - 40 %	5 - 10 %
> 40 %	10 - 15 %

Share of industry in employment (2012)

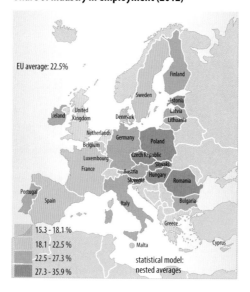

EU average: 22.5%

- 15.3 - 18.1 %
- 18.1 - 22.5 %
- 22.5 - 27.3 %
- 27.3 - 35.9 %

statistical model: nested averages

Source : Eurostat.

Pascal Orcier for the Robert Schuman Foundation, January 2013, © FRS.

Current Account in % of the GDP and Investments in R&D in Europe (2012)

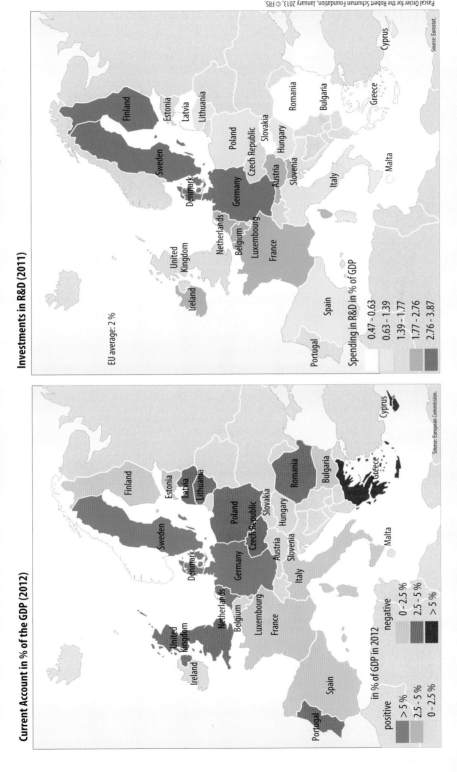

Current Account in % of the GDP (2012)

Investments in R&D (2011)

EU average: 2 %

Spending in R&D in % of GDP

0.47 – 0.63
0.63 – 1.39
1.39 – 1.77
1.77 – 2.76
2.76 – 3.87

In % of GDP in 2012

positive
> 5 %
2.5 – 5 %
0 – 2.5 %

negative
0 – 2.5 %
2.5 – 5 %
> 5 %

Source: European Commission.

Source: Eurostat.

Pascal Orcier for the Robert Schuman Foundation, January 2013, © FRS.

Research and Innovation in the European Union

Share of spending on research and innovation in % of GDP (2010)

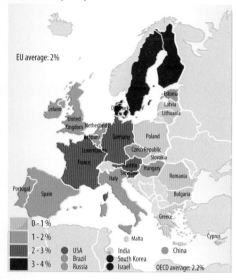

EU average: 2%

0 - 1 %
1 - 2 %
2 - 3 %
3 - 4 %

USA
Brazil
Russia

India
South Korea
Israel

China

OECD average: 2.2%

Summary Innovation Indicator (2011)

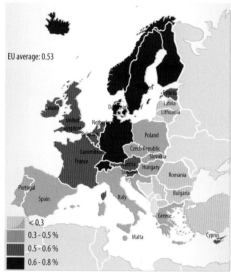

EU average: 0.53

< 0.3
0.3 - 0.5 %
0.5 - 0.6 %
0.6 - 0.8 %

Patents (2010)

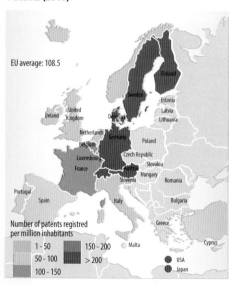

EU average: 108.5

Number of patents registred per million inhabitants

1 - 50
50 - 100
100 - 150
150 - 200
> 200

USA
Japan

Public spending in education in % of GDP (2009)

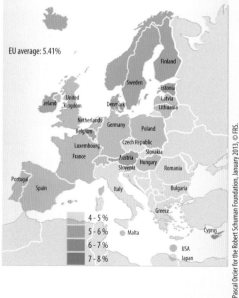

EU average: 5.41%

4 - 5 %
5 - 6 %
6 - 7 %
7 - 8 %

USA
Japan

Sources: Eurostat, GD Enterprise and Industry *Innovation Union Scoreboard*.

Pascal Order for the Robert Schuman Foundation, January 2013, © FRS.

Competitiveness and Governance
Governance Indicators (2011)
Control of Corruption

Rule of Law

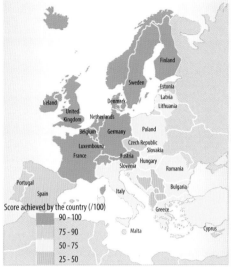

Government effectiveness

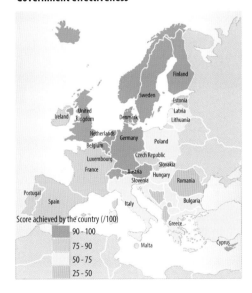

Source: World Bank.

Pascal Orcier for the Robert Schuman Foundation, January 2013, © FRS.

The Energy Issue in Europe (1)

Energy Import Dependence (2010)

Gas imports

Shale gas in Europe

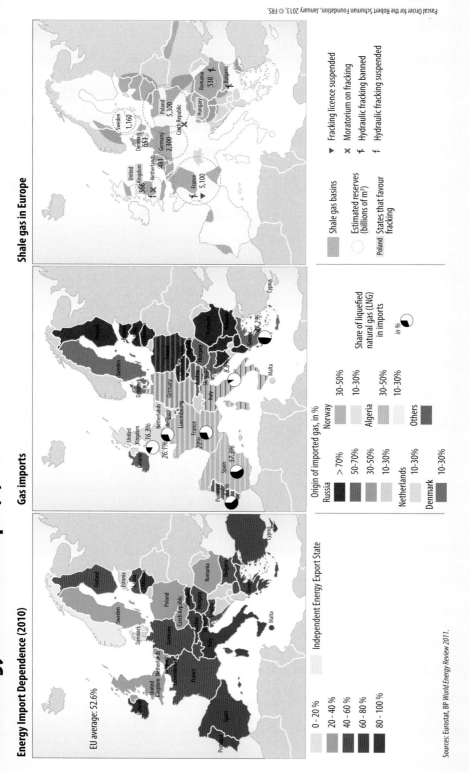

EU average: 52.6%

Energy Import Dependence (2010)

- 0 - 20 %
- 20 - 40 %
- 40 - 60 %
- 60 - 80 %
- 80 - 100 %

Independent Energy Export State

Gas imports

Origin of imported gas, in %

Russia	Norway
> 70%	30-50%
50-70%	10-30%
30-50%	Algeria
10-30%	30-50%
	10-30%

Netherlands
- 10-30%

Others

Denmark
- 10-30%

Share of liquefied natural gas (LNG) in imports

in %

Shale gas in Europe

- Shale gas basins
- Estimated reserves (billions of m³)
- Poland — States that favour fracking

▼ Fracking licence suspended
✕ Moratorium on fracking
Ⱶ Hydraulic fracking banned
Ⱡ Hydraulic fracking suspended

Sources: Eurostat, BP World Energy Review 2011.

Pascal Orcier for the Robert Schuman Foundation, January 2013, © FRS.

The Energy Issue in Europe (2)

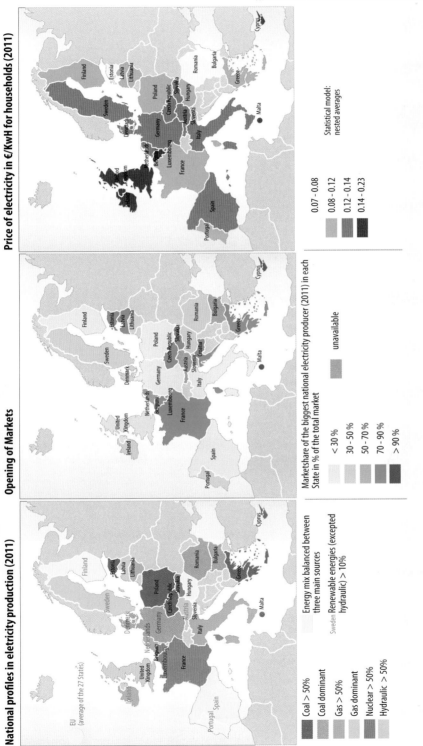

National profiles in eletricity production (2011)

Opening of Markets

Price of electricity in €/KwH for households (2011)

EU (average of the 27 States)

Coal > 50%
Coal dominant
Gas > 50%
Gas dominant
Nuclear > 50%
Hydraulic > 50%

Energy mix balanced between three main sources
Renewable energies (excepted hydraulic) > 10%

Marketshare of the biggest national electricity producer (2011) in each State in % of the total market

< 30 %
30 - 50 %
50 - 70 %
70 - 90 %
> 90 %
unavailable

Statistical model: nested averages

0.07 - 0.08
0.08 - 0.12
0.12 - 0.14
0.14 - 0.23

Sources: Eurostat, BP World Energy Review 2011.

Pascal Orcier for the Robert Schuman Foundation, January 2013, © FRS.

Intra-Community Trade, 2011

Share of intra-community trade

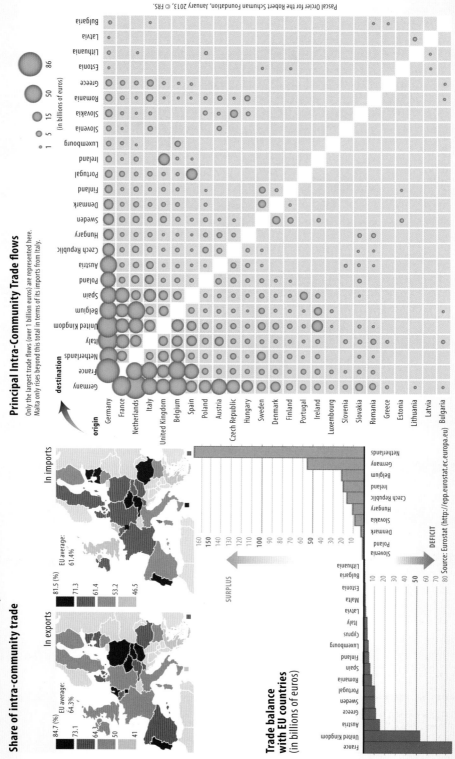

In exports

EU average: 64.3%

84.7 (%)	
73.1	
64.3	
50	
41	

In imports

EU average: 61.4%

81.5 (%)	
71.3	
61.4	
53.2	
46.5	

Principal Intra-Community Trade flows

Only the largest trade flows (over 1 billion euros) are represented here. Malta only rises beyond this total in terms of its imports from Italy.

(in billions of euros)

86   50   15   5   1

destination → / origin

Trade balance with EU countries (in billions of euros)

SURPLUS
160 150 140 130 120 110 100 90 80 70 60 50 40 30 20 10

Netherlands, Germany, Belgium, Ireland, Czech Republic, Hungary, Slovakia, Denmark, Poland, Slovenia, Lithuania, Bulgaria, Estonia, Malta, Latvia, Italy, Cyprus, Luxembourg, Finland, Spain, Romania, Portugal, Sweden, Greece, Austria, United Kingdom, France

DEFICIT
10 20 30 40 50 60 70 80

Source: Eurostat (http://epp.eurostat.ec.europa.eu)

Pascal Orcier for the Robert Schuman Foundation, January 2013, © FRS.

Europe and Globalisation: risks and assets

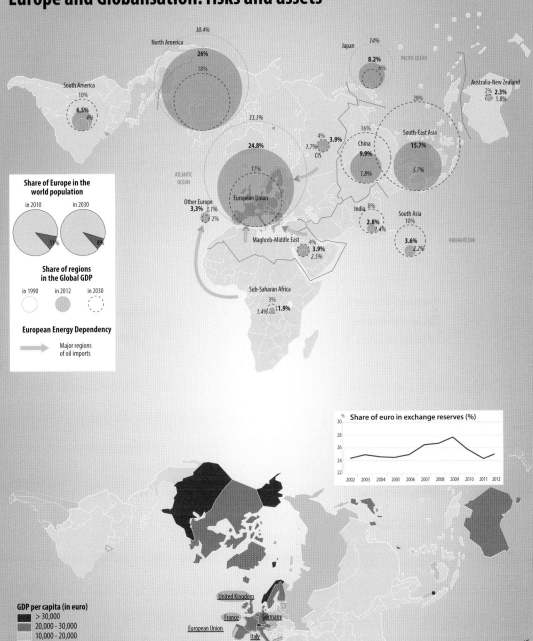

North America
30.4%
26%
18%

South America
10%
6,5%
4%

Japan
14%
8.2%
6%

Australia-New Zealand
2% **2.3%**
1.8%

33.3%
24.8%
17%

4% **3.9%**
1.7%
CIS

16%
China
9.9%
1.8%

28%
South-East Asia
15.7%
5.7%

PACIFIC OCEAN

ATLANTIC OCEAN

Other Europe
3,3% 3,1%
2%

European Union

India 8%
2.8%
1.4%

South Asia
10%
3.6%
2.2%

INDIAN OCEAN

Maghreb-Middle East
4%
3.9%
2.5%

Sub-Saharan Africa
3%
1.4% **1.9%**

Share of Europe in the world population

in 2010   in 2030

11%   8%

Share of regions in the Global GDP

in 1990   in 2012   in 2030

European Energy Dependency

→ Major regions of oil imports

Share of euro in exchange reserves (%)

2002 2003 2004 2005 2006 2007 2008 2009 2010 2011 2012

United Kingdom
France   Germany
European Union
Italy

GDP per capita (in euro)
- > 30,000
- 20,000 - 30,000
- 10,000 - 20,000

International status of the euro
- Euro area
- State whose currency is pegged against the euro by a fixed exchange rate

Over-representation in international organizations

France EU Member States which have a seat at the UN Council of Security
Germany G20 participants

EU Member States share of votes in the IMF
30.9 %

Euros in exchange reserves (value)

5,500,000
5,000,000
4,500,000
4,000,000
3,500,000
3,000,000
2,500,000
2,000,000
1,500,000
1,000,000
500,000

2002 2003 2004 2005 2006 2007 2008 2009 2010 2011

Sources: CEPII, COFER.

The USA and the EU: economy and demography

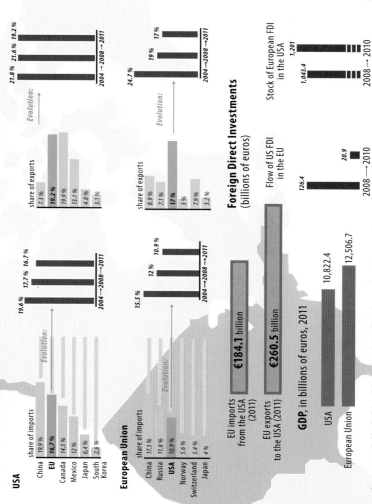

Trade in goods, major partners, 2010

USA

share of imports

China	19.9 %
EU	**16.7 %**
Canada	14.5 %
Mexico	12 %
Japan	6.4 %
South Korea	2.6 %

share of exports

	7.3 %
	19.2 %
	19.9 %
	13.1 %
	4.8 %
	3.1 %

Evolution:

19.6 % → 17.7 % → 16.7 %
2004 → 2008 → 2011

21.8 % → 21.6 % → 19.2 %
2004 → 2008 → 2011

European Union

share of imports

China	17.3 %
Russia	11.8 %
USA	**10.9 %**
Norway	5.6 %
Switzerland	5.4 %
Japan	4 %

share of exports

	8.9 %
	7.1 %
	17 %
	3 %
	7.9 %
	3.2 %

Evolution:

15.5 % → 12 % → 10.9 %
2004 → 2008 → 2011

24.7 % → 19 % → 17 %
2004 → 2008 → 2011

Foreign Direct Investments
(billions of euros)

EU imports from the USA (2011)
€184.1 billion

EU exports to the USA (2011)
€260.5 billion

Flow of US FDI in the EU

126.4 → 20.9
2008 → 2010

Stock of European FDI in the USA

1,043.4 → 1,201
2008 → 2010

GDP, in billions of euros, 2011

USA — 10,822.4

European Union — 12,506.7

Demography (millions of inhabitants)

2012
EU — 503
USA — 317
World Population — 11 %

2030
EU — 520
USA — 363.5
World Population — 10.7 %

Sources: compiled by the Robert Schuman Foundation (http://www.robert-schuman.eu/); eurostat; IMF (www.imf.org/); GD Trade (http://trade.ec.europa.eu/doclib/docs/2006/september/tradoc_113465.pdf); UNDP.

Pascal Orcier for the Robert Schuman Foundation, January 2013. © FRS.

The EU and World Trade in Globalisation: Trade in Merchandise, 2012

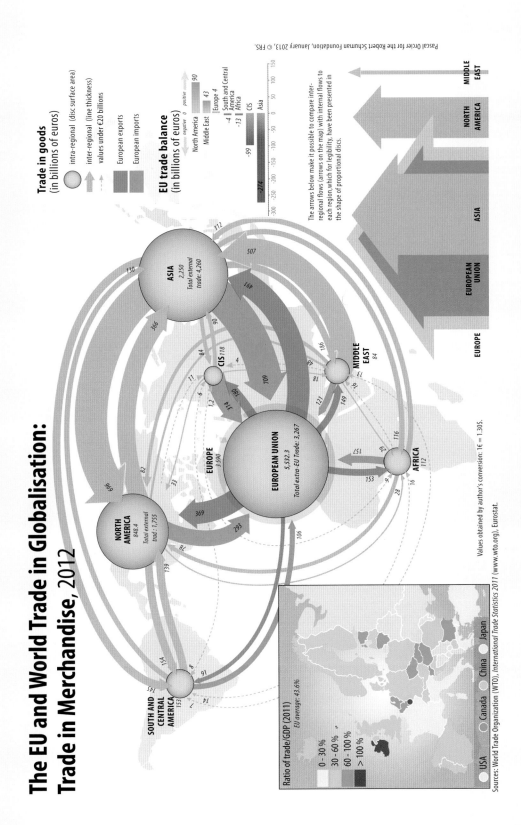

Trade in goods
(in billions of euros)

- intra-regional (disc surface area)
- inter-regional (line thickness)
- values under €20 billions
- European exports
- European imports

EU trade balance
(in billions of euros)

negative 0 positive

- North America 90
- Middle East 43
- Europe 4
- South and Central America
- Africa -4
- CIS -13
- Asia -99
- -274

The arrows below make it possible to compare inter-regional flows (arrows on the map) with internal flows to each region, which for legibility, have been presented in the shape of proportional discs.

MIDDLE EAST

NORTH AMERICA

ASIA

EUROPEAN UNION

EUROPE

Values obtained by author's conversion: 1€ = 1.30$.

ASIA
2,250
Total external trade: 4,260

CIS 118

EUROPE
3,590

EUROPEAN UNION
5,532.3
Total extra-EU Trade: 3,267

MIDDLE EAST
84

AFRICA
112

NORTH AMERICA
848.4
Total external trade : 1,755

SOUTH AND CENTRAL AMERICA
153

Ratio of trade/GDP (2011)
EU average: 43.6%

- 0 - 30 %
- 30 - 60 %
- 60 - 100 %
- > 100 %

○ USA ○ Canada ○ China ○ Japan

Pascal Orcier for the Robert Schuman Foundation, January 2013, © FRS.

Sources: World Trade Organization (WTO), *International Trade Statistics 2011* (www.wto.org), Eurostat.

The European Union in the World: trade agreements

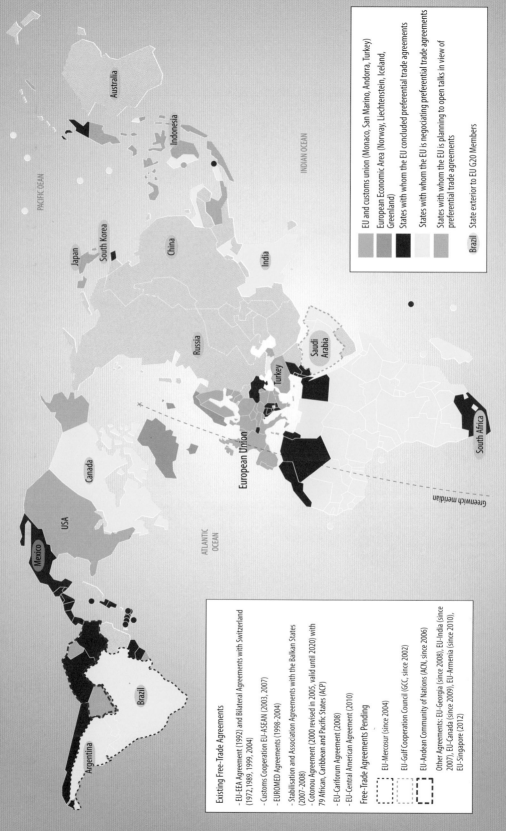

Pascal Orcier for the Robert Schuman Foundation, January 2013, © FRS.

PACIFIC OCEAN

ATLANTIC OCEAN

INDIAN OCEAN

Greenwich meridian

Australia

Indonesia

South Korea

Japan

China

India

Russia

Turkey

Saudi Arabia

South Africa

European Union

Canada

USA

Mexico

Brazil

Argentina

Legend:

- EU and customs union (Monaco, San Marino, Andorra, Turkey)
- European Economic Area (Norway, Liechtenstein, Iceland, Greenland)
- States with whom the EU concluded preferential trade agreements
- States with whom the EU is negociating preferential trade agreements
- States with whom the EU is planning to open talks in view of preferential trade agreements

Brazil   State exterior to EU G20 Members

Existing Free-Trade Agreements

- EU-EEA Agreement (1992) and Bilateral Agreements with Switzerland (1972, 1989, 1999, 2004)
- Customs Cooperation EU-ASEAN (2003, 2007)
- EUROMED Agreements (1998-2004)
- Stabilisation and Association Agreements with the Balkan States (2007-2008)
- Cotonou Agreement (2000 revised in 2005, valid until 2020) with 79 African, Caribbean and Pacific States (ACP)
- EU-Cariforum Agreement (2008)
- EU-Central American Agreement (2010)

Free-Trade Agreements Pending

- EU-Mercosur (since 2004)

- EU-Gulf Cooperation Council (GCC, since 2002)

- EU-Andean Community of Nations (ACN, since 2006)

Other Agreements: EU-Georgia (since 2008), EU-India (since 2007), EU-Canada (since 2009), EU-Armenia (since 2010), EU-Singapore (2012)

Sources: European Commission, GD Fiscality and custom union, International Labour Organization (www.ilo.org), GD Trade.

Critical regions and zones of interest

Legend:

- End of the crisis and transition
- State experiencing serious armed conflict
- States regarded as destabilizing
- Sectors subject to piracy
- Al-Qaeda's area of activity
- Zones not under control; sieges by guerillas or paramilitary groups
- Political transition and succession issues
- Political/Humanitarian crisis
- Tensions/Political contestation
- Closed Border
- Rebellion
- Frozen conflict
- Major attacks
- Strategic points
- Military base
- Presence of Western fleets

LIBYA

Map labels:

1,000 km 500 0

RUSSIA

KAZAKHSTAN

KYRGYZSTAN

UZBEKISTAN

TURKMENISTAN

TAJIKISTAN

Moscow 2010

Chechnya

Ingushetia

Vladikavkaz 2010

Russian Caucasus 2002-2010

Dagestan

Abkhazia

South Ossetia

Nagorny-Karabakh

BLACK SEA

Transnistria

TURKEY

Istanbul 2003-2010

Bosphorus

Dardanelles

Syrian refugees in Turkey

Sharing of the Caspian

IRAN

Iranian nuclear programme

Kashmir

Peshawar (5 attacks) 2009, 2011

Islamabad, 2009

Rawalpindi, 2009

Lahore 2010

Tensions on the Duran Line

AFGHANISTAN

Khost 2008

Al-Qaeda central

PAKISTAN

Baluchistan

Gwadar 2004

Karachi 2002

INDIA

Thar Desert

Ahmedabad 2008

Mumbai 2008

Pune 2010

Islands in the Persian Gulf

Hormuz

Abu Dhabi

OMAN

UNITED ARAB EMIRATES

QATAR

BAHRAIN

Riyadh 2003

SAUDI ARABIA

Nejd Desert

Nefud Desert

Jeddah 2009

Mecca

Medina

piracy

INDIAN OCEAN

Afar

In Afar 2009, 2010

Mossul

Kirkuk 2009, 2010

Aleppo 2009, 2010

SYRIA

Hama

Damascus 2006-2010

IRAQ

Baghdad 2006-2010

Hilla

Shiite rebellion 2009

KUWAIT

Zaïdit rebellion

Aden 2007

USS Cole, 2002

YEMEN

Al-Qaeda in the Arabic Peninsula (AQAP)

Bab el Mab

DJIBOUTI

Somaliland

Puntland

Bosasso 2008-2012

Mogadishu 2008-2012

Militias Al-Chabab

Kismayo 2008-2012

SOMALIA

ERITREA

Addis Ababa 2009

ETHIOPIA

Ogaden

LEBANON

Beirut

WEST BANK

West Bank

Gaza

Amman, 2005

Sharm el-Cheikh

JORDAN

Israeli raids on Gaza, 2012

CYPRUS

Akrotiri

Dhekelia

EGYPT

Cairo 2006, 2009

Suez

Rise in tension between Muslims and Copts

RED SEA

Tiflat, 2012

Nairobi 2009-2010

UGANDA

Kampala 2010

KENYA

Kenyan military intervention in Western Somalia since 16th October 2011. Kismayo, its objective, has been reached on 28th September 2012.

Situation on 19th December 2012
- 71 acts of piracy since 1st January
- 9 Ships held
- 147 Hostages held

LRA

Khartoum

Tensions in Kordofan and Blue Nile, resurgence of conflict between the two Sudans

SUDAN

SOUTH SUDAN

Juba

Darfur

CHAD

Ndjamena

CENTRAL AFRICAN REPUBLIC

Bangui

DEMOCRATIC REPUBLIC OF CONGO

Libreville

GABON

MEDITERRANEAN SEA

Benghazi

LIBYA

Challenge to security by armed militia

Tripoli

Misrata

TUNISIA

Djerba 2002

ALGERIA

Algiers 2007-2010

Tizi Ouzou Kabylia 2010

In Amenas 2013

SAHARA

south Algeria

Tuareg rebellion

NIGER

Agadez 2010

Niamey

Kidal

Gao

Tombouctou

MALI

Bamako

Al-Qaeda in the Islamic Maghreb (AQIM)

Polisario Front 2007

Western Sahara

MAURITANIA

Nouakchott 2009

SENEGAL

Dakar

isohyet 200

isohyet 600

limits of the Sahel

Platform for cocaine traffic

Western Africa: 27 incidents (kidnappings, murders, attacks) between 2003 and 2011

Proclamation of the independence of Azawad on 06/04/2012 and instauration of the charia in the north of Mali

French military operation with ECOWAS support against terrorists in North Mali, January 2013

Peace and ceasefire agreement in January 2013

Religious violences

Boko Haram

NIGERIA

Lagos

BURKINA-FASO

Ouagadougou

GUINEA

Conakry 600

GUINEA BISSAU

Bissau

Coups d'État in 2012

Abidjan

Accra

Tropic of Cancer

Equator

Casablanca 2003

MOROCCO

Madrid 2004

Gibraltar

London 2005

45°

Idea: Michel Foucher; design: Pascal Orcier, for the Robert Schuman Foundation, January 2013, © FRS.

World Security: European Union intervention and participation

Situation on 1st December 2012

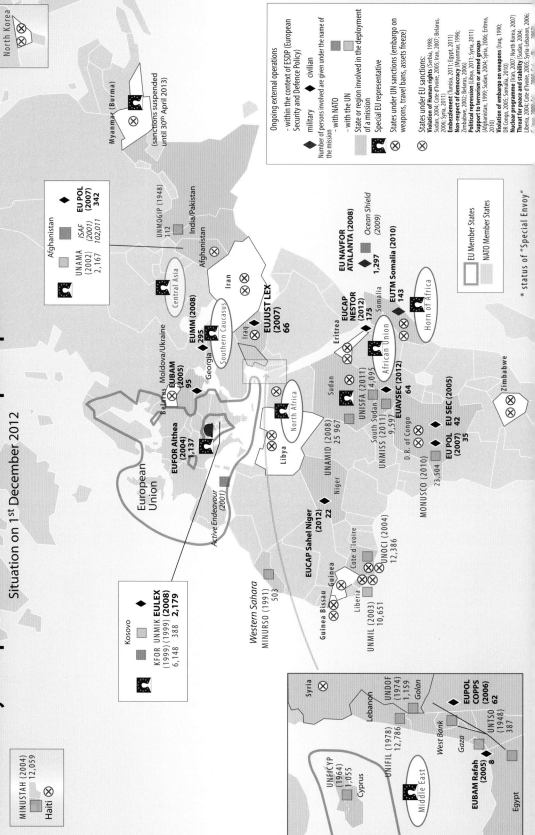

The EU and the Arab Revolutions

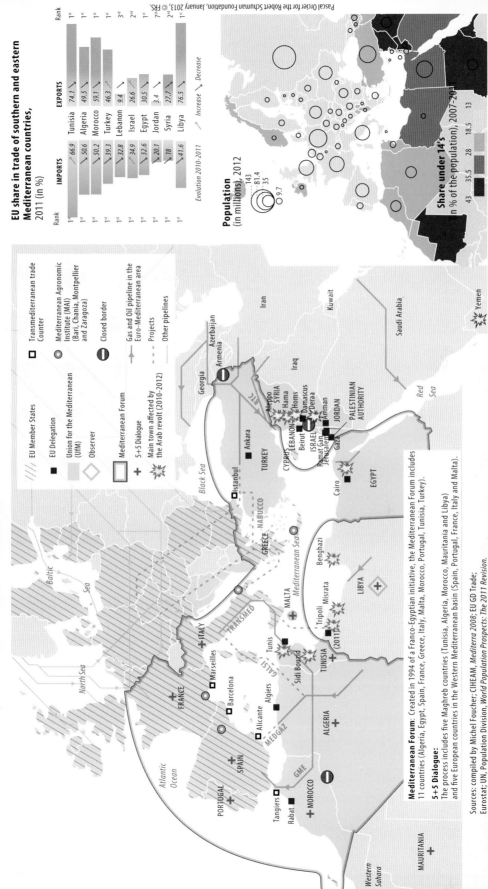

EU share in trade of southern and eastern Mediterranean countries, 2011 (in %)

	IMPORTS	Rank		EXPORTS	Rank
Tunisia	66.9 ↘	1st		74.1 ↗	1st
Algeria	50.6 ↘	1st		49.5 ↘	1st
Morocco	50.2 ↘	1st		59.1 ↗	1st
Turkey	39.3 ↘	1st		46.3 ↘	1st
Lebanon	32.8 ↘	1st		9.4 ↘	3rd
Israel	34.9 ↘	1st		26.6 ↘	2nd
Egypt	32.6 ↘	1st		30.5 ↗	1st
Jordan	20.1 ↗	7th		3.4 ↗	1st
Syria	18 ↘	2nd		27.7 ↘	2nd
Libya	41.6 ↗	1st		76.5 ↘	1st

Evolution 2010-2011   ↗ Increase   ↘ Decrease

Population (in millions), 2012
143 81.4 35 9.7

Share under 14's (in % of the population), 2007–20..
43 35.5 28 18.5 13

Transmediterranean trade Counter
Mediterranean Agronomic Institute (MAI) (Bari, Chania, Montpellier and Zaragoza)
Closed border
Gas and Oil pipeline in the Euro-Mediterranean area
Projects
Other pipelines

EU Member States
EU Delegation
Union for the Mediterranean (UfM)
Observer
Mediterranean Forum
5+5 Dialogue
Main town affected by the Arab revolt (2010–2012)

Mediterranean Forum: Created in 1994 of a Franco-Egyptian initiative, the Mediterranean Forum includes 11 countries (Algeria, Egypt, Spain, France, Greece, Italy, Malta, Morocco, Portugal, Tunisia, Turkey).

5+5 Dialogue:
The process includes five Maghreb countries (Tunisia, Algeria, Morocco, Mauritania and Libya) and five European countries in the Western Mediterranean basin (Spain, Portugal, France, Italy and Malta).

Sources: compiled by Michel Foucher; CIHEAM, Mediterra 2008; EU GD Trade; Eurostat; UN, Population Division, World Population Prospects: The 2011 Revision.

Pascal Orcier for the Robert Schuman Foundation, January 2013, © FRS.

Towards more women in Europe?

Pascale JOANNIN

2012 was not an extraordinary year for women in Europe. No women were elected as Head of State or of government, no women were appointed at the European Central Bank; a multitude of obstacles have been erected to undermine the European Commission's draft directive[1] which aimed to achieve a 40% quota of women on company boards – inequality between men and women has continued to grow[2] : there has been nothing to encourage our optimism.

Europe is still a male universe although the situation is slightly better in this part of the world than elsewhere. Women can only count on themselves if they are to be freed from the "confined" space that they have been granted or in which they have been restricted. They are not mistaken in this. After listening to decision makers' fine speeches, which are rarely followed by action, women have decided to organise.

Women's networks have grown. Not to swap interesting recipes or to talk house, but rather to define some strategies to disrupt the order established by men, which the latter guard jealously out of fear of being robbed of something. Women have done this mainly to show they exist, that they are worth as much as men and to let the latter know how to cohabit and share power.

Women and Power: towards new governance?

All of women's major victories have never happened by chance. No one has ever given them anything. Whatever they have achieved is owed to their perseverance and tenacity. That was true in the past, as it still is and will be in the future. Progress has been so slow that it will still take time before things really change. And these necessary developments cannot occur naturally, because impediments of all kinds are there to prevent progress being made. Sometimes destiny needs a helping hand ...

---

1. Commission Communication "The balance of men/women in business management positions: helping towards intelligent, sustainable, inclusive growth" COM(2012) 615 final, 14th November 2012 http://ec.europa.eu/justice/gender-equality/files/womenonboards/communication_quotas_fr.pdf

2. OECD report, "Male/Female Inequalities. It is time to act", 17th December 2012 http://www.oecd.org/fr/parite/agir.htm

If we are to change the existing imbalance between men and women the idea is gradually gaining ground that more restrictive measures are needed to overcome reticence and to "boost" the female profile in society. Women are more qualified than men but too few of them rise to leading positions. How can this situation be corrected? By quotas. But this word alone is enough to make some faint, annoy others or they lose their temper – it leaves no one indifferent.

Ten years ago quotas were introduced to remedy an evident under-representation of women in Parliamentary Assemblies. Several countries implemented them. It has to be admitted that this has boosted parity.

Just one example – there are more French women elected to the European Parliament (45.95%), where electoral law makes quotas obligatory, than to the National Assembly (26.34%) where the law is still just an incentive delivered to the political parties.

In spite of all the shouting about the introduction of quotas in several European States it seems difficult to go backwards on this. Firstly because the place of women is still relatively weak both in Parliaments (25.98% in the Union, 20.8% in the world) as well as within governments (27% in the Union) and that back-pedalling would be the worst thing that could happen and therefore detrimental to the instigator. It would also be bad because the method has been established in economic life.

In the face of the sorry lack of women in the management structures of major companies several European countries (Austria, Belgium, Denmark, Spain, France, Greece, Italy, the Netherlands, Portugal and Slovenia) decided to transpose the rule into the economic domain which now appears to producing results in the political sphere too. They have adopted laws to progressively make it obligatory via a quota system to have women on administrative boards. These laws only apply to companies that are floated on the stock exchange and do not concern the executive committees.

However in very little time the countries which introduced these measures have witnessed significant changes in their situation. As an example French companies floated on the stock exchange only had between 4 and 6% of women on their boards in the 1990's. The law of 27th January 2011 stipulated that companies had to open their boards to 20% of women within three years and to 40% within the next six years. In just two years these companies now have 16.6% of women on their boards[3]. This is not the only country that has achieved this. It is but a beginning.

Furthermore the European Commission is now addressing this issue. Basing itself on the fact that *"over the last decade, in spite of intense public debate and several pro-active initiatives, the male/female balance on company boards has barely developed in Europe,"* on 14th December 2012 it put forward a directive that set a minimum goal of 40% of the under-represented sex amongst non-executive administrators on company boards floated on the stock exchange in Europe by 2020 or by 2018 as far as public companies are concerned. European Commission Vice-President Viviane Reding recalls that *"the boards of the biggest European companies remain dominated by men and a glass ceiling is preventing talented women from rising to the highest positions. Women only comprise 15% of non-executive boards and 8.9% of executive boards."*

This proposal led to lively response and Ms Reding was even obliged to answer on two occasions to crush resistance both within the Commission and on the part of 9 Member States who opposed the quotas on principle[4].

It will be extremely difficult to go backwards now.

---

3. GMI Ratings' 2012 Women on Boards Survey, March 2012 http://library.constantcontact.com/download/get/file/1102561686275-86/GMIRatings_WOB_032012.pdf

4. Nine Member States reject quotas for women 17th September 2012 http://www.europolitics.info/business-competitiveness/nine-member-states-reject-quotas-for-women-artb342961-4.html

"Force fortune, hold on to your happiness and rise to the challenge. By watching you they will get used to the idea." – René Char

But we have to go further. Indeed more and more women are working: 62.5% in the European Union. They are more qualified than men: 58.9% of European university graduates are women. Slowly they have entered all professional sectors. But they still struggle to enter the highest spheres. Although they are not an answer to everything quotas have been useful. Without them women's progress would have been even slower.

Opening the doors to administrative boards is all very well but why should we limit this to companies on the stock exchange? Administrators' posts are also there to be taken in midcap or in small to medium sized companies (SMEs). And these companies need to be managed by men and women. A study[5] shows that administrative boards in France comprised 17.3% of the women in 2010 amongst SMEs, in comparison with 10.5% in big companies and 10.3% in intermediate-sized businesses. The average number was higher for women in family companies than amongst the others. Hence a great deal of work still has to be done.

Without expecting everything from quotas, women have decided to roll up their shirt sleeves and show what they are capable of. Initiatives had been taken everywhere across the world; from the Women's Forum, which in just a few years has become symbolic of women's "networking" worldwide, to hundreds of think-tanks run by women who have understood the very interest of this type of activity. It will be impossible to continue now as we have done in the past. Laws, debates, chats – the will is there to take matters forward, to help towards breaking the "glass ceiling". The Nordic countries are no longer alone in terms of showing off good figures, like Norway for example (36.3%) which launched the issue of women's participation on company boards in 2004. All of Europe is joining in ... And the movement is spreading further afield. We simply have to look at the situation in South Africa (17.4%).

Women no longer want to be intimidated and are rejecting unacceptable situations. During the renewal of the members of its board the European Central Bank[6], MEPs wondered why it had only appointed an exclusively male board until 2018 since it already has women on its Council. In the European Parliament they fought to win – in vain this time round, but everyone has now understood that in the future the institutions of Europe will have to respect the rules they have set themselves at least in order to achieve *"balance between men and women in the decision making process in economic and political life and in both public and private sectors."* It is time that this goal finally became a reality. For example the next time the Commission is renewed in 2014, it might be totally equal and have 14 women out of the 28 Member States which the European Union will then comprise.

Furthermore women are organising to counter fallacious arguments which state that there are no competent women available. Several initiatives have been launched to spot capable women and to promote them amongst those circulating untruths like this. Training schemes have been introduced to prepare women for administrators' posts, consultancies have developed activities to select women, thereby responding to the demand on the part of some businesses who want to appoint women to their boards.

---

5. 20 years of board development in France 1992-2010, Cahiers « Preuves à l'appui », October 2012 http://www.middlenext.com/IMG/pdf/Preuves_a_l_Appui_No3_vdef.pdf

6. Composition of the ECB's governing council since November 2012 : http://www.ecb.int/ecb/orga/decisions/govc/html/index.fr.html

These initiatives are now being copied. European business schools launched a database on 12th December 2012 "Global Board Ready Women"[7]. This list of 8000 members reveals that there are easily enough qualified women to contribute towards managing businesses in the 21st century and that it is time to break the glass ceiling which is preventing them from accessing managerial posts. This initiative has been supported by Viviane Reding.

Governance, be it European, national, political or economic has to be re-designed. It has to adapt permanently to global challenges that are set to the established order and our points of reference. From an international point of view China and other emerging countries are challenging the American and European positions; from an economic point of view the crisis is shaking certainty and the way we think about solutions to settle our problems. Finally from a professional and social point of view the presence of more women is making people think differently. Each of these phenomena is a vector for change.

Establishing a culture of equality implies changing mentalities and countering persistent stereotypes. This means mutual determination to succeed in this transformation: women are preparing for it by training, by putting themselves into question, by defining their relationship with power and by daring to assert what they believe in, their motivations and their ambitions. Men have to do the same and some are already working towards it; because we shall only be able to face future challenges together.

Across the world Europe is considered a model for women's rights. We cannot disappoint those who are watching us by failing to achieve true male/female equality.

This imperative should also be an integral part of the external policy which Europe undertakes to support democratisation and development movements. The example of the countries in the southern Mediterranean which experienced the Arab Spring in 2011 is immediately evident: Europe should condition its aid, which is the most important in the world, to the full respect of women's rights by these new regimes. It is a question of principle which serves the interests of these countries: without women reform will be more difficult.

Undoubtedly the battle is not as hard in Europe for women as it is for our neighbours on the other side of the Mediterranean. But it is of symbolic value. The progress we achieve serves as a model for them. Europe has to be exemplary. In sum, we have to dare.

Women are also daring to do more and more. They are convinced that to adapt to new world requirements businesses and society have to call on all types of talent including their own. They are complementary to men and can provide added value in terms of management and leadership. Their specificity can be an asset. Again we have to dare to rise to the challenge of placing women in all types of positions of responsibility. Modernity lies in an equal society: courage, diversity, adaptability, a better balance in governance between men and women are vital for the success of societies in the 21st century.

---

7. Launch of the Global Board Ready Women http://europa.eu/rapid/press-release_IP-12-1358_en.htm?locale=FR

ANNEXES
Women managers in companies

Country	% managers
Norway	40.1
Sweden	27.3
Finland	26.4
France	16.6
Denmark	15.6
UK	15
The Netherlands	14
Poland	13
Germany	12.9
Austria	10.8
Spain	10.2
Ireland	9.5
Belgium	9.4
Greece	8.8
Czech Republic	8.6
Hungary	5.9
Italy	4.5
Portugal	2.3
Latvia*	28
Slovenia*	19
Lithuania*	18
Slovakia*	14
Romania*	12
Bulgaria*	12
Luxembourg*	10
Estonia*	8
Cyprus*	8
Malta*	4
EU AVERAGE	13.46

Source : GovernanceMetrics International, Catalyst, European Commission*[8]

8.   http://ec.europa.eu/justice/gender-equality/gender-decision-making/database/business-finance/quoted-companies/index_en.htm

In the assemblies which are supposed to represent the entire population women are still under represented: according to the Inter-Parliamentary Union (IPU)[9] on 31st October 2012, of the 46 048 members of the parliaments in the world (lower and upper chambers together), there are only 9 939 women i.e. 20.8%.

The European Union (25.98%) is ahead of the Americas (23.8%), other European countries (21.9%), Sub-Saharan Africa (20.8%), Asia (18.5%), the Arab countries (14.9%) and the Pacific States (12.7%).

In terms of the number of women chairing one of the chambers of Parliament of the 39 women observed by the IPU, 14 are European, 11 of whom are from Member States (Austria, Belgium, Bulgaria, Estonia, Latvia, Lithuania, the Netherlands, Poland, Portugal, Czech Republic, UK). Women only represent 14.2% of the leaders of parliament.

Women within the 27 national parliaments
(lower or single chambers)

Rank	Member State	Parliament	Date of election	Total seats	Number of women	%
1	FINLAND	Eduskunta	2011	200	86	43.00
2	SWEDEN	Riksdag	2010	349	150	42.98
3	SPAIN	Congreso	2011	350	139	39.71
4	BELGIUM	La Chambre	2010	150	59	39.33
5	DENMARK	Folketinget	2011	179	70	39.11
6	THE NETHERLANDS	Tweede Kamer	2012	150	58	38.67
7	SLOVENIA	Zbor	2011	90	34	37.78
8	GERMANY	Bundestag	2009	620	204	32.90
9	PORTUGAL	Assembleia da Republica	2011	230	68	29.57
10	AUSTRIA	Nationalrat	2006	183	52	28.42
11	FRANCE	Assemblée Nationale	2012	577	152	26.34
12	LITHUANIA	Seimas	2012	139	34	24.46
13	POLAND	Sejm	2011	460	110	23.91
14	LATVIA	Saeima	2011	100	23	23.00
15	BULGARIA	Narodno Sabranie	2009	240	55	22.92
16	UK	House of Commons	2010	650	146	22.46
17	CZECH REPUBLIC	Poslanecka Snemovna	2010	200	44	22.00
18	LUXEMBOURG	Chambre des Députés	2009	60	13	21.67
19	ITALIY	Camera dei Deputati	2008	630	134	21.27
20	GREECE	Vouli	2012	300	63	21.00
21	ESTONIA	Riigikogu	2011	101	21	20.79
22	SLOVAKIA	Narodna Rada	2012	150	28	18.67
23	IRELAND	Dáil Éireann	2011	166	25	15.06
24	ROMANIA	Camera Deputatilor	2012	412	54	13.11
25	CYPRUS	House of Representatives	2006	56	6	10.71

9. http://www.ipu.org/wmn-f/world.htm

Rank	Member State	Parliament	Date of election	Total seats	Number of women	%
26	HUNGARY	Az Orszag Haza	2010	386	35	9.07
27	MALTA	Kamra Tad Deputati	2008	69	6	8.70
	TOTAL			**7197**	**1870**	**25.98**

Source : Robert Schuman Foundation ©

In the EU countries' governments women represent on average 27% of ministers and there is no more government where there are no women, even though 10 Member States only have one or two.

On 1st January 2013, 7 women are the Prime Minister of their country 3 of whom are in Europe – 2 in the EU (Germany, Denmark) and Iceland –, Australia, Bangladesh, Thailand and Trinidad and Tobago.

8 women are Presidents of their country, two of whom are in Europe – Lithuania, Kosovo-, Argentina, Brazil, Liberia, Costa Rica, Malawi and South Korea.

Women ministers* within the 27 governments

Rank	Member State	Date of the election	Ministers members of government*	Number of women	%
1	SWEDEN	2010	24	13	54.17
2	FRANCE	2012	21	11	52.38
3	DENMARK	2011	23	11	47.83
4	FINLAND	2011	19	9	47.37
5	AUSTRIA	2008	14	6	42.86
6	BELGIUM	2010	13	5	38.46
	THE NETHERLANDS	2012	13	5	38.46
8	GERMANY	2009	16	6	37.50
9	CYPRUS	2008	12	4	33.33
10	SPAIN	2011	14	4	28.57
	LATVIA	2011	14	4	28.57
12	LUXEMBOURG	2009	15	4	26.67
13	BULGARIA	2009	16	4	25.00
14	POLAND	2011	20	4	20.00
15	CZECH REPUBLIC	2010	16	3	18.75
16	UK	2010	22	4	18.18
17	MALTA	2008	12	2	16.67
	PORTUGAL	2011	12	2	16.67
19	ROMANIA	2012	19	3	15.79
20	ITALY	2008	13	2	15.38
21	IRELAND	2011	15	2	13.33
	LITHUANIA	2012	15	2	13.33

Rank	Member State	Date of the election	Ministers members of government*	Number of women	%
23	HUNGARY	2010	10	1	10.00
24	ESTONIA	2011	13	1	7.69
	SLOVENIA	2012	13	1	7.69
26	SLOVAKIA	2012	14	1	7.14
27	GREECE	2012	18	1	5.56
	TOTAL		**426**	**115**	**27.00**

Source : Robert Schuman Foundation©
* N.B.: The Prime Minister is counted but nor the delegate ministers nor the Secretaries of State.

There are more women in the European Parliament women (35.41%) than in the National Parliaments (25.98%).

Women in the European Parliament

	Member State	Number of European Deputies	Number of Women	%
1	Finland	13	8	61.54
2	Estonia	6	3	50.00
	Slovenia	8	4	50.00
4	Denmark	13	6	46.15
	Netherlands	26	12	46.15
6	France	74	34	45.95
7	Sweden	20	9	45.00
8	Ireland	12	5	41.67
9	Portugal	22	9	40.91
10	Spain	54	22	40.74
11	Slovakia	13	5	38.46
12	Germany	99	38	38.38
13	Belgium	22	8	36.36
	Hungary	22	8	36.36
	Romania	33	12	36.36
16	Latvia	9	3	33.33
	Bulgaria	18	6	33.33
	Cyprus	6	2	33.33
	Lithuania	12	4	33.33
20	Greece	22	7	31.82
21	Austria	19	6	31.58
22	United Kingdom	73	23	31.51
23	Italy	73	17	23.29

	Member State	Number of European Deputies	Number of Women	%
24	Poland	51	11	21.57
25	Czech Republic	22	4	18.18
26	Luxembourg	6	1	16.67
27	Malta	6	0	0.00
	TOTAL	**754**	**267**	**35.41**

Source : Robert Schuman Foundation ©
*NB: The leader of the Parliament is not counted.
Since 1ˢᵗ December 2011 18 seats are distributed amongst 12 Member States bringing the number of MEPs up to 754 until 2014.

The growing influence of topical issues in legislative activity: limited political, but innovative and responsive, initiative.

Jean-Baptiste LAIGNELOT and Nicolas DELMAS

It is now a well established fact that the immediacy of information and close connections between one point of the planet and another are forcing governments to act instantly. The European Union does not escape this rule. As a Union of law its response leads to legislative activity that suffers the tight constraint of topical issues. For example before the "Six Pack" had even entered into force on 13th December 2011,[1] in a bid to settle the euro crisis, the European Union and its Member States were organising the introduction of a new Treaty to restore the States' budgetary credibility.

Legislative production declined below previous levels in 2012. Indeed around forty acts were adopted in comparison with 60 in 2010 and 2011, which was already less than in 2009 (the last year of the previous legislature). Unsurprisingly the main areas of legislative activity in the time of crisis were in the following order: economy and finance, the fight to counter terrorism, the environment, the area of freedom, security and justice and the internal market.

Furthermore this assessment of legislative activity leads to some observations about the development of institutional balance in a context of crisis which naturally tends towards an accentuation of the position Member States occupy in the Union's decision making process. Hence the European Council continues its ascension, with the support of the Council, which is working ever faster whilst the European Parliament is now

---

1. Thus named because it comprises six legislative acts: five regulations (2011/1173/EU on the effective implementation of budgetary supervision in the eurozone; 2011/1174/EU establishing implementation measures in view of remedying excessive macro-economic imbalances in the eurozone; 2011/1175/EU modifying the Council's regulation 97/1466/EC on tightening supervision of budgetary positions as well as the supervision and coordination of economic policies; 2011/1176/EU on the prevention and correction of macro-economic imbalances; 2011/1177/EU modifying regulation 97/1467/EC that aims to speed up and clarify the implementation of the procedure governing excessive deficits) and one directive (2011/85/EU on the requirements applicable to Member States' budgetary frameworks).

playing a full role in legislative activity. Conversely the European Commission's monopoly over initiative seems to be under heavy pressure and is mainly exercised to achieve, except in terms of the major topical issues, minimalist proposals to adapt or consolidate existing legislation, bar a few interesting exceptions however.

Normative production mainly oriented towards settling the eurozone crisis

On 27th September 2012, the Treaty on the European Stability Mechanism (ESM) entered into force with Germany's ratification of it – following the conditional greenlight given by its Constitutional Court in Karlsruhe on 12th September. This was a treaty specific to the eurozone Member States, the goal being to raise funds (up to 700 billion €) on the financial markets in order to help the States experiencing problems.

But 2012 was marked above all by the adoption in March of a new intergovernmental treaty, the Treaty on Stability, Coordination and Governance (TSCG, also called the Budgetary Pact or "fiscal compact"), at present under ratification. It was signed by all of the Member States except for the UK and the Czech Republic. This treaty, in exchange for a commitment by the States to limit their structural deficit (the famous "golden rule") and to reduce their public debt, allows them to benefit if necessary from the European Stability Mechanism. It notably sets up the creation of an independent internal organ[2] to guarantee the sincerity of public accounts and the dispatch of draft budgets to the Commission so that it can analyse their conformity with the goals set out in the TSCG.

Furthermore the European Council of 18th and 19th October 2012 decided on guidelines in view of a banking union basing itself on a Commission proposal which the European Council initiated itself. This sets up granting the European Central Bank (ECB) the control of the banking establishments in the eurozone as well as within other Member States if they want to take part. On this basis the distribution of roles between the ECB and the national regulatory authorities is the focus of a great deal of discussion and in all likelihood it will lead to a reduction in the prerogatives planned for the ECB in this proposal in order to facilitate the integration of non-eurozone Member States, which do not have a representative within the ECB.

Hence a new enhanced cooperation agreement, the third in European history after the divorce and the patent, was launched on the establishment of a tax on financial transactions[3] receiving the approval of the Commission on 23rd October 2012. This example illustrates the States' concern of working together as much as possible, but to move forwards even though not everyone follows, in response to both budgetary and economic imperatives.

Other proposals are being discussed at the moment; for example the creation of a "Super Commissioner" who would have the right to veto over national budgets. The next few years will quite likely witness a continuation in the introduction of the instruments necessary for the stabilisation of the eurozone.

---

2. In France, this role will be given to the "Haut Conseil des Finances Publiques" (High Council for Public Finance).

3. France, Germany, Italy, Spain, Belgium, Portugal, Slovenia, Austria, Greece, Slovakia, Estonia. The Netherlands have said that they want to join the enhanced cooperation agreement.

The international environment also puts pressure on the EU's legislative activity:

Iran[4], Syria[5], Belarus[6], Eritrea[7], Somalia[8], Afghanistan[9], Côte d'Ivoire[10], all of these countries have witnessed conflict, which in 2012, justified the restrictive measures taken against certain authorities[11].

Indeed the Member States are working together within the European Union so that they have an even more detailed legislative arsenal to use against organisations or people who undertake activities that harm populations and threaten international peace. This cooperation generally finds support in the recommendations made by the UN Security Council.

The Union is thus trying to be seen as a responsible player in the international arena committed to the maintenance of peace.

Legislative production concerned with protecting the environment as well as the well being and health of citizens, workers and consumers.

The European Union continues to undertake an ambitious environmental policy. It has adopted three important directives: on the assessment of the impact of certain public and private projects on the environment[12], on electrical equipment waste[13] and on energy efficiency[14]. One directive has been proposed to respond to the risk of accidents involving dangerous substances[15]. Finally the Union has established minimal security prescriptions regarding workers' exposure to magnetic fields[16].

However, most of these texts are just the re-arrangement of existing documents, whether this takes the shape of codification, the recast or the more ambitious revision of certain parts of a previous text. The time of major legislative projects in the area of the environment or healthcare seems to be over or on hold at least: the Commission, and undoubtedly it is wise at this time – has preferred to place emphasis on consolidating

---

4. Regulation 2012/1067/EU by the Council on 14th November 2012 modifying regulation 2012/267/EU on the adoption of restrictive measures against Iran.

5. Implementing Regulation 2012/944/EU by the Council on 15th October 2012 implementing article 32, paragraph 1, of regulation 2012/36/EU on restrictive measures because of the situation in Syria.

6. Implementing Regulation 2012/1017/EU by the Council on 6th November 2012 implementing article 8 bis, paragraph 1, of regulation 2006/765/CE on restrictive measures against Belarus.

7. Implementing Regulation 2012/943/EU by the Council on 15th October 2012 implementing article 12, paragraph 1, and article 13 of regulation 2010/356/EU introducing some specific restrictive measures against some physical or moral people, entities or organisations because of the situation in Somalia.

8. Regulation 2012/942/EU by the Council on 15th October 2012 modifying regulation 2010/667/EU on certain restrictive measures against Eritrea.

9. Implementing Regulation 2012/705/EU by the Council on 1st August 2012 implementing article 11, paragraph 4, of regulation 2011/753/EU on restrictive measures introduced against certain groups and certain people, businesses, and entities in view of the situation in Afghanistan.

10. Regulation 2012/617/EU by the Council on 10th July 2012 modifying regulation 2005/174/EC by the Council imposing restrictive measures in view of the assistance associated with military activities in Côte d'Ivoire.

11. Sanctions adopted at European Union level against person or organisations which undertake activities that can damage international peace or security.

12. Directive 2011/92/EU by the European Parliament and the Council of 13th December 2011.

13. Directive 2012/19/EU by the European Parliament and the Council of 4th July 2012.

14. Directive 2012/27/EU by the European Parliament and the Council of 25th October 2012.

15. Directive 2012/18/EU by the European Parliament and the Council of 4th July 2012.

16. Directive 2012/11/EU by the European Parliament and the Council of 19th April 2012.

what exists already, and its action is oriented more to the supervision of the application of the law, notably via the prosecution of alleged infringements rather than towards new legislative proposals.

The drive to redesign the area of Freedom, Security and Justice

Two directives (on the minimal norms concerning the rights, support and protection of victims of crime[17] and on the fight to counter the sexual abuse and sexual exploitation of children[18]) were adopted in 2012, notably replacing two of the Council's framework decisions.[19].

This trend is due to grow in 2013 in anticipation of the changes caused in 2014 by the Lisbon Treaty within the area of freedom, security and justice. Indeed as of 2014 the area of freedom, security and justice will be fully subject to the supervision of the Commission, which will be able to launch infringement procedures against Member States. It will also be subject to the supervision of the Court of Justice in terms of interpretation and validity; the Court will also be able to condemn the States which fail in their duty even if this involves pre-2009 framework decisions. The vital issue of the UK's "opt-out" in this area should also have major consequences on legislative activity in 2013 but this was not the case in 2012, even though we can see that the Commission takes great care regarding its proposals.

Some significant progress for the internal market[20]

This year the legislator has mainly targeted businesses – hoping to strengthen common standards to promote trade and activities within the internal market. Hence three directives were adopted to facilitate business management[21].

Moreover the Union intervened in the area of intellectual property. A directive was adopted regarding orphan works[22], whilst a draft directive is under discussion at present within the European Parliament and the Council on collective rights management and multi-territorial licencing of rights in musical works for online uses. We should note that these are new initiatives which are not just the re-organisation of existing texts and deemed both desirable by professionals as well as the States so that the harmonisation of the internal market moves forwards in areas where it is felt necessary.

Hence negotiations on the finalisation of an enhanced cooperation agreement regarding a unitary European patent have moved forwards since the conclusions of the June 2012 European Council and have led us to think that a compromise between the Council and the European Parliament will soon be possible[23]; this should then enable the delivery of the first patents in 2014. We should note that it was on this issue that the European

---

17. Directive 2012/29/EU by the European Parliament and the Council of 25th October 2012.

18. Directive 2011/92/EU by the European Parliament and the Council of 13th December 2011.

19. The framework decisions 2001/220/JAI and 2004/68/JAI by the Council respectively.

20. As Michel Barnier recalled, "the internal market is the basement" of European integration".

21. Directive 2012/6/EU of 14th March 2012 on the annual accounts of micro-businesses, Directive 2012/17/EU of 13th June 2012 on the interconnection of central trade and businesses registers, Directive 2012/30/EU of 25th October 2012 on the coordination of guarantees demanded by the States.

22. Directive 2012/28/EU by the European Parliament and the Council on 25th October on certain authorised uses of orphan works; these are works for which it has been impossible to find the copyright owner. This directive should lead to a use of these works.

23. The Patent Package was the focus of a political agreement during the Council on 10th December and a favourable vote by the European Parliament on 11th December 2012.

Council intervened for the very first time in a legislative process to suggest – on the request of a Member State – a significant modification to the draft text, which had been the focus of an agreement between the Commission, the Council and Parliament. The European Council's involvement was discussed by the Parliament and delayed the entire enhanced cooperation agreement by several months.

Finally in February 2013 the Commission should be able to publish its re-written proposals on the regulation on brand law.

* * *

The crisis has clearly led the European Union to re-focus since 2010 on issues vital to the euro's survival; hence there has been reduced legislative activity, which is not necessarily to be regretted if it helps towards simplifying law. Nevertheless the political constraint exercised on the Commission's power of initiative at present may weigh on the smooth functioning of the Union a long term. A change to the treaties may be anticipated around 2015 and this will possibly be the opportunity to address delicate institutional issues[24]. It is the time for change but as Jean Monnet said *"men only accept change when necessary and they only see necessity in times of crisis."*

---

24. The merger of the posts of President of the Commission and of the European Council – his election would by direct, universal suffrage, reform of the Eurogroup, etc.

Europe and the Challenge
of "Peripheral Nationalism"

Magali BALENT

At a time when the European Union is fighting to preserve its cohesion and prevent the exit of the eurozone by one of its Member States, another challenge is threatening its integrity: the rise of "peripheral nationalism" in several European regions, which are defending a specific, discrete identity of the Nation-State to which they belong and as a consequence their right to self-determination. The recent electoral successes and declarations made by several European regionalist political parties bear witness to this: whilst the Neo-Flemish Alliance (N-VA) achieved scores that varied between 20 to 30% in the local elections in Flanders on 4th October 2012, pushed forward by its leader, Bart de Wever, as the Mayor of Anvers, Flanders' leading town; the Basque Nationalist Party (PNV) won the elections on 21st October in the parliament of the Basque Autonomous Community. In Catalonia, Artur Mas, the chair of the Generalitat and of the centre-right Catalan Nationalist Party – Convergencia i Unio (CiU) announced in September last to "his people" that he wanted to convene a referendum to give Catalonia "a State in its own right"[1]. Although the score achieved in the early elections on 25th November 2012 were disappointing (CiU dropped from having 62 to 50 regional seats), other more radical leftwing and far left parties, campaigning for independence (Esquerra Republicana de Catalunya and Candidatura d'Unitat Popular) improved their results. In Scotland the British Prime Minister, David Cameron confirmed one of the campaign promises made by the Scottish National Party (SNP) giving the green-light to the organisation of a referendum on Scotland's independence in the autumn of 2014. Finally the Northern League continues to be an influential political force in Italy in the wake of the excellent scores it achieved in the regional elections in March 2010 and its participation in several government coalitions under the presidency of Silvio Berlusconi. At present it governs the regions of Piedmont and Venetia, the richest in Italy. All of these autonomist claims are a real danger for the cohesion of the European Union and its future, and it is all the greater, since the attitude of the latter towards these regions of Europe, whose specific features it supports, is ambivalent.

Understanding the threat that these movements, asserting regionalist nationalism comprise for the future of the European Union entails a better understanding of what

---

1. Mathieu de Taillac, « Catalogne : le pari perdu d'Artur Mas », *Le Figaro*, 27th November 2012.

they are striving for and revealing the relations they entertain with the European Union which are ambiguous to say the least.

The Claims put forward by "Peripheral Nationalism"

Since the end of the Cold War the European Union has been the stage for the resurgence of nationalism and of the awakening of the peoples of Europe. This first involved the former communist countries in the East during the 1990's. The scission of Czechoslovakia into two Nation States, the Czech Republic and Slovakia, then the dislocation of the Federation of Yugoslavia (Croatia, Slovenia, Montenegro, Macedonia, Serbia, Kosovo) bear witness to this. Since 2008 the economic and social crisis has created the conditions for the rise of another form of nationalism which Frank Tétard qualifies as "peripheral" since it emerges within the Nation States, in regions which challenge the central State qualified as a "predator"[2]. Whilst "State built nationalism" of the 1990's caused the secession of nations that were "prisoner" of weak federation of States that had been built on the ruins of the multinational Empires of the 19th century, "peripheral nationalism" flourishes in Nation-States that have existed for a long time and which are members of the European Union. This nationalism is also the vector of specific demands.

A "nationalism of the privileged"[3]....

"Peripheral nationalism" is emerging in the wealthy regions of Europe. Hence Catalonia and the Basque Country in Spain alone represent 25% of the Spanish GDP. On average the GDP per capita is 25% higher than the EU average, an observation which proves true in Scotland, Flanders and Northern Italy[4]. This nationalism has irrupted against State imposed centralisation and because of the economic development of these "Eldorados" which have seen a gulf form between their excellent economic results and those of other regions, whose backwardness they do not want to assume. In Scotland where the GDP equals that of Ireland and Portugal, the resurgence of nationalism occurred at the same time as the discovery of oil in the North Sea in the 1970's; in Belgium, the reversal of the situation which existed in the 1960's between Flanders, which once lagged behind, and Wallonia, formerly the engine of the Belgian economy in the 19th century thanks to its heavy industries, revived Flemish nationalism[5].

The economic and financial crisis of 2008 awoke resentment as it accentuated the economic differential between these regions and the others, but also, paradoxically, it increased their debt which weakened them. Hence Catalonia has become the most indebted region of Spain (the regional debt in 2012 lay at 22% of the GDP, in comparison with 9.1% for Madrid and 10.7% for Andalusia)[6]. Now these regions are rejecting a situation in which they feel they are paying for the others, believing they have paid more to the State than they receive from it. This situation is however far from clear, as is the case in Scotland: between April 2009 and March 2010, the latter is said to have paid 50 billion € to the British State and received 74 billion[7]. In spite of this these parties

2. F. Tétard, *Nationalismes régionaux. Un défi pour l'Europe*, Paris, 2009, p. 26.
3. A. Dieckhoff, *La nation dans tous ses états : les identités nationales en mouvement*, Paris, Flammarion, 2002, p. 113.
4. *Eurostat regional yearbook* 2012, p. 18,http://epp.eurostat.ec.europa.eu/cache/ITY_OFFPUB/KS-HA-12-001/EN/KS-HA-12-001-EN.PDF
5. A. Dieckhoff, *op.cit.*, p. 78 et 84.
6. « La deudaespanolaalcanza el 75,9% del PIB y marca un nuevo record », *ABC.es*, 14th September 2012, http://www.abc.es/20120914/economia/abci-deuda-publica-espana-201209141037.html
7. Eric Albert Stirling, « Ecosse, la tentation indépendantiste », *Le Monde*, 26th March 2012.

are promoting the idea that independence will enable their region to recover the growth and social balance which typified them for so long.

The economic differential which is sometimes exaggerated for electoral ends[8], cannot explain everything. Indeed it is based on the feeling shared by a major part of the local population that they comprise a nation in their own right founded on strong identity markers. Hence behind this economic nationalism of the "privileged" as Alain Dieckhoff qualifies it, which runs through the separatist demands made by all of these regions, there hides a powerful cultural nationalism that is exacerbated by the crisis and which might also feed ethno-differentialist arguments.

…which reveals cultural nationalism

As Alain Dieckhoff indicates peripheral nationalisms take shape in "global societies"[9] with a strong identity profile. In Flanders and Catalonia identity is based on the claim of a language and culture distinct from those of the State. The latter are the source of "Catalanism", a trend of thought born in the 19th century which promotes the Catalan identity and opposes the hegemony of the Spanish language. Moreover, one of the first measures established by the Generalitat of Catalonia after achieving autonomous status in 2006 was to make the learning of Catalan obligatory and to impose this language on everyone taking exams to enter the civil service, notably for the judiciary. In Flanders the linguistic particularism was so acute that in 1963 it led to the introduction of a border separating the Belgian linguistic communities. This decision put an end to the supremacy of French, which had been the official language in Belgium until then.

Language is not the only identity referent however. In Scotland particularity involves more a specific culture, based on "institutions" that are specific to this British nation and as a result, which create identity: the Presbyterian Church, a judicial system based on civil law and an independent education system that privileges state establishments. It is also based on the specific nature of the Scottish territory, which is clearly defined geographically and which has forged its identity across history: is Scotland not bordered to the south by Hadrian's Wall, the northern most border of the Roman Empire built in 112AD, beyond which the Romans failed to assert themselves? Calling on history is however common to all of the nationalist parties who want to anchor their claims in the past and provide their particularisms with historical depth, so that they seem more legitimate. The major battles against the centralising State are brandished as founding moments of the "national" conscience: hence such is case with the battle of Stirling in Scotland led by William Wallace in 1297 against Edward I of England or the revolt of the Segadors (Catalonian reapers) in Catalonia against the fiscal measures of the Minister Olivares in 1640. Moreover it is not rare to see identity also being built on shared ethnic origin, thereby enhancing the homogeneity of the group *vis-à-vis* the rest of society. The founder of the Basque Nationalist Party (PNV), Sabino Arana highlighted the purity of the Basque blood in the 19th century, comparing the Basques to *"nobility exempt of any contamination by the Jews, the Moors and the heretics"*.[10] The Northern League also refers to the ethnic argument to define "the Padano Nation", rallying the region of the Pô Plain, whose populations are said to descend from the Celts, unlike the Latin peoples of

---

8. According to Michel Quévit, the nationalist demands in Flanders are less to do with the socio-economic situation in Wallonia than with electoral one-upmanship comprising the stigmatisation of the internal enemy to mobilise the electorate, as well as showing disdain for the Wallonian language and culture. M. Quévit, *Flandre-Wallonie, quelle solidarité ? De la création de l'Etat belge à l'Europe des régions*, Charleroi, Editions Asbl, 2010, p. 149-152.

9. *Ibid.*, p. 123.

10. A. Elorza, « Nationalisme basque : les chemins de la sécession », *Critique internationale*, n°11, April 2001, p. 3.

southern Italy[11]. More generally the ethnic argument is still present to a greater or lesser degree in the regionalist parties' discourse who oppose, in a Manichean manner, the nation they represent, described as dynamic and hard working, to the State to which they belong where the number of unemployed and socially assisted is constantly increasing.[12].

What place is there for "peripheral nationalism" in the European Union?

Whatever the aspirations of the nationalist parties, which vacillate between the desire for greater autonomy and separatist illusion, their demands still fall within the European context. Indeed unlike the parties which are qualified as "national-populist", for whom there is no more protective and natural realm for the individual than the Nation-State, the regionalist parties refer to two other community levels which are legitimate in their opinion: the region and Europe. They are no less a challenge to the European Union as they threaten, with their repeated call for secession, to fragment the European territory even further. We might then wonder what the European Union's response might be as it seems to hesitate before a situation with which it is not totally unfamiliar.

The regions and Europe, an ambiguous relationship

"Peripheral nationalism" declares itself openly pro-European. Repeating that their nation is prisoner within a State whose legitimacy they reject, they claim their historical membership of the European area, which in this sense seems to be an alternative. Hence the Scottish National Party contrasts the *United Kingdom which was the Union of the past* with *Europe which will be the Union of the future* adding that Scotland must now *"recover an active part in European affairs, as it did during the centuries prior to the 1707 treaty which separated it from the rest of Europe."*[13]. These parties advocate a Europe of regions stressing the vital role of the latter in the building of the European identity.[14].Hence the electoral programme of the Catalan party, CiU defends an independent Catalonia, a member of the EU in 2020[15]. But this attachment seems largely strategic, enabling some regionalist parties to short-circuit the State on which they depend and to promote their international credibility amongst their electorate.

Hence Europe is turned into a means for expression, which is as accessible as it is seductive since the EU supports regionalism. European law indeed grants a status to the regions of Europe: the creation of the FEDER in 1975 for the most impoverished regions, the European charter of regional, minority languages and the Committee of

---

11. On this subject see the work by Clothilde Champeyrache, *La Ligue du Nord. Un séparatisme à l'italienne. Racines et discours d'un parti politique*, Paris, l'Harmattan, 2002.

12. M. Quévit, *op.cit.*, p. 143.

13. The opinion of Allan MacCartney, MEP and spokesperson of the Scottish National Party (SNP) after the referendum in September 1997 for the establishment of the Scottish parliament. In Frédéric Chaix, *Histoire du nationalisme écossais*, Boulogne, Défi, 1998. As a reminder the Union Act of 1707 led to Scotland's annexation to the UK and the merger of the Scottish and English parliaments into one British parliament. This situation was changed by the Scotland Act of 1998 which after the 'yes 'to the referendum restored the Scottish Parliament and created a regional government.

14. On this subject see the N-VA's position in Flanders which defends an autonomous Flanders and demands that it be acknowledged "in the same way as the other countries and States, some of which are sometimes smaller than Flanders itself," N-VA's website http://international.n-va.be/fr/a-propos/faq#faq-ideo

15. This wish was expressed in the party's programme in the early general elections of 25th November 2012, in particular look at pages 23-30 http://estaticos.elperiodico.com/resources/pdf/9/4/1351429750849.pdf

Regions in 1992, turn these bodies into players in their own right alongside the States of Europe, granting legitimacy to their specific demands as a result. We should also add that the European Union allows the regionalist parties to compete in the European elections. The N-VA and the Basque Nationalist Party each have an MEP. The Catalan party CiU has two, whilst the Northern League has nine. The Union offers the regions arguments for them to free themselves from the tutelage of the country to which they belong and to adopt the behaviour of future sovereign nations. By helping towards the desacrilisation of the State and transferring a share of the States' powers towards other bodies, it seems that the European Union is a precious ally for "peripheral nationalism".

Given these secessionist demands, what can the European Union do?

And yet European legislation does not anticipate the scission of a Member State. This explains European leaders' embarrassment in the face of an unprecedented situation, which is threatening European integration that is built on the foundation of the Nation-State. Only the Treaty on European Union (TEU) stipulates in article 4.2 that the Union has to respect *"the vital functions of the State, notably those which aim to guarantee its territorial integrity."*[16] Legally the Union cannot interfere in the States' domestic policies. As a result European legislation includes nothing in the event of a unilateral declaration of independence of a region which would like to remain a Union Member. Only the TEU states that any new membership has to be approved unanimously by the Member States illustrating that the latter remain the only ones in control in this domain.[17] But can the States demand of the Union that it withdraw the rights from European citizens which they enjoyed previously, in a bid to punish them for having separated? On this issue, Viviane Reding, Vice-President of the European Commission for Justice, Fundamental Rights and Citizenship said at the end of September 2012 that "no law states that Catalonia should quit the Union if it became independent,"[18] before recanting in a letter dated 4th October saying that she would respect the institutional framework of the Union and the sovereignty of the States[19]. However the declaration of unilateral independence of Kosovo on 17th February 2008, acknowledged by 22 EU Member States, created a precedent in European history as it challenged the intangible principle of national sovereignty in Europe. But doesn't the Union's obstinacy to make Serbia accept this independence, an acceptance which now conditions the country's achievement of candidate status, make the situation even more difficult, in that it seems to insinuate that the Union is not hostile to this type of separatist initiative? It is significant that the States under secessionist threat are precisely those which have refused to acknowledge Kosovo to date.

Hence the Union has little room to manoeuvre. It can however count on the tactical nature of these secessionist claims, which comprises the achievement on the part of regionalist party leaders of greater autonomy by threatening the State with secession. The decline of the Catalan party CiU in the last general elections on 25th November 2012 is possible proof of this. In Scotland the polls indicate that only 1/3 of the Scots want

---

16. *Version consolidée du Traité sur l'Union européenne*, 2010, http://eur-lex.europa.eu/LexUriServ/LexUriServ.do?uri=OJ:C:2010:083:0013:0046:FR:PDF .

17. The method for the accession on the part of a new Member State is included in article 49 of the TEU.

18. Jean-Pierre Stroobants, « L'Union hésite sur l'attitude à adopter envers une région devenant indépendante », *Le Monde*, 16th October 2012.

19. Letter addressed by Viviane Reding to the Spanish Secretary of State for European Affairs, Inigo Mendez de Vigo on 4th October 2012: http://ep00.epimg.net/descargables/2012/10/30/a1688dfb-ca8854a8f4744bc6b58f1c15.pdf

independence[20], in Flanders, this figure totals 15%[21]. In this context might the solution for the Union lie in encouraging the States in question to anticipate greater autonomy and the transfer of wider sovereignty to the regions, thereby inviting the States to achieve on a national scale what it is promoting on a European level? We might hope that a development like this would break the secessionist spell and with it the danger of the balkanisation of the European Union.

* * *

The rise of "peripheral nationalisms" which dream of transforming their nation into a State reminds us that state building remains an important ideal for the peoples of Europe, at a time when globalisation has possibly led us to believe that Nation-States are part of the past. The European Union is now facing a not totally unfamiliar situation, which it has anticipated badly, because it is precisely a project that leads to the relativisation of national sovereignties. For the sake of coherence the Union would gain a great deal by providing opportunities for thought on how to settle the crisis thereby stepping out of a single frame of reference – i.e. the State – to focus more widely on what the citizens of Europe want – expectations which it will necessarily have to take on board and support.

---

20. Yves Bourdillon, « Les indépendantistes surfent sur la crise de surendettement en Europe », *lesechos.fr*, 17th October 2012, http://m.lesechos.fr/international/les-independantistes-surfent-sur-la-crise-de-surendettement-en-europe-0202329856319.htm

21. « La scission, farfelue ou non ? », *lalibrebelgique.be*, 9th July 2012, http://www.lalibre.be/actu/belgique/article/748618/la-scission-farfelue-ou-non.html

The Europeans, the Crisis and the World

Pascal PERRINEAU

The economic and financial crisis, which has been in full swing in Europe for the last four years has established in most of these countries expectations that are marked by a distinct note of pessimism. In the spring Eurobarometer 2012[1], 60% of those interviewed believed that in terms of the impact of the crisis on the employment market "the worst is yet to come" (cf. map 1). Of course pessimism is at its highest in the countries most affected by the crisis: Portugal (78%), Greece (77%), Spain (72%), Italy (62%) but the opinions of the most prosperous countries such as Finland, Luxembourg and even the UK are also marked by a high rate of pessimism. At 59%, France still lies within the European average. However seven countries, including five in Central and Eastern Europe avoid these morose forecasts to some extent: Slovakia (49%), Latvia (49%), Denmark (45%), Austria (44%), Estonia (44%), Romania (42%) and Bulgaria (40%). In these more "optimistic" countries, the unemployment rate is relatively low (Austria and Denmark) or also high (Latvia, Bulgaria). Economic and social indicators of well-being are not the only means to illustrate what the Europeans think of the crisis. Of course the attitude of the most impoverished social categories is marked by pessimism: 66% of the unemployed, 61% of workers, 65% of those who left school at 15 or under believe that "the worst is yet to come" but this also applies to 51% of students and 58% of executives. In 2012, pessimism about the effects of the crisis seems to be "the best shared thing in the world". In all age categories and in all social classes pessimism rules. It peaks (71%) amongst Europeans who believe that "globalisation is not an opportunity". The overall attitude to globalisation is often more decisive in understanding the opinion of the crisis than categories of sex, age and social class.

If we leave the area of the perception of the effects of the crisis on employment behind and try to define its impact on the daily life of European households, the disparity between countries in the centre and the north of Europe and the countries in the south and the east is high. When asked "whether their present situation prevents them from anticipating projects in the future" and whether it forces them to "live on a day to day basis", 35% of those interviewed in Europe answer that this is the case for themselves and their families. In eight countries this response corresponds more or less to half and even more of the population: Greece (68%), Malta (67%), Cyprus (55%), Hungary (54%), Bulgaria (54%), Portugal (53%), Spain (49%) and Ireland (49%). However in seven

---

1. *Eurobarometer Standard 77*, Spring 2012, "The Europeans, the European Union and the Crisis".

countries nearly half of those interviewed declare "that they have a long term vision of what their household would be like in one or two year's time": Sweden (54%), Luxembourg (51%) Germany (50%), Denmark (50%), the Netherlands (50%), Austria (47%), Finland (47%). Only the countries in the centre and the north of Europe, which have been spared from the crisis somewhat, foresee a relatively positive scenario vis-à-vis their future, whilst the countries in the south and the east, which have often suffered greater economic and financial turbulence, put forward much weaker, more uncertain forecasts.

Given this crisis, the effects of which are perceived with an acute sense of concern, Europeans do not feel totally helpless since a majority of them believe that the national and international institutions can "act effectively in response to the effects of the financial and economic crisis." Amongst these institutions feature the European Union and the national governments, which are deemed to be the most effective. The European Union and the national government are also quoted by 21% of those interviewed, then follows the IMF (15%), the G20 (14%), the USA (7%). When Europeans are asked to estimate the effectiveness of the action taken by some of these players since the start of the economic crisis, 37% believe that their government's action has been effective, 36% opt for the USA and 33% the European Union. As far as the latter is concerned (cf. map 2: "The EU's effectiveness in countering the crisis"), its action is lauded more outside of the eurozone (39% against 32% across all of the zone euro countries), particularly in three countries of Eastern Europe - Poland (50%), Bulgaria (54%) and Romania (58%). However it is in Greece (14%), Cyprus (13%), Spain (22%) and in the UK (22%) that the European Union's action is judged most severely. Except for the UK all countries are more than reticent about the real or supposed virtues of globalisation.

It is clear that attitudes regarding the major "Other" in globalisation are decisive in the way Europeans perceive and take on board the crisis, Europe and the world[2]. Most of the European countries which see globalisation negatively are at the top of the pessimism hit-parade as far as the crisis is concerned: Greece, Portugal, Romania, Latvia, Italy and Spain are all countries which see the effects of crisis on households extremely negatively and also believe that globalisation is not an "opportunity for economic growth" (cf. map 3 "Globalisation represents an opportunity for economic growth"). Although 56% of those interviewed in Europe believe that globalisation "represents an opportunity for economic growth," only 44% of the French think so – only the Greeks are less in number to see it as an "opportunity". Although we can see how the default of the Greek economy has led to this perception, it is not as easy to understand the reasons for the negative opinion the French have of the possible economic virtues of globalisation. The French are amongst the most negative, together with the countries most sorely affected by the economic and financial crisis (Greece, Portugal, Italy, Spain) and their opinion is extremely different from the opinions of the countries in the centre and north of Europe, where the vision of globalisation as a vector of economic is the most developed. 87% of the Danes, 82% of the Swedes, 76% of the Dutch, 71% of the Finnish, 70% of the Hungarians, 68% of the Slovakians, 64% of the Estonians, 63% of the Belgians and Germans, likewise 62% of the British share the feeling that "globalisation represents an opportunity for economic growth".

The same applies to globalisation, as far as appreciating whether it "helps towards development of poor countries" is concerned. Although 45% of Europeans share this opinion (64% of the Danes, 62% of the Swedes, 61% of the Slovaks, 60% of the Estonians, 54% of the Dutch, 54% of the Finns, 53% of the Czechs, 51% of the Austrians), only a large third do so in Greece (34%), in Latvia (37%), in Spain (37%) and in France (34%).

The same applies also to the idea that globalisation can "protect us from price increases". Only 26% of Europeans believe that globalisation helps protect us from

---

2. The opinion data relative to the perception of globalisation are excerpts from *Eurobarometer Standard 73*, "Public Opinion in the European Union" November 2010.

inflation. But this diagnosis is severest in France: only 12% of the French think that glo-balisation helps to counter price increases, 76% believe the contrary. France is amongst the 27 in the EU where belief in the anti-inflationist virtues of globalisation has fallen the most. A strong majority of Europeans (60%) also believe that "globalisation increases social inequalities". But again the perception of globalisation which "takes away", "worsens" and which provides nothing positive, beats all records in Greece (81%) and in France (76%). Unlike some countries with a liberal tradition (the UK, the Netherlands) or those in Eastern Europe, which grant some virtues to economic opening (Romania, Lithuania), France and Greece see globalisation as a process that is only to the benefit of the large trans-nationals and absolutely not the citizens. This view dominates in the European Union where 62% of those interviewed agree with the idea that "globalisation only benefits the major trans-nationals and not the citizens." Only the Romanians (48%), the Danes (46%), the Dutch (45%), the Swedes (45%) and the Maltese (38%) do not fall within this majority. But as per usual this impression is overwhelming and affects more than three quarters of those interviewed in Greece (81%) and France (77%) as well as in Slovenia (79%). In the opinion of an often extremely wide majority of French, globali-sation appears to have no virtues at all.

Interviewed at a decisive electoral moment in May-June 2012, 60% of the French said that "for a country like France globalisation represents a danger because it threatens its businesses and its social model." Only 39% of those interviewed believe that globalisation is an opportunity because "it opens up markets abroad and promotes modernisation" (Post-electoral survey, after the Presidential election 2012 CEVIPOF, by Opinionway on 18th May to 2nd June 2012). This positive vision of globalisation only wins a majority within the higher, qualified social categories and which enjoy a high standard of living - amongst practising Catholics who know what a trans-national company is and finally amongst Nicolas Sarkozy and Eva Joly's electorate.

Table 1: the perception of globalisation in France.

Question : For a country like France, is globalisation rather:

	A chance, because it opens the foreign markets and pro-motes modernisation		A danger, because it threatens its busi-nesses and its social model
	39%		60%
Leading executives., independents	56%	18-24 years	55%
Higher education graduates.	52%	Workers	72%
vote Sarkozy	62%	Public sector workers.	65%
vote Joly (Green Party)	54%	vote Mélenchon	82%
Practising Catholics.	52%	vote Hollande	62%
6000€ and +	53%	vote Le Pen	80%
		No religion	64%

Source : Opinionway survey CEVIPOF, 18th May-2nd June 2012

However within the popular classes, in the public sector and also amongst the young, people who do not practice a religion and voters on the left and the far right ... it is the view that globalisation poses a threat that wins the day.

The dominant idea of globalisation as a threat, which is an integral part of the "French particularity" requires explanation. The feeling of a *deminutio capitis* runs deep in a country which for centuries has been accustomed to having "the leading role". In December 2010 already 62% of the French interviewed on the position their country occupies in the "world economic competition" believed that France was "faring badly". In the same survey[3], 16% of the Australians, 17% of the Dutch, 18% of the Germans, 21% of the Brazilians, 28% of the Chinese, 44% of the British, 50% of the Americans, 51% of the Poles and 55% of the Italians think that about their country. French pessimism and the feeling of impotence are fed by the nostalgia of a "powerful past"[4]. Another source of pessimism is *"revolutionary passion"* which of all passions remains resolutely French and which – to quote François Furet, fosters *"an infinite ability to produce children and men who hate the social and political regime in which they are born, hating the air they breathe, whilst they live on it and they have never known anything else"[5]*. The economic, social and political regime is now turning towards the outside but many French reject this and demand protection. In an IFOP survey undertaken for *La Croix* in April 2012, 60% of those interviewed believe that from an economic point of view *"the opening of France and Europe's borders to goods from countries like China and India and the opening of these countries to French products"* is a *"bad thing for France"*. From this standpoint a wide majority of the French both on the left and the right demand the implementation of strict protectionist policies.

This globalised world, which is rejected, resembles France and its model less and less. The hiatus between the world and France is particularly difficult to overcome in a country that is supposed to be universalist. But this universalism finds it increasingly difficult to position itself in the globalised world. This difficulty is more acute because the French universal model is anchored in an extremely strong national identity, which, in its unity, is relatively incapable of taking on diversity. As Mona Ozouf notes, the political nation *à la Française* is *"self-confident and dominant, (and) has never favoured the cultural nation"[6]*. For this political nation all types of pluralism are *"either aesthetic archaism or political subversion."* Often allergic to domestic diversity, France adopts the same attitude to diversity on the outside. But globalisation is the vector of great cultural, economic, financial, judicial and even political diversity. For all of these reasons France possibly finds it all the harder to take the world as it is, to take opening as it comes and otherness for what it is: it is simply otherness and not a threat to its identity *per se*.

---

3. Survey « Regards croisés sur la mondialisation dans dix pays », by IFOP for *La Croix* amongst a sample of 6023 people representative of inhabitants aged 18 and over in ten countries. Survey undertaken between 8th to 23rd December 2010.

4. Cf. Pascal Perrineau, Le pessimisme français : nature et racines, *Le Débat*, n°166, September to October 2011, p. 79-90. Interview with Pascal Perrineau, La France in the boudoir, http://www.parislike.com/FR/snoopy-pascal-perrineau.php.

5. François Furet, La passion révolutionnaire au XXe siècle. Essai sur le déclin du communisme, *La Révolution française*, Gallimard, 2007, p.951.

6. Mona Ozouf, *Composition française. Retour sur une enfance bretonne*, Gallimard, 2009, p.14.

VI

The European Union in figures

Alain FABRE – Gerald STANG

This annex provides the reader with a series of statistics that paint an economic and social portrait of the European Union. It uses the latest data available at the time of writing, mostly from 2011 and early 2012. As far as data sources permit, we have provided a comparison with the United States, Japan and some emerging economies (Brazil, Russia, India and China).

List of abbreviations:

EU: European Union. The 27 Member States are Austria, Belgium, Bulgaria, Cyprus, Czech Republic, Denmark, Estonia, Finland, France, Germany, Greece, Hungary, Ireland, Italy, Latvia, Lithuania, Luxembourg, Malta, the Netherlands, Poland, Portugal, Romania, Slovakia, Slovenia, Spain, Sweden and the United Kingdom.

PPP: purchasing power parity. According to the French National Institute for Statistics and Economic Studies (INSEE), "PPP is a money conversion rate used to express the purchasing powers of different currencies in common units. This rate expresses the ratio between the quantity of monetary units required in different countries to purchase the same "basket" of goods and services." The rate used for PPP standardisation is calculated by the statistical institutes providing the data. The rate varies from one year to another, which explains certain differences with the previous editions of the Schuman Report.

R&D: research and development.

Country abbreviations

DE	Germany	GR	Greece	PT	Portugal	CA	Canada
AT	Austria	HU	Hungary	CZ	Czech Republic	US	United States
BE	Belgium	IE	Ireland	RO	Romania	CN	China
BG	Bulgaria	IT	Italy	UK	United Kingdom	IN	India
CY	Cyprus	LV	Latvia	SK	Slovakia	TR	Turkey
DK	Denmark	LT	Lithuania	SI	Slovenia	RU	Russia
ES	Spain	LU	Luxembourg	SE	Sweden	BR	Brazil
EE	Estonia	MT	Malta			W	World
FI	Finland	NL	Netherlands	EA	eurozone		
FR	France	PL	Poland	EU	European Union		

Contents

2. Restoring Financial Stability and Control of Public Finances

1. The EU in the New World Order

1.1. The Demographic Weight of the EU and the Member States

1.1.1 Population of the EU and international comparisons (1990 - 2010 and projections)

	Population (in millions of inhabitants)			Share of world population (2010)	Share of EU population (2010)	Fertility rate (2005-2010)	Internationial migrant stock (as % of population)		Net migration (2005-2010)
	1990	2010	Projection for 2030				1990	2010	
Austria	7.7	8.4	8.6	0.1%	1.7%	1.38	10.3%	15.6%	160,000
Belgium	9.9	10.7	11.2	0.2%	2.1%	1.79	8.9%	9.0%	200,000
Bulgaria	8.8	7.5	6.5	0.1%	1.5%	1.46	0.2%	1.4%	-50,000
Cyprus	0.8	1.1	1.3	0.0%	0.2%	1.51	5.7%	14.0%	44,166
Czech Republic	10.3	10.5	10.8	0.2%	2.1%	1.41	4.1%	4.3%	240,466
Denmark	5.1	5.6	5.9	0.1%	1.1%	1.85	4.6%	8.7%	90,316
Estonia	1.6	1.3	1.3	0.0%	0.3%	1.64	24.3%	13.6%	0
Finland	5.0	5.4	5.6	0.1%	1.1%	1.84	1.3%	4.2%	72,634
France	56.7	62.8	68.5	0.9%	12.5%	1.97	10.1%	10.3%	500,000
Germany	79.1	82.3	79.5	1.2%	16.4%	1.36	7.5%	13.2%	550,000
Greece	10.2	11.4	11.6	0.2%	2.3%	1.46	4.1%	10.0%	154,004
Hungary	10.4	10.0	9.6	0.1%	2.0%	1.34	3.3%	3.7%	75,000
Ireland	3.5	4.5	5.4	0.1%	0.9%	2.10	6.5%	20.1%	100,000
Italy	56.8	60.6	60.9	0.9%	12.1%	1.38	2.5%	7.4%	1,998,926
Latvia	2.7	2.3	2.1	0.0%	0.5%	1.41	24.2%	14.9%	-10,000
Lithuania	3.7	3.3	3.1	0.0%	0.7%	1.41	9.4%	3.9%	-35,495
Luxembourg	0.4	0.5	0.6	0.0%	0.1%	1.62	29.8%	34.2%	42,469
Malta	0.4	0.4	0.4	0.0%	0.1%	1.33	1.6%	3.7%	5,000
Netherlands	14.9	16.6	17.3	0.2%	3.3%	1.75	8.0%	10.6%	50,000
Poland	38.1	38.3	37.8	0.6%	7.6%	1.32	3.0%	2.2%	55,644
Portugal	9.9	10.7	10.3	0.2%	2.1%	1.36	4.4%	8.6%	150,002
Romania	23.2	21.5	20.3	0.3%	4.3%	1.33	0.6%	0.6%	-100,000
Slovakia	5.3	5.5	5.5	0.1%	1.1%	1.27	0.8%	2.4%	36,684
Slovenia	1.9	2.0	2.1	0.0%	0.4%	1.39	8.9%	8.0%	22,000
Spain	38.9	46.1	50.0	0.7%	9.2%	1.41	2.1%	13.8%	2,250,005
Sweden	8.6	9.4	10.4	0.1%	1.9%	1.90	9.1%	13.9%	265,649
United Kingdom	57.2	62.0	69.3	0.9%	12.4%	1.83	6.5%	10.4%	1,020,211
EU	**471.0**	**500.4**	**515.8**	**7.3%**		**1.55**	**5.6%**	**9.3%**	**7,887,689**
United States	253.3	310.4	361.7	4.5%		2.07	9.3%	13.9%	4,954,924
Canada	27.7	34.0	39.8	0.5%		1.65	16.2%	21.1%	1,098,444
Russia	148.2	143.0	136.4	2.1%		1.44	7.8%	8.7%	1,135,737
China	1145.2	1341.3	1393.1	19.5%		1.64	0.0%	0.1%	-1,884,102
Japan	122.3	126.5	120.2	1.8%		1.32	0.9%	1.7%	270,000
India	873.8	1224.6	1523.5	17.8%		2.73	0.9%	0.5%	-2,999,998
Brazil	149.7	194.9	220.5	2.8%		1.90	0.5%	0.4%	-500,000
World	5306.4	6895.9	8321.4			2.52	3.0%	3.1%	

Source: UN, World Population Prospects, 2010 Revision
Data collected and collated for the Robert Schuman Foundation, © FRS

Between 1990 and 2010, the population of the EU increased from 471 million to 500 million people, an increase of 6.2%. Over the same period, the world's population increased by 30% to nearly 7 billion people. The relative decline of the European population is relevant not only in comparison with the growing global population, driven by areas such as India and Africa. The USA also has the demographic regime of a young country, experiencing population growth of 22.5% between 1990 and 2010. By 2030, the USA will experience only limited relative demographic decline (dropping to 4.3% of the world population in 2030 from 4.8% in 2010) while the decline will be much more pronounced in Europe: in 2030, the EU will represent 6.2% of the world population, compared with nearly 9% in 2010 (a drop of 2.8%).

The contribution of natural population growth to European demographic strength is limited. Across the EU, the fertility rate averaged 1.55 in 2010, which is much lower than the world average (2.52) or growing areas like India (2.73). On this issue, the case of the USA deserves to be re-emphasized, as the fertility rate (2.07) is almost at the low water mark required to ensure the renewal of the population (2.1). Low fertility is a common trend in the developed Western world; the European rate is similar to that recorded in Canada. Within the EU, fertility rates are particularly low in countries such as Germany, Italy and Spain (1.36, 1.38 and 1.41 respectively), and do not differentiate between Catholic and Protestant countries. However, more respectable levels of fertility are found in Ireland (2.10), France (1.97), Sweden (1.90), Denmark (1.85), Finland (1.84) and the Netherlands (1.75). All these countries have active family policies and allow families to avoid a stark choice between professional and family life.

Over the last twenty years, immigration has played a larger role in the evolution of the European population. Total net immigration between 2005 and 2010 reached nearly 8 million people. Between 1990 and 2010, the proportion of migrants in the population has increased dramatically throughout Europe, rising from 5.6 to 9.3%, an increase of 66%. Over the same period, the USA saw the proportion increase from 9.3 to nearly 14%, a jump of 49%. What is also striking is the fact that the traditional host countries of migrants have not experienced significant change. In France, the migrant population in 2010 constituted 10% of the population, which was the same as in 1990. Similar situations exist in Belgium (9% in 2010) and the Netherlands (10.6%). In contrast, countries with historically low migration rates have seen dramatic changes in the space of twenty years. This is true of countries such as Germany (a jump of 76% in the migrant proportion of the population) and Austria (51%), where the migrant population is now close to 15% of the total. The transformation has been much greater in countries such as Italy where the share of migrants has tripled, thanks to large flows – nearly 2 million between 2005 and 2010 – that have increased the migrant share from 2.5 to 7.4% of the population, though this is still below the European average. Spain recorded the most dramatic increase, with a gain of 2.25 million people between 2005 and 2010. In twenty years, the share of migrants has increased from 2 to nearly 14% of the population, a seven-fold jump.

1.1.2 Aging population in the EU and international comparisons (2010)

	Median age (2010)	Old-age dependency ratio* (2010)	Share of population aged			Life expectancy (2005-2010)
			under 15 years	15 to 64 years	65 years or over	
Austria	42	26	15%	68%	18%	80
Belgium	41	27	17%	66%	17%	80
Bulgaria	42	25	14%	69%	18%	73
Cyprus	34	16	18%	71%	12%	79
Czech Republic	39	21	14%	71%	15%	77
Denmark	41	25	18%	66%	16%	78
Estonia	40	25	15%	67%	17%	74
Finland	42	26	17%	66%	17%	79
France	40	26	18%	65%	17%	81
Germany	44	31	13%	66%	20%	80
Greece	41	28	15%	67%	19%	80
Hungary	40	24	15%	69%	17%	74
Ireland	35	17	21%	67%	12%	80
Italy	43	31	14%	66%	20%	81
Latvia	40	26	14%	68%	18%	72
Lithuania	39	23	15%	69%	16%	71
Luxembourg	39	20	18%	68%	14%	79
Malta	39	20	15%	71%	14%	79
Netherlands	41	23	18%	67%	15%	80
Poland	38	19	15%	72%	14%	76
Portugal	41	27	15%	67%	18%	79
Romania	38	21	15%	70%	15%	73
Slovakia	37	17	15%	73%	12%	75
Slovenia	42	24	14%	70%	16%	79
Spain	40	25	15%	68%	17%	80
Sweden	41	28	17%	65%	18%	81
United Kingdom	40	25	17%	66%	17%	80
EU	**41**	**26**	**16%**	**67%**	**17%**	**79**
United States	37	20	20%	67%	13%	78
Canada	40	20	16%	69%	14%	81
Russia	38	18	15%	72%	13%	68
China	35	11	19%	72%	8%	73
Japan	45	35	13%	64%	23%	83
India	25	8	31%	64%	5%	64
Brazil	29	10	25%	68%	7%	72
World	29	12	27%	66%	8%	68

* Number of persons aged 65 years or over per 100 persons aged between 15 and 64 years

Source: UN, World Population Prospects, 2010 Revision
Data collected and collated for the Robert Schuman Foundation, © FRS

At the threshold of the 2010s, Europe continues to age in a world that remains young. The median age around the world is 29 years old; in the EU, it is 41. It is especially notable in the emerging world (25 in India, 29 in Brazil), but also in the USA (37). In Japan, by contrast, the median age is 45 years old. These differences are reflected in the structure of the population: the proportion of Europeans aged less than 14 years is 16%, versus 27% globally and 20% in the USA. The share of the population aged 65 and over is less than 8% globally, but rises to 13% in the USA and 17% in the EU. The difference in median age between the developed world and the rest of the planet is related to life expectancy. Globally, life expectancy averages 68 years. Russia matches the world average and India is below it (64 years) but people in Europe and the USA live almost 10 years past the average.

Within the EU, the situation is not homogeneous. Countries such as Germany, Austria and Italy have quickly aging population structures: those below the age of 14 now represent less than 13% of the population in Germany and 14% in Italy. For France, Denmark, Finland, the Netherlands and the United Kingdom, those below the age of 14 constitute around 17-18% of the population. The proportion of the population aged 65 years and over reaches 20% in Germany and Italy, which are gradually heading towards a situation like Japan (23%). Greece (19%) is in a similar situation. In the rest of the EU, the trend is in the same direction but less pronounced. Countries that maintain demographic vitality – France, Scandinavia and the Netherlands – have approximately 17% of the population in this oldest cohort.

1.1.3 Age structure of the EU compared to the world (2010)

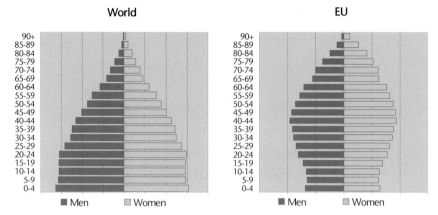

Source: UN, World Population Prospects, 2010 Revision
Data collected and collated for the Robert Schuman Foundation, © FRS

The population pyramids clearly highlight the divergence of an aging Europe from a young world. Generations of baby boomers who had contributed to the economic vitality of the old continent during the 'trente glorieuses', the boom years from 1945 to 1975, have gradually slipped from the world of production; rather than net contributors, they are becoming net beneficiaries in the form of pensions. This evolution constitutes a real metamorphosis of the European continent in a world that is also changing. In the balance between workers and dependents, demographic changes are not everything; overly deterministic interpretations should be avoided. Labour productivity remains much higher in Europe, for example (see 3.3.2 below), than in the world as a whole. Aging does not, in itself, ineluctably lead to economic loss or the loss of Europe's political role in the world. Demographic developments, instead, strengthen the case for a redefinition of a European strategy in a world that is not as "European" as it was in the sixteenth century, but in which the old continent will not disappear.

1.2. The Economic and Financial Weight of the EU, the Member States and other Centres of Economic Power

1.2.1 Distribution of global GDP at purchasing power parity (2012)

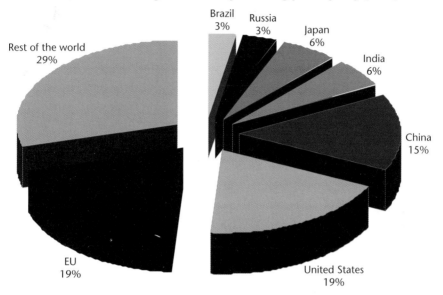

Brazil
3%

Russia
3%

Japan
6%

India
6%

Rest of the world
29%

China
15%

EU
19%

United States
19%

Source: IMF, World Economic Outlook, October 2012
Data collected and collated for the Robert Schuman Foundation, © FRS

Analysis of trends in demographics and wealth can help us understand the nature of changes in the world over the past decade. It is true that the BRICS (Brazil, Russia, India, China and South Africa) have experienced breath-taking economic growth and have, in 15 or 20 years, made changes that Europe and the USA required much more time to achieve. Nevertheless, the West – defined as the combination of the USA and Europe – represents 38% of the wealth produced in the world though it contains only 12% of the global population. China, whose rise is still the dominant issue of the past 15 years, produces 15% of global wealth while its population is 20% of the world total.

What is striking about this data is the fact that in the USA, since 1919, and in China over the last decade, the wealth produced is seen as part of a discussion about power, while Europe disclaims the connection between the two.

1.2.2 GDP of EU Member States at purchasing power parity and world ranking (2012)

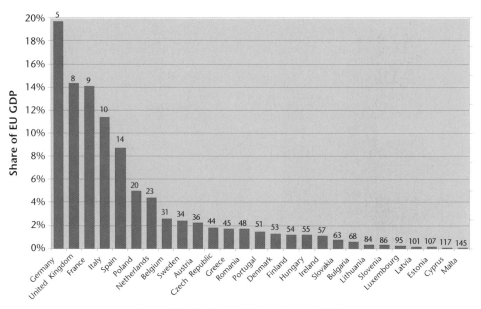

Source: IMF, World Economic Outlook, October 2012
Data collected and collated for the Robert Schuman Foundation, © FRS

The economic weight of the EU is very much connected with its largest Member States. In fact, the largest seven states – Germany, Spain, France, Italy, the Netherlands, Poland and the United Kingdom – account for almost 80% of EU GDP. This is both an advantage – the ability of nation states to directly influence their primary place in the world's economic and political life – and disadvantage – their inability to agree on a European strategy for the world.

This configuration also poses organizational problems within the Union; in an EU that is both enlarged and concentrated, how to define a balance between the weight of large states and the rights of small states? The changing world of the 2010s will require urgent resolution of this contradiction.

1.2.3 Market capitalisation of the world's leading financial centres (2007 - 2011)

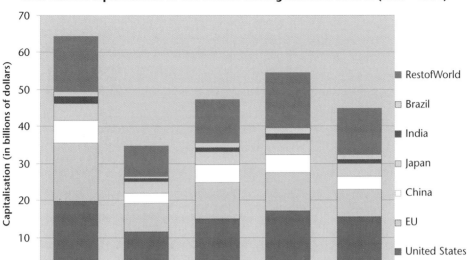

Source: World Development Indicators database, World Bank
Data collected and collated for the Robert Schuman Foundation, © FRS

After four years of crisis, the market capitalisation of the world's leading financial centres has still not regained its 2007 level. The recovery that started after 2008 seems to have been interrupted, with 2011 recording a decline compared to 2010 levels. While markets in the USA seemed better able to resist the tense and uncertain financial climate of 2011, European markets experienced a clear decline.

Regardless, despite strong growth in emerging economies and the fact that the financial crisis remains unresolved, markets in the USA and Europe continue to constitute the largest share of total global market capitalization (55%).

1.2.4 Distribution of GDP between sectors (1990 and 2010)

	Agriculture		Industry		Services	
	as % of GDP in 2010	Change since 1990	as % of GDP in 2010	Change since 1990	as % of GDP in 2010	Change since 1990
Austria	1.5	-59%	29	-10%	69	8%
Belgium	0.7	-66%	22	-31%	78	16%
Bulgaria	5.4	-69%	31	-36%	63	87%
Cyprus**	2.1	-70%	20	-24%	78	17%
Czech Rep.***	2.5	-59%	38	-22%	59	32%
Denmark	1.2	-70%	22	-15%	77	9%
Estonia***	3.4	-81%	30	-25%	67	58%
Finland	2.9	-54%	29	-13%	68	13%
France*	1.8	-58%	19	-30%	79	15%
Germany	0.9	-41%	28	-25%	71	16%
Greece***	3.4	-67%	19	-23%	78	19%
Hungary	3.5	-76%	31	-21%	65	41%
Ireland*	1.0	-89%	32	-8%	67	19%
Italy	1.9	-46%	25	-21%	73	13%
Latvia	4.1	-81%	22	-53%	74	132%
Lithuania	3.5	-87%	28	-9%	68	62%
Luxembourg	0.3	-79%	13	-53%	87	22%
Malta	1.9	-45%	33	-41%	65	61%
Netherlands	2.0	-55%	24	-19%	74	12%
Poland	3.5	-57%	32	-37%	65	56%
Portugal	2.4	-72%	23	-19%	75	19%
Romania	7.1	-70%	26	-48%	67	153%
Slovakia	3.9	-48%	35	-41%	61	83%
Slovenia	2.5	-56%	32	-26%	66	27%
Spain	2.7	-51%	26	-23%	71	17%
Sweden	1.8	-51%	26	-14%	72	10%
United Kingdom	0.7	-60%	22	-36%	78	21%
EU	**1.5**	**-58%**	**26**	**-23%**	**73**	**15%**
Euro area	**1.5**	**-55%**	**26**	**-19%**	**72**	**13%**
United States	1.2	-43%	20	-28%	79	13%
Canada	1.9	-33%	32	2%	66	0%
Japan	1.2	-45%	27	-27%	71	18%
Russia	4.0	-76%	37	-24%	59	69%
China	10.1	-63%	47	13%	43	37%
India	17.7	-39%	27	2%	55	24%
Brazil	5.3	-35%	28	-27%	67	25%

*=2009; **=2008, ***=2007

Source: World Development Indicators database, World Bank
Data collected and collated for the Robert Schuman Foundation, © FRS

Around the world, economic growth results in a transfer of activity and employment from agriculture to industry and services. This development, which Europe has seen since 1770, is being extended to the whole world. The Chinese takeoff, which has its origins in the late 1970s but is most evident since the 1990s, reflects basically the same transformation. In twenty years, the transformation has been dramatic with agriculture dropping to only 10% of GDP and services rising to account for 43%. Industry remains the main component of China's GDP (47%). This Chinese situation contrasts with the situation observed in India. India is distinguished by having the majority of its economy related to services (55%) but also by the relative importance of agriculture (18%), which breaks with the traditional pattern of having economic take-off based on industry. Indian industry accounts for only 27% of GDP.

The economy in the USA is now concentrated in services, which constitute nearly 80% of economic activity. Industry generates 20% of economic activity, having shrunk 28% in the space of 20 years, while agriculture has experienced a contraction of 43% since 1990 and by 2010 represented only 1.2% of the wealth produced in the USA.

While the accelerated globalization of the last twenty years has meant a kind of relative decline of industry, or a movement of "deindustrialization", in the West, Europe has distinguished itself from the USA by its ability to contain these changes, knowing that industrial trade accounts for two thirds of total trade worldwide. For both the EU and the eurozone, industry constituted 26% of GDP in 2010. The share of agriculture (1.5%) is slightly higher than that observed in the USA; however the share of services (72%) is significantly lower than in the USA because of the less dramatic decline in European industry in the global economy.

Within the Union, the situations are obviously mixed. While the common agricultural policy (CAP) has been a for long time, and is still, important electoral terrain, agriculture represents less than 1% of GDP in the United Kingdom and does not even exceed 4% in the east – Poland (3.5%), Slovakia (3.9%). In France, which has been traditionally attached to the CAP, agriculture contributes only 1.8% of GDP.

Every EU country has experienced a decline in the share of industry in the economy. In almost all EU countries, this erosion has remained moderate. Industry in Germany (28% of GDP) is 2 percentage points above the EU average, while Finland is 3 points above the average (29%). Spain and Sweden are at exactly the EU average while in Italy (25%), the Netherlands (24%), Portugal (23%) and the United Kingdom (22%), industrial erosion remains moderate. Except for the very special and easily explainable case of Luxembourg, France and Greece (19% each) appear as exceptions, having now the lowest industrial contribution to GDP in the EU. It is important to note that France particularly stands out because the change in industry's share in GDP since 1990 (-30%) is 7 points worse than the average European change in that time.

1.3. The EU in International Trade

1.3.1 Development of world trade (2005 - 2012)

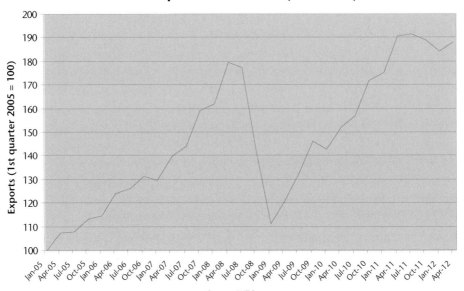

Source: WTO
Data collected and collated for the Robert Schuman Foundation, © FRS

After a brilliant and sustained expansion between 2005 and mid-2008, global trade shrank by about a third between summer 2008 and the first quarter of 2009. The rebound began in the spring of 2009 and was particularly strong during the ensuing months to regain the pre-crisis level at the beginning of 2011. After a very strong increase of 13.6% in 2010, trade increased by 6.6% in 2011 and 4.5% in 2012.

1.3.2 The EU in international trade (2011)

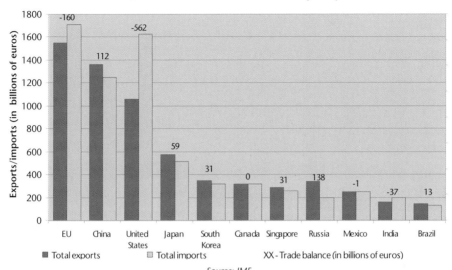

Source: IMF
Data collected and collated for the Robert Schuman Foundation, © FRS

While the EU and the USA have a similar share of world GDP, they are different in terms of international trade. The EU is the world's leading foreign trade zone with nearly 15% of world exports, though this takes into account intra-EU trade. Other major centres of world trade are China (14%) and the USA (11%). In 2011, the USA recorded a heavy current account deficit (-$500 billion, or 4% of GDP) against a deficit of $200 billion or 1.5% of GDP in Europe. The Chinese surplus was approximately $200 billion.

1.3.3 Where do European imports come from?
The main suppliers of the EU (2011)

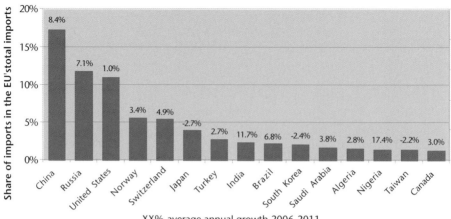

XX%-average annual growth 2006-2011

Where do European exports go?
The main customers of the EU (2011)

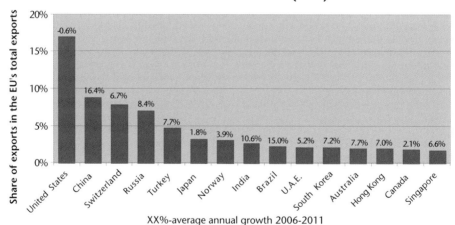

XX%-average annual growth 2006-2011

Source: Eurostat
Data collected and collated for the Robert Schuman Foundation, © FRS

Schematically, the EU gets its imports from China, Russia and the USA. The weight of Russia and Norway in imports reflects the importance of energy supplies in European imports. The EU's leading markets for exports are the USA (16%), China (9%), Switzerland (8%) and Russia (7.5%). While trade with the USA changed little between 2006 and 2011, the same period was marked by a faster pace of trade with Asia. With new emerging countries, trade with the EU is lively and oriented in a direction favourable to the EU: with China, exports (+16.4%) grew almost twice as fast as imports (+8.4%); with Brazil, exports increased by 15% against 6.8% for imports; with Russia, there was also a faster increase in exports than imports (+8.4% against 7.1%) whereas with India, trade increases have been balanced in both directions.

**1.3.4 Foreign direct investment (FDI) of the EU
and international comparisons (stocks in 2011)**

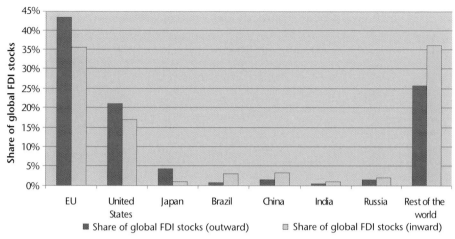

Source: Eurostat
Data collected and collated for the Robert Schuman Foundation, © FRS

The central role of the EU in a globalised economy appears even more clearly when analysing foreign direct investment (FDI). The EU represents 43% of outward FDI stocks compared with 22% for the USA. The EU accounts for more than 35% of inward FDI stocks, compared with 17% for the USA. In 2011, the EU accounted for more inward FDI stocks than the USA, Japan, Brazil, China, India and Russia combined.

1. 4. The External Action of the EU

1.4.1 Military expenditure in the EU and international comparisons (2011)

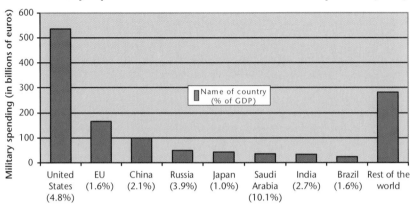

1.4.1a Military expenditure of EU Member States (2011)

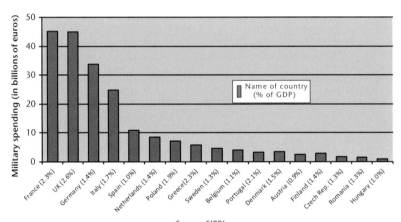

Source: SIPRI
Data collected and collated for the Robert Schuman Foundation, © FRS

In terms of military spending, there is the USA, and then there is everybody else. With military spending of more than $520 billion, the USA spends 4.8% of its GDP on military expenditures, accounting for 40% of the world total. Europeans spend a third of what the USA does, totalling 1.6% of GDP. New emerging countries such as China have been increasing military spending: military spending in China increased by 170% in the last 10 years, totalling nearly $100 billion in 2011 (2.1% of GDP). Russian military spending reached $50 billion in 2011 (4% GDP), and is planned to total $750 billion by 2020.

Despite being addressed in various treaties and initiatives, both bilateral and multilateral, European defense struggles to detach from national imperatives. A review of military spending in the EU shows that if there is European military action, it must be done by the United Kingdom and France. These two states each spent $45 billion in 2011, representing 2.6 and 2.3% of their GDP, respectively. Germany, which has begun to send troops abroad since the early 1990s (ex-Yugoslavia, Afghanistan, etc.), still fails to play a military role to match its economic weight. In the 2011 Libya conflict, France and the United Kingdom acted with German abstention in the UN. France, which joined the integrated command of NATO in 2008, and the United Kingdom, with its special partnership with the USA, will continue to play a role on the international stage.

1.4.2 Leading arms exporters (2004 - 2011)

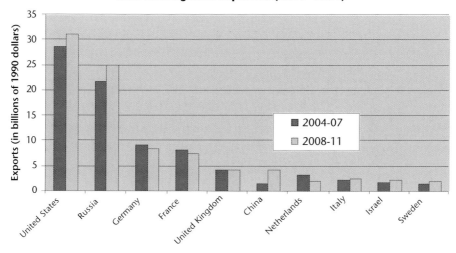

Source: SIPRI
Data collected and collated for the Robert Schuman Foundation, © FRS

Arms sales are closely related to the logic of power. With nearly $25 billion in arms exports between 2008 and 2011, Russia intends to maintain an asset inherited from the USSR, despite the weakness of its economy 20 years after the collapse of communism. The USA remains the undisputed leader in an area where they are able to combine very effectively the power of their economy with their political stature as a great power in world politics. Europeans, especially France and Germany but also, to a lesser extent, the United Kingdom, play a significant role in this area. The cumulative arms exports of these three countries come close to matching Russia's total arms sales.

1.4.3 Official development assistance (2000, 2006 and 2011)

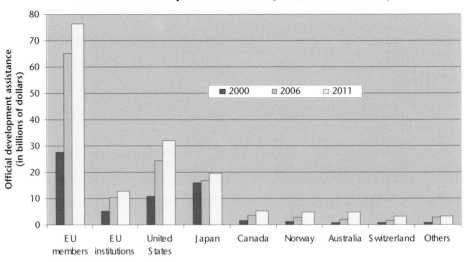

Source: OECD
Data collected and collated for the Robert Schuman Foundation, © FRS

In terms of development, the EU, whether the Member States or EU institutions, makes the greatest aid contribution with an ODA total of nearly $90 billion. Despite the financial crisis and struggles with public finances, the European effort grew by approximately $10 billion between 2006 and 2011. By comparison, aid from the USA is approximately half of the European amount.

2. Restoring Financial Stability and Control of Public Finances

2.1. The Crisis in Public Finances

2.1.1 Deficits and public debts of EU Member States and international comparisons (2012)

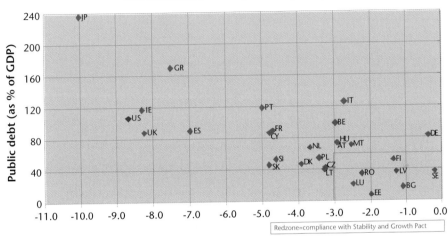

Public deficit (as % of GDP)

Source: IMF
Data collected and collated for the Robert Schuman Foundation, © FRS

The effects of the financial crisis of 2008-2009, whether as a result of automatic stabilizers – the lack of offset for diminishing revenues due to the decline in activity – or as a result of the stimulus packages in its wake, led all OECD countries to situations of severely widened deficits and greatly increased public debt. In the USA, the deficit reached 10% of GDP and public debt has surpassed 100% of GDP. Across the EU, public debt jumped to 83% of GDP, and in the eurozone to 90% of GDP. Public deficits widened to an average of 6% of GDP in the eurozone and 7% in the whole EU.

Across the EU, whether from eurozone countries or non-eurozone countries like the United Kingdom, plans for the reduction of deficits that have been in place since 2010, have taken at the same time a general nature and a magnitude hitherto unknown. In the case of the eurozone countries, the fact that economies are linked by a fixed exchange rate removes, by definition, the use of devaluation as a means of adjustment. Deficit reduction measures were implemented under pressure from the markets, marked by soaring interest rates on the debt of developing countries and an explosion of interest rate differences with German public debt, the reference market for the eurozone.

Overall, in 2012, deficits fell sharply even as the contraction in GDP led to a reverse trend of deterioration in deficit/GDP and debt/GDP ratios. This resulted in a lack of clarity regarding the effects of the deficit cuts, with Keynesian experts dreading the start of a vicious circle. The deficits/GDP ratio was reduced at a rate slower than the absolute deficit values. The deficits of the eurozone dropped from 6 to 4% of GDP from 2011 to 2012. In the cases of Greece and Spain, their European partners had to agree to a two-year extension for getting government spending plans back in balance to meet the desired deficit/GDP objectives. Regarding the debt/GDP levels, with the exception of Germany, where higher growth than its partners reduced its debt ratio from 83 to 80% of GDP, most Member States still, despite adjustment programs, continue to have worsening debt/GDP ratios.

However, the changes that have been made, despite their painful economic and social effects, especially in terms of unemployment, have actually had the effect of allowing states to control their deficits and see the beginnings of the virtuous effects that were expected. Italy ended the year 2012 with a deficit down to about 2.9% of GDP, compared with 3.9% in 2011; combined with the effects of the relaxation of European monetary policy, this policy has reduced Italy's interest rate differential with Germany from 575 points in 2011 to 200 in 2012, which greatly facilitates the return to budget balance. In Spain, where in just one year, 2012, the reduction of the structural deficit reached 5.25% of GDP, exports are growing more quickly than in Germany (17% vs. 12% growth since 2008). A return to positive growth in the second half of 2013 should see strengthening economic trends translate into improvements in national accounts.

2.1.2 Rate of public expenditure (2012)

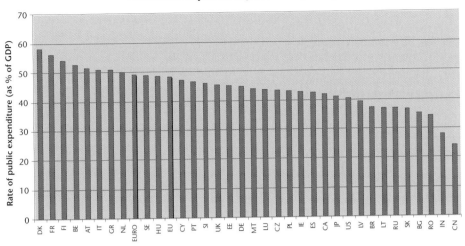

Source: Eurostat
Data collected and collated for the Robert Schuman Foundation, © FRS

With the combined effects of the contraction of the economy and states' efforts to cushion the impact of the crisis, public spending increased as a proportion of GDP in the USA and Europe. But this is an area where Europe is different. In the USA, total public spending accounted for 42% of GDP, which is below the 49% average found in the EU and in the eurozone.

While, the return to balanced budgets comes with the cost of a heavier tax burden, Europeans have realized, if only because of the impossibility of increasing debt loads, exhaustion of Keynesian strategies targeted managing growth by adjusting public spending. In fact, following the examples of reforms in Sweden in the mid 1990s, and Germany from 2003, economic strategies now common in Europe involve reducing deficits and conducting structural reforms aimed primarily to create a more flexible labour market (Italy, Spain, Portugal, etc.). There are also strategies with the medium-term goal of reducing rates of expenditures and the return to balanced budgets is naturally facilitated when expenditure rates are lower.

Hence the importance of the differences in rates of public expenditure in Europe for the coherence of interdependent economic policies. These differences plagued the functioning of the eurozone for the last ten years, including the gap in public spending between France and Germany, which account for 46% of GDP in the eurozone, and have become a key concern for European growth. While France ranks second in the EU in its rate of public expenditure (56%) behind Denmark (58%), France ranks first in the eurozone, 8 points above the eurozone average, while Germany is 2 points below. In France, public expenditure as a percentage of GDP has grown continuously for 10 years as the crisis has accelerated; Germany pursued a reduction in government spending during the same period. The effects of the crisis on countries such as Spain (42% of GDP) and Italy (51%) are in large part due to the combined effects of expenditure rigidity and a contraction of economic activity. In Italy, public expenditure decreased from 51.9% of GDP in 2009 to 49.9% in 2011. In Spain, the rate of public spending, driven by the crisis from 41.5% of GDP in 2009 to 46.3% in 2010, has begun a downward trend (45.2% in 2011). The medium-term trend in both countries is of declining public expenditure, as it is in most European countries. Outside the eurozone, the trend is the same: the United Kingdom has one of the most drastic policies in the EU for reducing public spending.

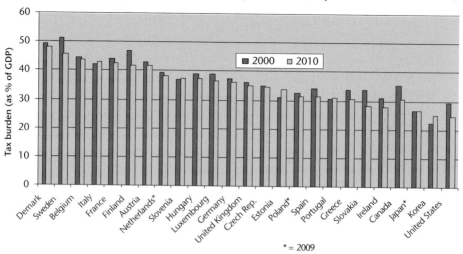

2.1.3 Tax burden (2000 and 2010)

* = 2009

Source: OECD
Data collected and collated for the Robert Schuman Foundation, © FRS

The counter-party to public spending is taxation. The tax burden does not exceed 25% in the USA and is a little over 30% in Canada. In Europe, taxes are much higher than in North America. With the exception of the southern EU countries and Poland, where the tax burden is around 30%, the largest European countries have tax rates of around 38-42%. Sweden (45%) and Denmark (49%) are exceptions.

However, data from 2009/2010 must be analyzed with some caution when analysing trends before and after the crisis: the 2009/2010 period corresponds to a period of significant contraction in economic activity, during which plans for deficit reduction and increased taxes were just beginning to be put in place.

Government programs implemented in 2011-2012 and those announced for 2013 include significant increases in all tax rates which should lead to a marked increase, at least temporarily, of the tax burden.

2.1.4 Development of public debt (1999, 2007 and 2012)

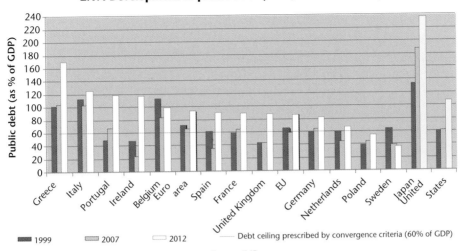

Source: IMF
Data collected and collated for the Robert Schuman Foundation, © FRS

The impact of the crisis is strongly reflected in enlarged public debt: public debt increased by 20% of GDP in the eurozone between 2008 and 2012. The biggest increase took place in Greece, where the debt has increased from 112% of GDP in 2008 to 170% in 2011. Italy, which had managed to reduce its public debt ratio from 120 to 106% between 1999 and 2008, saw their efforts wiped out by the crisis. At the end of 2012, the debt was expected to reach 124% of GDP. Germany, which had managed to balance its accounts (-0.1% of GDP) in 2008 and stabilize debt at 67% of GDP, suffered a marked deterioration of its fiscal situation with a debt ratio of 82.5% in 2010. This improved to 80% in 2011 due to improved control of its public accounts. Spain, which had obtained a very good deficit and debt performance prior to 2008, saw its efforts ruined by the explosion of the housing bubble and its impact on the balance sheets of the country's banks. Public debt rose from 40 to 70% of GDP between 2008 and 2011. France, which is in a situation of structurally degraded public finances, underwent significant additional worsening of its debt situation. Already at close to 70% of GDP before the crisis, the debt ratio is close to 90% in 2012. Finally, the United Kingdom, which had a debt level significantly lower than that of its EU partners in 2008 (52% of GDP) experienced the highest growth of public debt, which increased sharply to 85% of GDP in 2011: a leap of +33% of GDP.

2.1.5 Share of the public sector employment in the labour force (2000 and 2008)

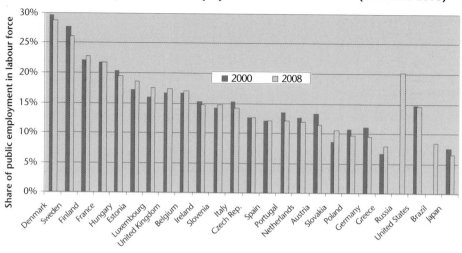

Source: OECD
Data collected and collated for the Robert Schuman Foundation, © FRS

Most European governments going through deficit reduction programs have included an element of staff downsizing (United Kingdom, Italy, etc.). Apart from the Nordic countries – Denmark, Sweden and Finland – where public sector employment fell slightly (about 2.5%), from a high level, between 2000 and 2008, France appears to be the country where the public sector constitutes the largest proportion of the total labour force. It has 500,000 more public employees than Germany with a population that is 17 million lower. As a proportion of the labour force, the gap is 12 points: 22% in France versus 10% in Germany in 2008. In some European countries (the United Kingdom, Belgium, Ireland and Italy), the rate of public sector employment was near 15%. In a reversal from expected stereotypes, southern Europe seems not particularly prone to swelling the numbers of public employees. In Spain and Portugal, the rates are close to those of the Netherlands and Austria at around 12-13%. In Greece, the proportion of employees in the public sector in 2008 was 7.5%. In Greece, it was the rising pay for officials (+110% between 2000 and 2010), which was the cause of the loss of control of public accounts.

2.2. The Crisis in Banking and Finance

2.2.1 Divergence in market interest rates in the eurozone (2008 - 2012)

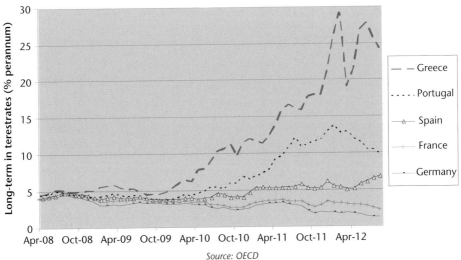

Source: OECD
Data collected and collated for the Robert Schuman Foundation, © FRS

The debt of each state of the eurozone is now a debt of the entire eurozone! Until 2009, there was appreciation in the financial markets for the debt of eurozone members. This situation had not only led to an absence of rate differences but also to a new paradigm for global finance in the 2000s: a highly liquid financial market with connections to Western financial systems, particularly American, and external surpluses in emerging economies, coupled with highly accommodative monetary policy in the USA. Somehow, the absence of a risk premium between Greek debt and German debt was based on the idea that market liquidity was supposed to be available at any time, removing any solvency risk.

The financial crisis shattered the prevailing configuration in which a convergence of interest rates was accepted despite growing economic differences – government budget balances, economic growth rates, unemployment rates, trade balances – which had held from creation of the euro to the financial crisis of 2008. If one could give an overview of what has happened since the crisis, one could say that after a period of very pronounced distrust between governments and markets in which spreads – the difference in interest rates on government bonds – grew between German debt and the debt of the southern states and Ireland, the eurozone eventually reached a point, since the end of 2011, where it was able to recover a significant portion of its credibility with financial markets. These markets passed through successive phases of apprehension over government finances. After driving governments to enact extremely stringent adjustment policies, markets have finally begun to worry about the impact of these policies on growth and therefore on the ability of eurozone states to meet their financial commitments with this spiral of uncertainty feeding worry of a possible risk of implosion of the single currency.

The return to a more relaxed financial climate in 2012, due to a combination of factors, has reduced market fears. Despite technical and political difficulties, the states of the region were finally able to respond to market fears about the risk of collapse of the single currency, with much of the differences in rates corresponding to a premium for the risk of being paid in national currency. Ultimately, states have demonstrated their political and financial ability to protect the weakened states of the eurozone (Greece, Ireland, Spain and Portugal). Credibility was also found in most states, particularly the most vulnerable of the large states, France, to continue on the road toward order in public finances, despite a stagnant economy or recession. Finally, there has been a reversal of market expectations, following the changes initiated in 2008 by Jean-Claude Trichet, President of the European Central Bank, and continued by his successor Mario Draghi, that added credibility to the message that "the euro is irreversible." It is with this perspective that in late August 2012 the European Central Bank launched the Outright Monetary Transactions (OMT) program by which the central bank commits itself to buy unlimited public debt of the countries of the eurozone pursuing reform plans.

In fact, the strength of European policy since the end of the year 2011 in particular, has been to bind together deficit reduction, the implementation of structural reforms and the easing of monetary policy. Setting monetary policy reforms without connection to reforms only served to weaken European credibility by sending a message of plans to exit the crisis through inflation. The perfect example of this strategy is Italy, which was unable to rely solely on European solidarity, but strengthened the course of its reforms and deficit reduction policy, and was able to see its interest rate spread drop from 525 to 200 basis points. Italian government 10-year bonds, that had risen to 7.5% in late 2011, dropped below 4.5% in late 2012. Spain has also found greater market credibility with interest rates dropping to 5.2%. French debt, which offers investors ideal liquidity conditions, has benefited from strong demand from investors with interest rate of 2.04%, a premium of only 64 points difference with Germany (1.4%). This reduction reflects the differing rates of success within the eurozone in overcoming financial crisis and repressing market worries over the risk of rupture of the single currency. The rate reduction also contributes strongly to deficit reduction efforts and lowers the cost of reforms.

2.2.2 Key interest rates of the ECB, US Federal Reserve and Bank of England (2007 - 2012)

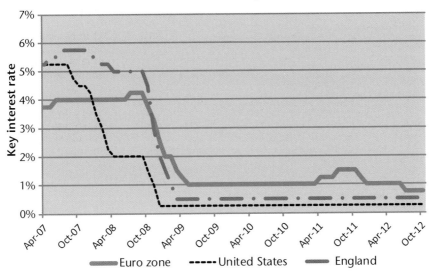

Sources: ECB, United States Federal Reserve and Bank of England
Data collected and collated for the Robert Schuman Foundation, © FRS

2.2.3 Unconventional monetary policy measures of the ECB, the US Federal Reserve and the Bank of England (2007 - 2012)

European Central Bank		
Date	Action	Effect / Amount
Sept. 2008	Start of special term refinancing operations	ongoing
Oct. 2008	Switch to fixed rate, full allotment refinancing	ongoing
June 2009	Long Term Refinancing Operation, 1 year maturity	€ 442 billion
July 2009 - June 2010	First Covered Bond Purchase Programme	€ 60 billion
Oct. 2009	Long Term Refinancing Operation, 1 year maturity	€ 75 billion
Dec. 2009	Long Term Refinancing Operation, 1 year maturity	€ 97 billion
May 2010	Securities Markets Programme	Decided by the governing council
Oct. 2011	Long Term Refinancing Operation, 1 year maturity	€ 57 billion
Nov. 2011	Second Covered Bond Purchase Programme	€ 40 billion
Dec. 2011	Long Term Refinancing Operation, 3 year maturity	€ 489 billion
Dec. 2011	Loosening collateral requirements	
Dec. 2011	Reducing reserve requirements from 2% to 1%	
Feb. 2012	Long Term Refinancing Operation, 3 year maturity	€ 530 billion
Sept. 2012	Outright Monetary Transactions (OMT) - purchase of public debt securities maturing within three years	Unlimited sterilised purchases - fully compensated by selling other securities

United States Federal Reserve		
Date	Action	Effect / Amount
Dec. 2007 - Mar. 2010	Term Auction Facility (TAF): liquidity auction under loosened collateral requirements	1 month loans of varying sizes
Nov. 2008	Purchase of $100 billion of government-sponsored corporate debt and $500 billion of Mortgage Backed Securities (MBS)	$600 billion
Mar. 2009 - June 2010	Term Asset-Backed Securities Loan Facility (TALF): similar to TAF, but collateralized by asset-backed securities	Longer term loans of varying sizes
Jan. 2009 - Mar. 2010	Expansion of purchasing programme for debt of the Government Sponsored Enterprises (GSEs), Fannie Mae and Freddie Mac	$200 billion
Jan. 2009 - Mar. 2010	Expansion of MBS purchase programme	$1250 billion
Jan. 2009 - Mar. 2010	Purchases of longer term Treasury securities	$300 billion
Nov. 2010	Additional purchases of longer term Treasury securities	$600 billion
Sept. 2011	Extending average maturity of Treasury holdings by selling short term (<3 years) and purchasing long term (6-30 years) Treasury securities. Also called "Operation Twist".	$400 billion (gross, $0 net)
June 2012	Expansion of Operation Twist program	$267 billion (gross, $0 net)
Sept. 2012	Expansion of MBS purchase program	$40 billion per month

Bank of England		
Date	Action	Effect / Amount
Apr. 2008 - Jan. 2009	Special Liquidity Scheme (SLS): banks swap high quality asset-backed securities for UK Treasury Bills. Closed January 2012	£185 billion
Jan. 2009	Extended maturity of discount window	ongoing
Mar. - Nov. 2009	Quantitative easing: purchase of mainly Gilts - UK government debt	£200 billion
Oct. 2011	Additional purchases of Gilts	£75 billion
Feb. 2012	Additional purchases of Gilts	£50 billion

Source: ECB, United States Federal Reserve and the European Parliament, Directorate General for Internal Policies, Paper IP/A/ECON/NT/2012-04
Data collected and collated for the Robert Schuman Foundation, © FRS

2.2.4 Balance sheet expansion of the ECB, the US Federal Reserve and the Bank of England (2007 - 2012)

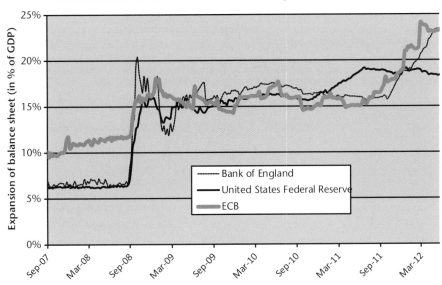

Sources: ECB, United States Federal Reserve and Bank of England
Data collected and collated for the Robert Schuman Foundation, © FRS

Since the beginning of the 2008-2009 financial crisis, the ECB has accelerated its transformation towards being a full central bank on the model of international central banks such as the US Federal Reserve and the Bank of England. The announcement by ECB President Mario Draghi on September 6, 2012 of the ECB's decision to accept unlimited debt of the states of the eurozone (to support their bank refinancing operations) is a milestone and marks a near completion of this transformation, which is essential to build the ECB as a European institution in its own right. The ECB, however, conducts its operations according to a logic quite different from that of the Fed. It uses the policy rate as a macro-economic guide considering both inflation and growth. But the 2008 crisis exposed the lack of means for regulating bank liquidity. Faced with the drying up or paralysis of the interbank market following the collapse of Lehman Brothers in 2008, and again in the summer of 2011, the ECB found itself at the forefront of ensuring bank liquidity. Hence the activation of "unconventional" techniques, which differ from "conventional" rate-modifying price interventions, to ensure the normal operation of bank liquidity. These intervention techniques were initiated from the beginning of the 2008 crisis and took on their full extent as the consequences of the Greek crisis impacted bank balance sheets.

While the ECB has no legal right to directly acquire government debt, it acted on these assets through the channel of support to banks. In May 2010, as part of the Securities Markets Program (SMP), it intervened by buying Greek bonds. In 2011, it stepped up its interventions in this respect, increasing its intervention program from €74 to 211 billion. In December 2011 and February 2012, the ECB conducted two long term financing operations for purchase of assets of up to 3 years maturity in amounts of €489 and 529 billion. It also lowered the level of reserve requirements of banks by €100 billion. Finally, in September 2012, under the Outright Monetary Transactions (OMT) program, the ECB began purchases of unlimited debt of eurozone states. In direct consequence of this metamorphosis, the ECB's balance sheet has increased from €1450 to €3100 billion between mid-2008 and mid-2012. Coupled with the reduction of fiscal deficits of eurozone states, these changes in European monetary policy have led to a relaxation of market rates. Rates on European sovereign debt returned to significantly reduced and consistent levels. At year-end 2012, the Spanish rate returned to 5.4%, as compared to 7.5% in mid-summer, while Italian rates dropped from 6.6 to 4.5%. Portugal has seen its rates melt, with yields on 10-year securities dropping from 17.2% to 7.49% during the same period. As for the Irish rate, they experienced the most dramatic decline, reaching year-end 2012 at 1.89% as compared to 23.2%

in July 2011. Germany is still the best risk in the eurozone (1.35%) but the other big states of the monetary union have also benefited from historically low yields. Favoured by the high liquidity of the securities to which they apply, yields on French government debt fell to 1.87%, for a 0.52 point spread with the German Bund. In total, 2012 saw a real convergence of intervention methods used by the ECB to match those of the Fed and the Bank of England, which widely and heavily used quantitative easing techniques. This convergence is also evident in rates: the key interest rate of the ECB (refi) was lowered in July by 25 basis points from 1% to 0.75%. It was set at 3.25% on the eve of the crisis in 2008. At the end of 2012, the ECB rate was only 0.5% above the rate of the FED (0.25%) and 0.25% above that of the Bank of England (0.50%).

2.2.5 Changes in the money supply in the eurozone (1999 - 2012)

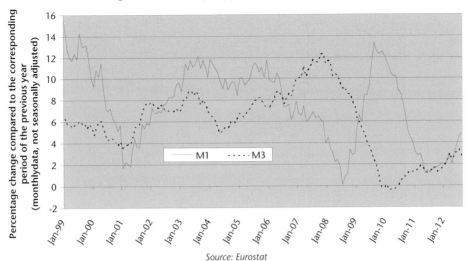

Source: Eurostat
Data collected and collated for the Robert Schuman Foundation, © FRS

The OMT program announced by the ECB at the start of September 2012 impacted the evolution of the broad money supply (M3), reducing the need for liquidity cushions used by large institutional investors to cover the risks related to financial tensions in the eurozone. At the end of 2012, the growth rate of the money supply was in a slight acceleration phase, reaching an annual rate of change of 3.9%, as compared with 2.9% in the summer. The average annual rate of M3 for 2012 was 3%. Its narrow component, M1, also saw accelerated growth. At the end of 2012, its annual rate of change was 6%. Term deposits (M2-M1) operated at a rate of 1.7% and the negotiable component (M3-M2) saw slightly negative or zero change. On the counterparty side of the money supply, the credit growth rate for eurozone residents was moving at a slow pace (+0.5%): the growth of credit to governments was at an annual rate close to 9%, while the private sector saw a decline in the range of -0.7 to -0.9% on an annual basis. This sluggish evolution applied to both housing loans to households (1.3%) and those to companies (-2%).

2.2.5a Inflation in the eurozone (1999 - 2012)

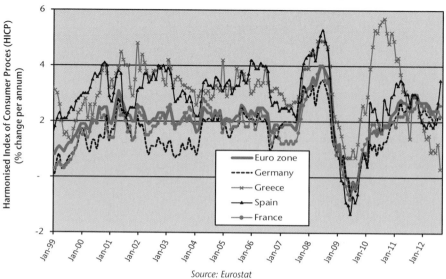

Source: Eurostat
Data collected and collated for the Robert Schuman Foundation, © FRS

Highly dependent on changes in energy prices, consumer prices in the eurozone were rising at the rate of 2.2% at year end 2012. This development marks a significant slowdown compared to 2011 when consumer prices were rising at the rate of 3%. Forecasters expect that this rate will fall below 2% in 2013. Energy prices could support this trend. Rising at an annual rate of 12% in late 2011, the energy price slowdown was clear at the end of 2012 (5.8%).

2.2.6 Exchange rate of the euro against major currencies (2000 - 2012)

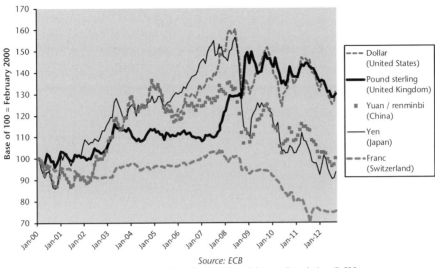

Source: ECB
Data collected and collated for the Robert Schuman Foundation, © FRS

The effective exchange rate of the euro has significantly decreased (-14% between 2009 and summer 2012) since the beginning of the global financial crisis of 2008. This trend has been interrupted since the end of summer 2012: by the end of 2012, the effective exchange rate of the euro grew by 2% compared to its level in July 2012. The change in the trend was also apparent for developments in bilateral exchange rates: based on the observed data in the summer of 2012, the euro had depreciated by 10% against the pound sterling, nearly 12% against the yen and 13.5% against the US dollar, compared to its level in 2011. Between summer and the end of 2012, the euro has been rising against these currencies: +6.5% against the yen, +4% against the dollar and +1.8% against the pound sterling.

2.2.7 Cross-exposure of banking systems (2011 and Q1 2012)

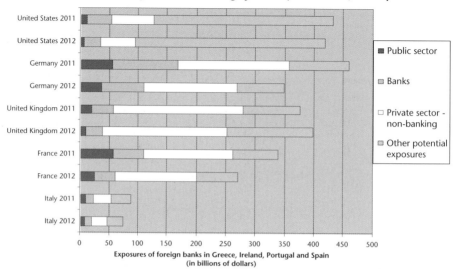

Source: Bank for International Settlements
Data collected and collated for the Robert Schuman Foundation, © FRS

Macroeconomic risks which affected the balance sheets of banks in the eurozone, especially in 2010 and 2011, were substantially reduced in 2012 due to the easing of financial tensions in the latter part of the year. As the emblematic example of the risks that the European banking system faced, Spain had been suffering from investor flight: capital transfers out of the country and a return of public debt securities to the balance sheets of central banks of the eurozone. From the moment when Europe had the means to solve the problem, with the agreement of the European Council of 28 June to provide the Spanish banking sector with a credit line of €100 billion and the ECB announcement of its intention to act as lender of last resort, the capital flight reversed. The overall exposure risks across banking systems were strongly mitigated. The Spanish banking sector has been able to complete its restructuring with the assistance of the European Stability Mechanism (ESM): €37 billion in aid was released in December 2012 for savings banks nationalized by the Spanish State and the "defeasance" (bad bank) structure, the Sareb, designed to accommodate €45 billion of toxic assets, was provided with €2.5 billion in resources by the ESM. During 2012, the eurozone thus managed to regain control of the risks to which it was exposed as a result of the crisis in the banking systems of the peripheral states (Portugal, Greece, Ireland and Cyprus). The announcement by the Council in June 2012 to launch a banking union under the auspices of the ECB has also allowed the entire European financial sector to reconnect with a high degree of stability.

2.2.8 Development of stock markets (2000 - 2012)

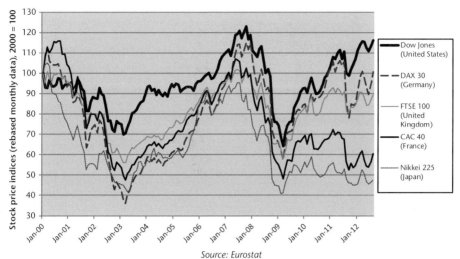

Source: Eurostat
Data collected and collated for the Robert Schuman Foundation, © FRS

While the major international stock markets have not fully recovered to their 2007 levels near-ly 5 years after the crisis, 2012 has nevertheless seen consolidation of the process of recovery. The strong reduction of monetary and financial tensions in Europe has contributed to the disappea-rance of unfavourable positions on the values of the European banking sector. This reversal has helped the recovery in the financial sector, as well as the overall market, with improvements in the non-financial sector proving more moderate. This dichotomy has not occurred in the USA, where financial stocks were little changed, while non-financial stocks suffered a slowdown. Overall, risk aversion measures have still not disappeared, but a significant recovery in corporate earnings, including in the USA, combined with lower yields on risk-free assets, could lead to a revision of this situation in 2013.

2.3. Reducing Internal Economic Disparity in the EU

**2.3.1 Real growth rates of EU Member States
and international comparisons (2011 and 2012)**

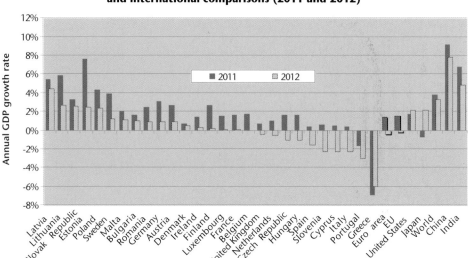

Source: IMF, World Economic Outlook, October 2012
Data collected and collated for the Robert Schuman Foundation, © FRS

Throughout the global economy, the year 2011 saw a strong first half in the wake of a sharp rebound in activity that began in 2010. This followed a significant reduction in activity in 2009, which was partly due to effects carried over from the previous year, as well as a change in activity calculated from a reduced base. The slowdown in the pace of activity seen in 2010 was due not only to the gradual easing of cyclical factors but also to the development of strong fiscal pressures, especially in the summer of 2011. Faced with the need to reduce their domestic demand, the countries of the EU as a whole, far beyond the circle of Member States of the eurozone, followed restrictive fiscal policies which affected the entire international economy. For the USA, whose aim is to correct their fiscal imbalances by stimulating growth through expansionary monetary policy, and which was the only large economy to see an increase of activity in 2012 compared to 2011, the year was still marked by the persistence of a real estate market paralyzed by imbalances. The EU has chosen a policy closely linking monetary easing – it is the same in the United Kingdom and in the eurozone – and very large budget deficits. Under these conditions, as a result of the reduction in domestic demand, growth in Europe in 2012 remained low or negative following a sluggish 2011.

However, while the general trends are weak, contrasts are very significant from one country to another and even from one region to another. The recession especially hit those countries forced to react in an emergency with a significant reduction in domestic demand. In this hardest hit first subset were the countries of southern and eastern Europe, like the Czech Republic and Hungary, as well as the Netherlands and the United Kingdom. A second subset includes those countries with growth below 1%: Germany, France, Belgium, Finland, Denmark and Romania. Finally, Europe has a third subset of countries which saw significant growth: the Baltic States, Poland and Sweden.

At the start of 2013, the slow growth trend from 2012 looks poised to continue, though forecasters expect economic activity to accelerate towards the third quarter. Stimulus programs underway in most European economies, with an aim of fiscal consolidation, should start to produce the expected results. The first signs of improvement will be seen by an increased contribution to GDP growth from foreign trade that has developed from improved competitiveness, and which should produce ripple effects throughout the entire economy. These changes are already visible in the economies of southern Europe.

2.3.2 Index of industrial production (2005 - 2012)

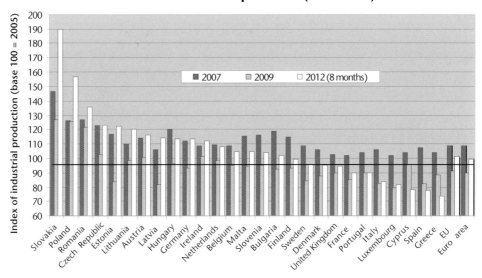

Source: Eurostat
Data collected and collated for the Robert Schuman Foundation, © FRS

Across the EU, and in the eurozone, 2009 saw a sharp contraction in industrial production due to a sudden drop in economic activity resulting from the financial crisis. Faced with the need to reduce domestic demand, Europe is struggling after more than four years to attain the levels of industrial production achieved in 2007. The industrial heart of the EU centred on Germany – the Czech Republic, Austria, Hungary, Poland, Romania and Slovakia – has restored production to pre-crisis levels and even exceeded them. A similar situation has played out in Ireland, which took full advantage of its adjustment efforts and restored its competitiveness. Mediterranean countries and the United Kingdom have not returned to pre-crisis levels but have seen a pronounced reduction of domestic demand. Italy exemplifies this situation. France is not facing a reduction in domestic demand but rather an inability of industry to meet the demand.

2.3.3 Savings, investment and consumption in the EU
and international comparisons (2007 and 2011)

	Savings		Investment		Household consumption	
	in % of GDP					
	2007	2011	2007	2011	2007	2011
Austria	27.3	25.6	21.4	21.4	52.9	54.4
Belgium	26.9	22.8	21.7	20.7	50.9	52.6
Bulgaria	8.8	24.8	28.7	20.9	69.0	60.7
Cyprus	10.0	12.3	22.1	16.3	67.2	66.5
Czech Republic	24.7	20.7	27.0	23.9	47.7	50.8
Denmark	24.7	24.1	21.7	17.2	48.4	48.5
Estonia	22.9	25.8	35.5	21.7	54.1	51.1
Finland	27.1	19.7	21.3	19.6	50.4	55.5
France	20.6	18.1	20.9	20.1	56.5	57.7
Germany	26.8	23.9	18.4	18.1	55.9	57.4
Greece	9.1	4.4	26.6	15.1	69.6	74.6
Hungary	15.0	20.5	21.8	17.9	55.0	53.0
Ireland	20.9	12.0	25.6	10.1	47.3	48.7
Italy	20.8	16.4	21.5	19.6	58.6	61.3
Latvia	17.6	24.5	34.1	21.3	62.4	61.9
Lithuania	16.2	16.8	28.1	17.8	64.3	63.4
Luxembourg	n.d.	n.d.	20.8	19.0	32.0	31.3
Malta	n.d.	9.2	21.6	14.8	61.7	61.1
Netherlands	28.8	26.4	20.0	17.7	46.2	45.0
Poland	19.4	17.4	21.6	20.3	60.5	61.2
Portugal	12.7	10.9	22.2	18.1	65.3	66.3
Romania	20.2	24.7	30.2	24.6	66.9	62.0
Slovakia	22.2	21.5	26.2	23.1	56.1	57.5
Slovenia	27.4	20.3	27.8	18.5	52.5	57.8
Spain	21.0	17.8	30.7	21.1	57.4	58.3
Sweden	28.9	26.1	19.6	18.4	46.7	47.8
United Kingdom	16.0	13.2	17.7	14.2	63.5	64.3
EU	**21.5**	**18.9**	**21.3**	**18.5**	**57.0**	**58.0**
Euro area	22.9	19.7	21.8	19.2	55.9	57.4
United States	14.6	12.2	19.4	15.2	69.7	71.2
Japan	27.2	20.8	22.6	20.7	57.3	60.4

Source: Eurostat
Data collected and collated for the Robert Schuman Foundation, © FRS

There is a significant difference between the EU and the USA in the relative balance among consumption, savings and investment. Consumption accounts for over 71% of GDP in the USA while in the EU it is around 58% – a difference of 13%. The ability of the USA to issue the main global reserve currency alleviates the constraint of being forced to finance from the savings of economic agents including households. As a result, the gross savings rate reached 12.2% of GDP in the USA in 2011 whereas it amounted to 19% within the EU. The latter does not follow a homogeneous pattern in all states. Household consumption exceeds 60% of GDP in Greece, Portugal, Italy, Poland and the United Kingdom. Countries such as Denmark, Sweden, the Netherlands, Ireland and the Czech Republic had consumption as a proportion of GDP below 50%. Contrary to widespread opinion, Germany belongs to the group of EU countries in which consumption exceeds 55% of GDP. With 57% of its GDP devoted to consumption, Germany's situation was not significantly different from that of France (58%). Spain, Belgium, Austria, Finland and Slovakia also belong to this intermediate group.

As a result of the crisis, the investment rate declined in Europe, but only moderately. It fell between 2007 and 2011, from 21.3% to 18.5%, while the decline was more pronounced in the USA, falling from 19.4% to 15.2% during the same period. France directed a greater share of GDP to investment than Germany did in 2011: 20% versus 18%. In Italy, the crisis had a limited impact on investment (19.6% against 21.5%), as it did in Finland, Belgium, Poland and Sweden. In contrast, the effects of the crisis and remediation efforts weighed heavily on investment in Spain, where it was influenced by the decline in residential investment, dropping from 30.7% to 21.1% GDP. Greece suffered a setback of similar magnitude: 26.6% versus 15.1%. The change in Ireland was even more pronounced: from 2007 to 2011, investment fell from 25.6% of GDP to 10.1%.

2.3.4 Development of residential property prices (2004 - 2011)

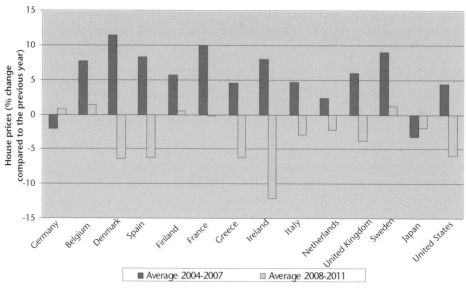

Source: OECD
Data collected and collated for the Robert Schuman Foundation, © FRS

With the notable exception of Germany, which saw a contraction, property prices rose sharply in the major EU countries prior to the crisis. In most countries, prices increased from 2004 to 2007 at an average annual rate of about 5%. In Spain, Belgium, Ireland and Sweden, the growth rate hovered around 7%. In France and Denmark, the growth rate reached 10% or more. This trend ended with the cyclical downturn in 2008, when a downward trend in prices became widespread, except in Germany where they grew moderately. For Spain, Denmark and Greece, the decline in prices occurred at an average annual rate of more than 5%. In Ireland, the average annual decline reached 12%. The decline was small in Italy, and near zero in France.

2.3.5 Household debt in EU Member States (2000 - 2010)

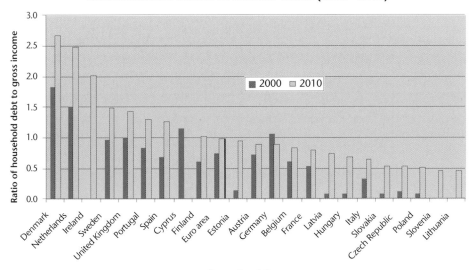

Source: Eurostat
Data collected and collated for the Robert Schuman Foundation, © FRS

Household indebtedness in the EU is the result both of the increase in residential investment and changes in consumer financing. Compared to Americans, household debt is lower in Europe. Overall, debt in 2010 neared 100% of gross income, while ten years ago, this level was approximately 70%. Large countries such as France and Italy are below this level despite an increase due to the crisis. In Germany, the level even declined. However, in some parts of Europe, household debt is significant. It exceeds 100% of gross household income in Spain and the United Kingdom. In Ireland, the Netherlands and Denmark (which holds the European record at 250%), it is over 200%.

2.3.6 Taxation in EU Member States (2010)

	Implicit tax rates on:		
	Consumption	Labour	Capital
Austria	21.4	40.5	24.1
Belgium	21.4	42.5	29.5
Bulgaria	22.8	24.4	20.7**
Cyprus	18.8	27.0	31.1
Czech Republic	21.1	39.0	16.7
Denmark	31.5	34.8	43.8*
Estonia	25.6	37.0	9.1
Finland	25.2	39.3	28.4
France	19.3	41.0	37.2
Germany	19.8	37.4	20.7
Greece	15.8	31.3	16.5*
Hungary	27.2	39.4	17.5
Ireland	21.6	26.1	14.0
Italy	16.8	42.6	34.9
Latvia	17.3	32.5	7.4
Lithuania	18.2	31.7	6.8
Luxembourg	27.3	32.0	n/a
Malta	18.9	21.7	n/a
Netherlands	27.0	36.9	12.5
Poland	20.2	30.1	20.5
Portugal	17.4	23.4	30.7
Romania	18.9	27.4	n/a
Slovakia	17.7	32.0	15.9
Slovenia	24.1	35.0	22.5
Spain	14.6	33.0	27.2
Sweden	28.1	39.0	34.9
United Kingdom	18.4	25.7	38.9*
EU	**19.7**	**36**	**n/a**
Euro area	**19.2**	**38.1**	**27.5**
* 2009; ** 2007			

Source: Eurostat
Data collected and collated for the Robert Schuman Foundation, © FRS

In the open European economy, consumption taxes are characterized by minimal differences. The implicit tax rate on consumption stood at around 20% throughout the EU. The differences are small: Germany (19.8%), France (19.6%), the Czech Republic (21.1%), Belgium (21.4%), Poland (20.2%) and the United Kingdom (18.4%). However, there is a tendency to under-tax consumption in southern Europe: Portugal, (17.4%), Italy (16.8%), Greece (15.8%) and Spain (14.6%). Conversely, the tendency is to over-taxation in northern Europe: Denmark (31.5%), Sweden (28.1%), the Netherlands (27%) and Finland (25.1%).

For labour taxation, the variation around the European average (36%) is similar to that observed for consumption. In Ireland, the United Kingdom, Portugal, Greece and Poland rates are significantly below the average. They are very similar and moderate in Germany, the Netherlands, Slovakia, Slovenia and Denmark. There is a tendency to overtax labour – 40% or more – in Austria, Sweden, the Czech Republic, Finland, Italy, Belgium and France.

The taxation of capital – including residential property – shows the greatest implied tax differentials throughout the EU. Rates range from 43.8% in Denmark to 12.5% in the Netherlands. Contrary to popular opinion, the United Kingdom is among the states with among the highest implicit tax rates (39%). France and Italy are also close to the average in Europe: they apply rates of 37 and 35% respectively. In Austria (24%) and especially in Germany (20.7%), capital is taxed less. Spain (27%) and Finland (28%) belong to an intermediate category.

2. 4. Solidarity in the Face of Crisis

2.4.1 Financial assistance to Member States of the eurozone

	Bilateral EU loans - disbursements	European Financial Stabilisation Mechanism (EFSM) / European Financial Stability Facility (EFSF)	European Stability Mechanism (ESM)	IMF	Total
	in billions of euros				
Greece 1st plan (2010-11)*	53.1			19.9	73.0
Greece 2nd plan (2012-15)		144.7		28.0	172.7
Ireland (2010-13)	4.9	40.2		22.6	67.7
Portugal (2011-14)		54.2		27.8	82.0
Spain (2012-13)**			39.5		39.5
Total	58	239.1	39.5	98.3	434.9

* Of a total amount available of €80 billion in bilateral loans and €30 billion in IMF loans

** Of a total amount available of €100 billion. The first €39.5 billion were disbursed to the Spanish Fund for Orderly Bank Restructuring (FOBR).

Sources: IMF Country Reports No. 12/57 No. 12/264 and No. 12/292
Data collected and collated for the Robert Schuman Foundation, © FRS

The eurozone crisis has highlighted the critical nature of financial solidarity as a factor in the stability of a monetary union. With the Greek debt crisis and Ireland's difficulties in 2010, the eurozone had the necessary instruments to deal with shocks that affected some of its members and had the potential to weaken the single currency. The European Financial Stability Facility (EFSF) was created in May 2010 for a period of three years. It comprised a €750 billion fund to cope with the European financial crisis, of which €440 billion came in the form of government guarantees. This rescue mechanism was supplemented by up to €60 billion from the commission under the European Financial Stability Mechanism (EFSM) and €250 billion from the IMF. It operates through the capital markets. The EFSF intervened on behalf of Ireland, Portugal and Greece in the context of its second aid plan (2012). Established by a treaty signed in July 2011 and launched in September 2012, the European Stability Mechanism (ESM) will follow the EFSF from 2013 onward. It will have a permanent lending capacity of €700 billion of which €80 were paid in at its implementation. The first aid plan for Greece amounting to €110bn was adopted in May 2010 and was organized in the form of bilateral loans. In total, taking into account the funds allocated to Spain to clean up its banking system, total EU interventions under the financial solidarity of the eurozone reached close to €435 billion at the end of 2012.

2.4.2 The cost of solidarity between Member States of the eurozone

	Bilateral loans to Greece (1st plan)	Maximum guaranteed commitment to the EFSF	Maximum guaranteed commitment to the ESM	Capital paid-in to ESM
	in billions of euros			
Germany	22.3	211.0	190.0	21.7
France	16.8	158.5	142.7	16.3
Italy	14.7	139.3	125.4	14.3
Spain	9.8	92.5	83.3	9.5
Netherlands	4.7	44.4	40.0	4.6
Belgium	2.9	27.0	24.3	2.8
Greece	-	21.9	19.7	2.3
Austria	2.3	21.6	19.5	2.2
Portugal	2.1	19.5	17.6	2.0
Finland	1.5	14.0	12.6	1.4
Ireland	1.3	12.4	11.1	1.3
Slovakia	0.4	7.7	5.8	0.7
Slovenia	0.4	3.7	3.0	0.3
Estonia	0.0	2.0	1.8	0.2
Luxembourg	0.2	2.0	1.4	0.2
Cyprus	0.2	1.5	1.3	0.2
Malta	0.1	0.7	0.5	0.1
Total	80.0*	780.0**	700.0	80.0

EFSF = European Financial Stability Facility

ESM = European Stability Mechanism (replaces EFSF)

* Of which 53.1 billion were disbursed

**Total effective = 726.0 (taking into account the programs of Greece, Portugal and Ireland)

Sources: www.esm.europa.eu, www.efsf.europa.eu and European Commission,
Directorate-General for Economic and Financial Affairs, Occasional Paper 68, August 2010.
Data collected and collated for the Robert Schuman Foundation, © FRS

Interventions by each of the 17 states of the eurozone are based on their share of European Central Bank capital. This applies in bilateral operations as well as the terms and conditions of intervention for the EFSF and the ESM. In the crisis of the eurozone which concerned the "peripheral" countries of the monetary union, these operations ultimately amounted to transfers from large states at the centre – Germany, France and Italy. These states, including Germany, are themselves faced with very high debt ratios. Hence the link between the development of these devices and the widespread austerity programs within the eurozone. In any case, this formula has proven to be a success. The ESM was able to obtain funds at market rates for countries whose situation deprived them of direct access to international investors: Ireland is a prime example of how European solidarity allowed a Member State to recover, particularly through exports, to restart the growth of its economy.

3. Towards a Growth Strategy: the Imperative of Competitiveness

3.1. The Challenges of Employment and Aging

3.1.1 GDP per capita and average annual GDP growth rate before and after the crisis

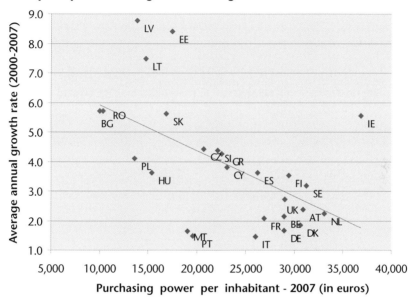

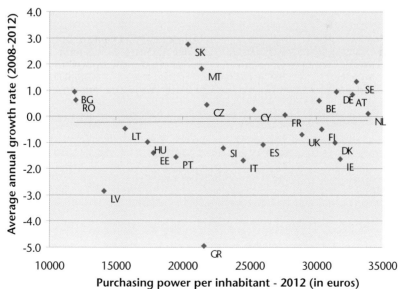

Source: Eurostat
Data collected and collated for the Robert Schuman Foundation, © FRS

The EU is in a region of the world where the standard of living of the population is generally high. In 2011, average per capita GDP (based on purchasing power parity – PPP) in the EU reached $27,820. It remains substantially below the USA level ($42,257), a difference of 34%, Canada ($35,709), which it trails by 22% and, even after ten years of stagnation, Japan ($30,680), which it lags by 9%. But per capita GDP remains well above that of the large emerging countries: it exceeds China by almost four times, is more than two and a half times that of Brazil and twice that of Russia. The difference with the performance of other major developed areas is in large part due to the disparity in performance and living standards between western and eastern Europe, which still exists nearly a quarter of a century after the end of communism despite tremendous progress. However, the dynamics at work should lead to a more nuanced judgment of developments between the two parts of Europe. The countries of Eastern Europe are experiencing a significant increase in the growth rate of GDP per capita. Over the past decade, Poland, which has established itself as a new leading European player, had an annual increase of 4.3% in GDP per capita. For the same period, the annual increase in the standard of living was 4.6% in Slovakia, 2.9% in the Czech Republic and 4.3% in Romania. In contrast, increases were more moderate for the western part of the continent: the annual change in the standard of living rose 2.4% in Sweden, 1.3% in Austria, 1.1% in Germany and 0.9% in the Netherlands. In the remainder of the western region, the gains were very low: 0.5% in France and Spain, 0.2% in Denmark and even a decline of 0.4% in Italy.

3.1.2 Unemployment in EU Member States and international comparisons (2007 and 2012)

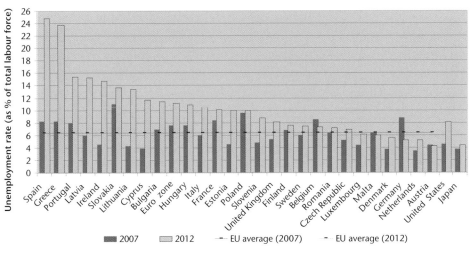

Source: Eurostat
Data collected and collated for the Robert Schuman Foundation, © FRS

The unemployment rate, already at 10% of the active population in 2011, continued to grow in 2012, standing at 11% for the EU and close to 11.7% for the eurozone at the end of 2012. The rise in unemployment resulted from the general decline in economic activity and there was a sharp contraction owing to the rigidities of the labour market in a number of Member States. In Europe, the unemployment trend remains upward while the reverse trend has already begun in the USA where the unemployment rate fell to 7.7% in late 2012. In Northern and Eastern Europe, the overall situation is stable. The unemployment rate fell below 8% in the United Kingdom: by the end of 2012 it had dropped to 7.7% from 8.3% in 2011. It decreased slightly in Germany, to 5.4% versus 5.7% a year earlier. In Belgium, the increase was limited to 7.5% versus 7.2% in 2011. The Netherlands saw a similar situation: 5.5% in 2012 versus 4.8% in 2011. In the Scandinavian countries, the unemployment rate was stable at around 7.5% (Denmark, Sweden and Finland). Norway had close to full employment (3%), unchanged from 2011. Despite a higher growth rate than the western region, the eastern part of Europe experienced limited changes in the unemployment rate between 2011 and 2012. It went from 10 to 10.4% in Poland, 11.1 to 10.8% in Hungary; it did not change in Slovakia (14%). It increased but remains at a manageable level in the Czech Republic, going from 6.5 to 7.3%. In western Europe, unemployment trended upward. For France and southern Europe, current levels and recent trends are concerning. In France, where it was already at 10% in late 2011, the unemployment rate rose again in 2012 to 10.7%. Likewise in Italy, where the increase is more pronounced: it jumped in one year from 8.8 to 11.1%. Portugal saw a similar increase from an already higher base: 16.3% in 2012 versus 13.7% in 2011. With its unemployment rate (22.7%) already the highest in the EU in 2011, Spain experienced a further marked deterioration in its unemployment situation (now 26.2%). Finally Greece, which has undergone a contraction of 25% of GDP since 2008, emulated the Spanish rate: 25.4% in 2012 versus 18.4% in 2011.

3.1.3 Youth unemployment in EU Member States and international comparisons (2007 and 2012)

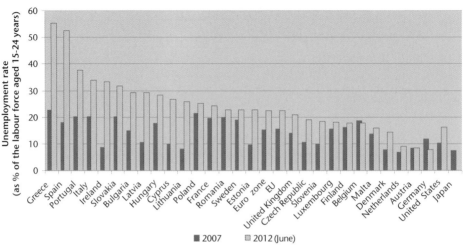

■ 2007   ▣ 2012 (June)

Source: Eurostat
Data collected and collated for the Robert Schuman Foundation, © FRS

To understand the pattern of unemployment rates in Europe, it is important to point out how it reflects the conditions of access to the labour market. Thus, the rate of youth unemployment is one of the most illustrative accounts of barriers to entry into the professional world. In the EU, the unemployment rate for young people (under 25 years) stood at 23.4% in 2012 versus 22% in 2011; in the eurozone, it was 24% in 2012 vs. 21% in 2011. In this respect, the disparities are even more marked than for the general population. The unemployment rate for young people was slightly higher than for the overall labour force in Germany (8%) and Austria (8.5%). The young experienced a moderate deterioration of their situation in the Netherlands (10% versus 8.2% in 2011). In the rest of Europe, being young imposes a higher barrier to entering the labour market. In Belgium and Finland, the unemployment rate for young people is 19%. In the other Scandinavian countries, it ranges from 13.7% in Denmark to 23% in Sweden. France's rate is above that of the Scandinavian countries (25.5%). Youth in eastern European countries faced an unemployment rate of around 30%: 27% in Poland, 30% and in Hungary and Slovakia. However, Romania (23%) and the Czech Republic (20.7%) have roughly the average European or slightly below. In southern Europe, barriers for young people entering the labour market were particularly high. For those under the age of 25, unemployment rates were around 36.5% in Italy and 39% in Portugal. The labour market is virtually closed to them in Spain (56%) and Greece (57%). The unique situation of quasi-exclusion of young people from the labour market in southern Europe justifies the measures taken by southern European governments to try and reduce the rigidities of the labour market.

3.1.4 Labour market of EU Member States (2011)

	Employment rate (15 to 64 years)				Employment rate (15 to 24 years)	Employment rate (55 to 64 years)
	Total	Change since 2000	Men	Women		
Austria	72.1	5.3%	77.8	66.5	54.9	41.5
Belgium	61.9	2.3%	67.1	56.7	26.0	38.7
Bulgaria	58.5	16.1%	60.9	56.2	20.1	43.9
Cyprus	68.1	3.7%	74.7	61.6	29.3	55.2
Czech Republic	65.7	1.1%	74.0	57.2	24.7	47.6
Denmark	73.1	-4.2%	75.9	70.4	57.5	59.5
Estonia	65.1	7.8%	67.7	62.8	31.5	57.2
Finland	69.0	2.7%	70.6	67.4	40.4	57.0
France	63.9	2.9%	68.2	59.7	29.9	41.5
Germany	72.5	10.5%	77.3	67.7	47.9	59.9
Greece	55.6	-1.6%	65.9	45.1	16.3	39.4
Hungary	55.8	-0.9%	61.2	50.6	18.3	35.8
Ireland	59.2	-9.2%	63.1	55.4	28.2	50.0
Italy	56.9	6.0%	67.5	46.5	19.4	37.9
Latvia	61.8	7.5%	62.9	60.8	27.2	51.1
Lithuania	60.7	2.7%	60.9	60.5	19.7	50.5
Luxembourg	64.6	3.0%	72.1	56.9	20.7	39.3
Malta	57.6	6.3%	73.6	41.0	44.7	31.7
Netherlands	74.9	2.7%	79.8	69.9	63.5	56.1
Poland	59.7	8.5%	66.3	53.1	24.9	36.9
Portugal	64.2	-6.1%	68.1	60.4	27.2	47.9
Romania	58.5	-7.1%	65.0	52.0	23.8	40.0
Slovakia	59.5	4.8%	66.3	52.7	20.2	41.4
Slovenia	64.4	2.5%	67.7	60.9	31.5	31.2
Spain	57.7	2.5%	63.2	52.0	21.9	44.5
Sweden	74.1	1.5%	76.3	71.8	40.5	72.3
United Kingdom	69.5	-2.4%	74.5	64.5	46.4	56.7
EU	**64.1**	**1.4%**	**70.1**	**58.5**	**33.6**	**47.4**
Euro area	**64.2**	**4.2%**	**70.3**	**58.2**	**33.5**	**47.1**
United States	66.7	-10.1%	71.4	62	n/a	60.0
Japan	70.1	2.0%	80.2	60.3	n/a	65.1

Source: Eurostat
Data collected and collated for the Robert Schuman Foundation, © FRS

The employment rate of the working age population is 64% in Europe (in both the EU and the eurozone) while it reaches 70% in Japan. The rate in the USA is a little higher (67%) than the European average. In Europe, there is a gap of 12 points between men and women; in the major countries of the eurozone, the gap is around 8 to 10 points. Outside Bulgaria (+16%), the largest gains in the employment rate of people aged 15-64 between 2000 and 2011 were seen in Germany (+10.5%), Poland (+8.5%) and Italy (+6%). The employment rate over the decade grew moderately in countries such as France (3%), the Netherlands (+2.7%), Finland (+2.7%) and Spain (+2.5%). In some countries, the employment rate dropped, either moderately, as in the United Kingdom (-2.4%) or more significantly, as in Denmark (-4%) and Portugal (-6.1%). The fall has been spectacular in Ireland (-9.2%). The degree of performance in employment coincides fairly well with the progress on unemployment. The rates for 15-64 year-olds are between 70 and 75% in the United Kingdom, Scandinavia, Germany and Austria. At the 60-70% level are countries such as Belgium, France, Portugal, the Czech Republic, Poland and Slovakia. In the 50-60% bracket, we find Italy, Spain, Greece and Hungary. For the edges of the labour market – both young and old – there are high participation rates in Germany, Austria, Scandinavia, the Netherlands and the United Kingdom. In these countries, employment rates at both age limits are around 45% for youth and 60% for seniors. In France, Italy, Spain and Portugal, but also in eastern Europe – Poland, Czech Republic and Hungary – the lower employment levels of youth and seniors primarily reflects the obstacles to the fluidity of the labour market.

3.1.5 Poverty and inequality in EU Member States and international comparisons (2010/2011)

	Income inequality			Poverty	
	Gini coefficient (2011)	Ratio between the income of the richest and poorest 20% of the population (2011)	Gender wage gap (2010)	At-risk-of-poverty rate (threshold: 50% of national median equivalised disposable income) (2011)	At-risk-of-poverty or social exclusion (threshold: 60% of national median equivalised income) (2011)
Austria	26.3	3.8	25.5	7.1	16.9
Belgium	26.3	3.9	8.6	8.3	21.0
Bulgaria	33.2*	5.9*	15.7	16.0	49.1
Cyprus	29.1*	4.4*	21.0	8.4*	23.6*
Czech Republic	25.2	3.5	25.5	5.1	15.3
Denmark	27.8	4.4	16	7.5	18.9
Estonia	31.9	5.3	30.9***	10.9	23.1
Finland	24.8	3.7	19.4	6.0	17.9
France	29.9*	4.5*	16	7.5*	19.3*
Germany	29.0	4.5	23.1	9.7	19.9
Greece	32.9*	5.6*	22***	12.4*	27.7*
Hungary	26.9	3.9	17.6	7.4	31.0
Ireland	33.2*	5.3*	12.6	7.8*	29.9*
Italy	31.2*	5.2*	5.5	11.6*	24.5*
Latvia	35.2	6.6	17.6	13.5	40.1
Lithuania	32.9	5.8	14.6	14.1	33.4
Luxembourg	27.2	4.0	12.0	6.7	16.8
Malta	27.4	4.1	6.1	8.2	21.4
Netherlands	25.8	3.8	18.5	5.2	15.7
Poland	31.1*	5.0*	5.3	10.5	27.2
Portugal	34.2	5.7	12.8	11.1	24.4
Romania	33.2	6.2	12.5	16.1	40.3
Slovakia	25.9*	3.8*	20.7	7.8*	20.6*
Slovenia	23.8	3.5	4.4	7.7	19.3
Spain	34.0	6.6	16.7	15.2	27.0
Sweden	24.2	3.6	15.8	7.6	16.1
United Kingdom	33.0*	5.4*	19.5	9.8*	23.1*
EU	**30.5***	**5.3**	**16.4**	**9.9***	**23.4***
Euro area	**30.2***	**6.0**	**16.8**	**9.8***	**21.5***
United States	37.3**	n/a	20.4**	17.3*	n/a
Japan	32.9*	n/a	20.1**	15.7*	n/a
Canada	31.9*	n/a	30.7**	11.4*	n/a

*2010, **2009, ***2008

Source: Eurostat
Data collected and collated for the Robert Schuman Foundation, © FRS

Europe is the world region with the lowest level of inequality. While women earn 17% less than men, this discrepancy is less pronounced than in the USA or Japan, where the difference reaches 20%. Within the EU, the disparity is strong in Germany and Austria – 23 and 25% respectively. Smaller discrepancies exist in the Scandinavian countries (~16%) due to their longstanding commitment to gender equality. Catholic countries in the EU, unlike what stereotypes may predict, perform significantly better than their Protestant partners. In Portugal and Ireland, the gap is less than 13%. Italy is the most egalitarian country with respect to the income gap between men and women, with a difference of only 5.5%. In the EU, the richest 20% of individuals receive income five times higher than the poorest 20%. Most major European countries – France, Germany, Italy and the United Kingdom – are at approximately that level or are slightly below it. Spain and Romania are exceptions.

3.1.6 Social challenges of aging populations in the EU (2010/2011 and forecasts)

	Life expectancy at 65 years (2011*)	Average exit age from the labour market (2010*)	At-risk-of-poverty rates for retirees (2011*)	Public expenditure on pension systems (as % of GDP)	
				2010	Projections for 2050
Austria	20.1	60.9	14.9	12.7	14.0
Belgium	19.6	61.6	17.3	10.3	14.7
Bulgaria	15.8	64.1	30.7	9.1	10.8
Cyprus	19.3	62.8	41.1	6.9	15.5
Czech Republic	17.6	60.5	6.7	7.1	10.2
Denmark	18.8	62.3	14.3	9.4	9.6
Estonia	17.9	62.6	14.9	6.4	5.3
Finland	19.9	61.7	17.5	10.7	13.3
France	21.4	60.2	8.4	13.5	14.2
Germany	19.8	62.4	14.0	10.2	12.3
Greece	19.7	61.5	19.0	11.6	24.0
Hungary	16.6	59.7	4.2	11.3	13.2
Ireland	19.4	64.1	10.6	4.1	8.0
Italy	20.4	60.4	12.3	14.0	14.7
Latvia	16.6	62.7	11.3	5.1	5.8
Lithuania	17.0	59.9	14.8	6.5	10.4
Luxembourg	19.8	59.4	3.9	8.6	22.1
Malta	19.9	60.5	17.6	8.3	12.0
Netherlands	19.8	63.5	6.4	6.5	10.3
Poland	17.9	59.3	13.2	10.8	9.1
Portugal	20.1	62.6	17.9	11.9	13.3
Romania	16.1	64.3	11.1	8.4	14.8
Slovakia	16.8	58.8	6.7	6.6	9.4
Slovenia	19.3	59.8	18.4	10.1	18.2
Spain	20.9	62.3	15.9	8.9	15.5
Sweden	20.0	64.4	18.9	9.6	9.0
United Kingdom	19.7	63.0	22.9	6.7	8.1
EU	**19.3**	**61.5**	**13.9**	**10.2**	**12.3**
Euro area	**20.0**	**61.4**	**12.5**	**n.d.**	**n.d.**
*or the most recent year available					

Source: Eurostat
Data collected and collated for the Robert Schuman Foundation, © FRS

Increasing life expectancy in Europe, combined with the low birth rate, has led to an aging population. This is a structural change which European economic and social systems will have to face over the course of the twenty-first century. Europeans at age 65 now have a life expectancy of 20 years. The first response to this challenge has been to increase the age of retirement. In many countries, the retirement age is over 60 years. The average age of exit from the workforce is now around 62 years in Germany, Spain, Portugal and Belgium. In countries such as the Netherlands, Sweden and the United Kingdom, the end of working life is closer to 63 or 64. For France, Italy, Poland, Slovenia and the Czech Republic, the retirement age is earlier, at around 59 or 60 years old. It is not improbable that reforms adopted in recent years will still be insufficient to contain increasing pension costs as a proportion of GDP. The changes made in Germany should be sufficient to address the expansion of pension costs up to 12% of GDP in 2050 from 10% in 2010. In Poland and the Czech Republic, public expenditure on pensions should remain constant at 10% of GDP by mid-century. In France, public pension spending already stood as the highest in the EU in 2010, at 13.5% of GDP, and is predicted to increase moderately by 2050 to 14.2%. For Italy, Belgium and Spain, the proportion will be around 15% in 2050. In Greece, the burden is predicted to double between 2010 and 2050 from 12 to 24%.

3.1.7 OECD's Better life index (2011)

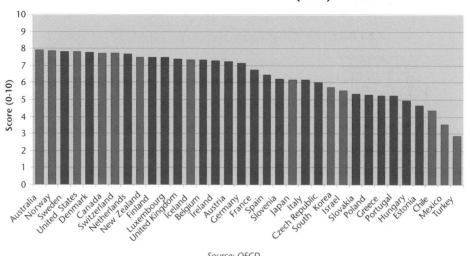

Source: OECD
Data collected and collated for the Robert Schuman Foundation, © FRS

Since the late 1960s, sociologists have questioned the qualitative effects of quantitative changes. "Nobody falls in love with a growth rate", was the slogan as the war boom came to an end. In France, the Stiglitz Commission was tasked by the government to analyze the links between growth and well-being in the age of globalization. Per capita GDP takes little account of social realities: by comparing the GDP per capita of Qatar and Germany, what can one really discern from the data? With their unique histories in a continent divided only 25 years ago between two opposing economic systems, the countries of Europe do not yet share the same patterns in the growth of economic wealth. The OECD's Better Life Index measures a broader range of variables and found that among the best-ranked countries are the Scandinavian countries, Australia and Canada. At the other end of the spectrum of OECD countries, Greece, Portugal and Romania are ranked closer to South Korea, either because of lower initial levels of development or because of pressure from the current crisis. Major European countries – the United Kingdom, Germany and France – have middle rankings.

3.2. The Challenge of Human Capital

3.2.1 Public and private expenditure on education (2009)

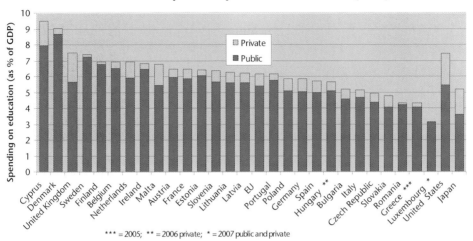

*** = 2005;   ** = 2006 private;   * = 2007 public and private

Source: Eurostat
Data collected and collated for the Robert Schuman Foundation, © FRS

Education expenditure in Europe, at 5.8% of GDP, is higher than that of Japan, but significantly lower than the level in the USA (7.5% of GDP). Public spending is the predominant component of the overall effort, amounting to 5.1% of GDP, compared with 0.75% of GDP by the private sector. The United Kingdom maintains both higher public expenditures than the EU average (5.4%), as well as much greater private involvement (1.7% of GDP) than its EU partners. In this area, the eastern European countries are not left behind when compared to their western partners: Poland's public and private spending rates relative to GDP exceed those of Germany and are slightly below those of France. Scandinavian countries are characterized by an effort that is almost entirely public and much higher than that of their EU partners.

3.2.2 Life-long learning (2011)

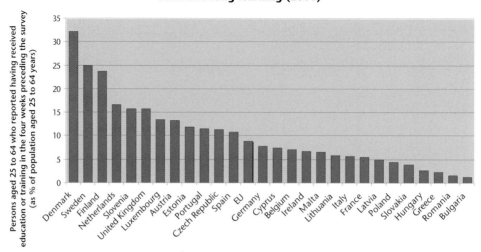

Source: Eurostat
Data collected and collated for the Robert Schuman Foundation, © FRS

In an economy that emphasizes knowledge and skilled labour as keys to the growth of high value-added activities, education efforts must be followed up and extended by continuous training. The countries putting the greatest emphasis on education spending are often those who also spend significant amounts on training: the Scandinavian countries, the United Kingdom and the Netherlands.

3.2.3 R&D expenditure in EU Member States and international comparisons (2010)

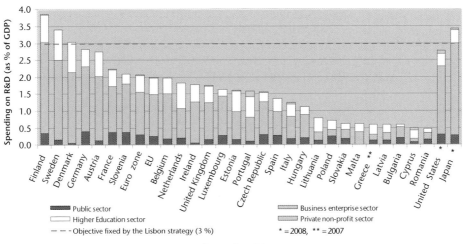

Source: Eurostat
Data collected and collated for the Robert Schuman Foundation, © FRS

In a global economy where technology plays a key role in the hierarchy of power and economic vitality, the EU compares poorly with Japan and the USA. In these countries, spending on R&D is 3.4 and 2.8% of GDP, respectively, while spending is slightly below 2.0% of GDP in the EU. A comparison of European performance shows very clear differences between northern Europe and Germany, with among the highest spending levels in the world and the rest of the EU where R&D spending is still very limited. Leading the European field is Finland, where R&D amounted to 4% of GDP, with a much larger share of the effort coming from the private sector (2.8% of GDP) than the public sector (0.36%). Sweden, with R&D spending totalling 3.6%, and Denmark, at 3%, follows a similar pattern. The dominant economy of the continent, Germany, has put forth an impressive R&D effort at 2.8% of GDP, with the public sector less involved (0.41%) than the private sector (2%). Austria is similar to Germany, whereas in the Netherlands (1.8%), spending is significantly lower, especially for businesses (0.9%), which is roughly half of the German amount. France is one notch below its main partner at 2.2%. This is not only the case in the private sector (1.3%) but also for the public sector (0.36%). Southern countries had significantly lower expenditures: Italy faces vexing problems of general productivity, spending only 1.27% of GDP on R&D due to the weakness of the efforts of the private sector (0.65%). Spain and Portugal had a similar situation. The countries of Eastern Europe can rely on their comparative advantages in labour costs, but their R&D efforts have been weaker.

3. 3. The Imperatives of Competitiveness and Innovation

3.3.1 Unit labour costs (2000 - 2011)

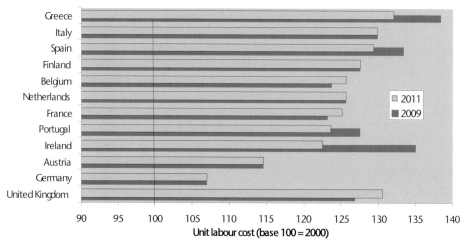

Source: ECB
Data collected and collated for the Robert Schuman Foundation, © FRS

The disparities in growth rates and trade balances among countries, both within the EU and beyond, have had a decisive impact on labour productivity. Germany, which pursued social welfare reform and labour market flexibility, has managed to constrain unit labour costs to a total increase of 7% since 2000. At the other end of the spectrum, Greece has seen labour costs rise by about 38%. This situation has exacerbated the crisis in the eurozone since the Greeks had to pursue policies to contain these costs: despite the decline in unit labour costs of 4.5% between 2009 and 2011, Greece is still 31% above their 2000 level. Countries affected by the eurozone crisis are facing the need to correct the excessive increase in unit labour costs: after seeing an increase of 35% in Ireland from 2000 to 2009, unit labour costs were reduced by 8% from 2009 to 2011, a trend that has helped rebalance the country's foreign trade. Over the last two years, Portugal and Spain followed similar paths (down about 4% in both countries). Italy saw a continuous decline in relative productivity during the 2000s, allowed its unit labour costs to grow by 30% in 10 years, and has not managed to reduce them between 2009 and 2011. Unlike its major partners of the eurozone, France actually recorded an increase in unit labour costs from 2009 to 2011 (up by 2.5%), while from 2000 to 2009, unit labour costs increased by 23%. This increase was three times the rate of Germany and is one of the major causes of the performance discrepancy between the two largest economies in the eurozone. Free from the constraints of a fixed exchange rate like the other members of the eurozone, the United Kingdom has nonetheless followed the same pattern of increasing unit labour costs: from 2000 to 2009, they increased by 27% and have continued in this direction. In 2011, they were 31% higher than in 2000.

3.3.2 Labour productivity (2000 and 2011)

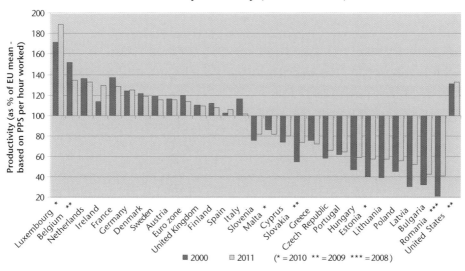

Source: Eurostat
Data collected and collated for the Robert Schuman Foundation, © FRS

If we consider the average European labour productivity indexed at 100, we can measure the position of each country in relation to the Union as a whole. As expected, because of their long years as market economies, the western part of Europe has productivity levels above the average, while the eastern part, subject to 45 years of communist rule, has productivity below the EU average.

Observed over a decade, developments in labour productivity provide a number of lessons. Integration into the EU under liberal economic terms has seen the countries of Eastern Europe reduce their deviation from the EU average. Poland, which had labour productivity at 40% of the average in 2000, is now at 55% of the EU average. The Czech Republic, due to its industrial tradition, was at 60% of the EU average in 2000 and has continued to converge, reaching 70% today.

As expected when measuring countries relative to a common mean, the inverse process has been occurring in parts of Western Europe as their historical productivity gap over the east has been narrowed. While Germany's relative labour productivity has remained largely unchanged at 20% above the EU average, and Ireland has enjoyed strong growth, there have been relative declines in France, though its labour productivity remains higher than Germany's, and especially in Italy where relative productivity has dropped from a level of around 18% above the EU average in 2000 to a level almost identical to the EU average today. In the southern countries of the eurozone, Greece, from a level below the average, has slowly increased its relative productivity while Portugal, from a lower position, and Spain from a position close to the average, have improved their relative performances

3.3.3 Trade balances of Member States of the eurozone (2011)

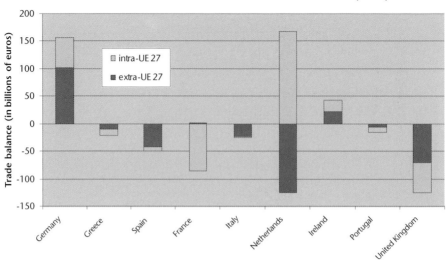

Source: Eurostat
Data collected and collated for the Robert Schuman Foundation, © FRS

With the exception of the United Kingdom, the EU in 2011 is divided between a northern zone (Germany, the Netherlands and Ireland) which generates trade surpluses and a southern zone that records deficits. Germany had a €100 billion accumulated trade surplus outside the EU and a €50 billion surplus within the EU. The Netherlands has a trade deficit outside of Europe but a surplus with their EU partners. Southern EU countries mainly suffer from their trade deficits with the rest of the world. France, which has a zero trade balance in Europe, suffered a deficit of more than €70 billion outside Europe. In Italy, the total trade deficit – about €25 billion – is almost completely accounted for by extra-European energy trade, while Spain has a similar issue. Greece has similar trade deficits with the two trading zones – the EU and outside the EU – while in Portugal, a deficit in intra-European trade dominates its overall trade balance.

The argument often advanced regarding the role of the euro in the degradation of European trade balances does not account for the situation in the United Kingdom which combines large deficits with the EU and with the world. The United Kingdom is facing a trade deficit of €65 billion with its EU partners and a deficit of €50 billion with non-European countries.

3.3.4 Exports of high technology products (2011)

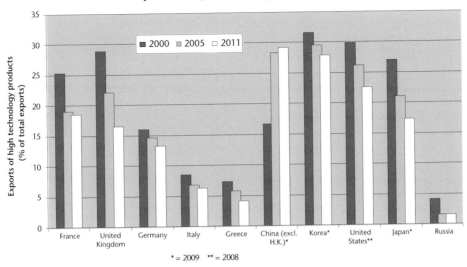

* = 2009   ** = 2008

Source: Eurostat
Data collected and collated for the Robert Schuman Foundation, © FRS

South Korea and the USA are leaders in exports of high technology products, with high tech accounting for more than 20% of their exports. Japan has seen its position crumble: while high technology accounted for 27% of its exports in 2000, this dropped to 17% by 2009. The spectacular evolution within China has seen high technology increase from 16 to 28% of its total exports between 2000 and 2011. These numbers must, however, be qualified by the fact that the Chinese export data includes value added elsewhere in the supply chain, including in the USA. The value-added content of Chinese exports in high technology is considerably lower. The high technology export numbers show here do not reflect the comparative advantages of this type of Chinese products but its place in the international division of production processes.

For the EU, the share of high technology products in total exports is near 15%. It has, however, world leaders within the continent. The high tech share of German exports (13% of total) is significantly lower than levels in Japan (17%) and the USA (22%). Even France (18.6%), the Netherlands (17.3%), the United Kingdom (16.5%), the Czech Republic (16.2%) and Sweden (13.9%) are ranked higher than Germany. One should, however, qualify any apparent specialization of these countries in high technology R&D. The total amount of all German exports is 2.5 times that of France, so its high-tech exports are still 1.7 times those of France.

3.3.5 Summary of competitiveness and innovation indicators

	Global Competitiveness Index (2012)	Ease of Doing Business Index (2012)	Summary Innovation Index (2011)	Patent filings by residents (2010)	European high-tech patents (2009)	Share of high-tech exports in total exports (2011)
	ranking out of 144 countries	ranking out of 185 countries	on a scale from 0 to 1	per million inhabitants	per million inhabitants	in %
Austria	19	29	0.60	289	13.7	11.2
Belgium	17	33	0.62	57	18.5	7.7
Bulgaria	62	66	0.24	32	0.3	3.8
Cyprus	58	36	0.51	4	0.6	14.9
Czech Republic	39	65	0.44	82	0.7	16.2
Denmark	12	5	0.72	293	15.7	9.3
Estonia	34	21	0.50	63	1.5	14.9
Finland	3	11	0.69	323	19.7	8.0
France	21	34	0.56	227	17.7	18.6
Germany	6	20	0.70	576	19.5	13.0
Greece	96	78	0.34	64	0.6	4.2
Hungary	60	54	0.35	65	0.7	20.8
Ireland	27	15	0.58	164	7.1	20.7
Italy	42	73	0.44	146**	4.3	6.4
Latvia	55	25	0.23	79	1.3***	6.7
Lithuania	45	27	0.26	33	0.6	5.6
Luxembourg	22	56	0.60	156	2.0	24.8
Malta	47	102	0.34	29	4.9***	30.1
Netherlands	5	31	0.60	156**	18.7	17.3
Poland	41	55	0.30	84	0.7	5.2
Portugal	49	30	0.44	47	0.8	3.0
Romania	78	72	0.26	64	0.3	9.1
Slovakia	71	46	0.31	43	0.1	6.6
Slovenia	56	35	0.52	215	3.7	5.3
Spain	36	44	0.41	77	2.5	4.8
Sweden	4	13	0.76	234	22.2	13.9
United Kingdom	8	7	0.62	249	8.6	16.5
EU	**n/a**	**n/a**	**0.54**	**n/a**	**9.5**	**15.4**
United States	7	4	0.67*	783	26.2***	22.6***
Japan	10	24	0.64*	2276	42.7***	17.4**
Canada	14	17	n/a	133	24.8***	8.0**
China	29	91	n/a	219	n.d.	29.2**
India	59	132	n/a	6**	n.d.	6.2**
Brazil	48	130	n/a	14	n.d.	3.0**

* 2010; ** 2009, ***2008

Data collected and collated for the Robert Schuman Foundation, © FRS

In terms of competitiveness, the EU includes a number of champions and a wide variety of different situations. The EU has five of the most competitive countries among the world's top ten: Finland, Sweden, the Netherlands, Germany and the United Kingdom. But many of its members hold medium rankings (Belgium, Austria and France) and some have alarming rankings (Spain, Italy and Portugal). Ireland was ranked low in terms of competitiveness but rises to 15th place in the world for ease of doing business. The best countries in the EU for ease of doing business are Denmark and the United Kingdom, though they are still ranked lower than the USA (fourth place worldwide). The impressive performance of US patent productions is due to the size of the economy. In relative terms, they trail the Japanese. In Europe, only Germany rises to the inner circle of the best international patent producers.

3.4. The Challenges of Resource Scarcity and Climate Change

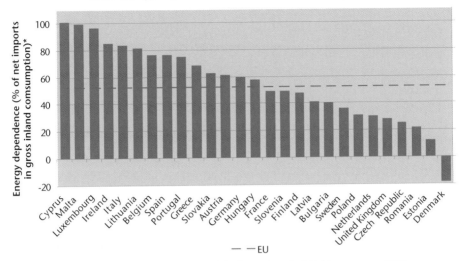

3.4.1 Energy dependence of EU Member States (2010)

* The energy dependence rate is defined as net imports divided by gross consumption.

Source: Eurostat
Data collected and collated for the Robert Schuman Foundation, © FRS

During the 20 years since the signing of the Kyoto Protocol (1992), Europe has sought the development of a sustainable energy model. This concern reflects the phenomenal surge in energy demand from emerging markets which is keeping global demand structurally elevated. After the Fukushima accident in March 2011, Germany announced its intention to phase out nuclear power by 2022. All these factors underline the importance of European energy dependence. Inextricably entangled in this discussion are technical constraints, economics and power relations. Russian influence poses to its European neighbours, especially Germany, a strong political constraint. Despite the pronouncements of the new government, France, which has the cheapest electricity in Europe thanks to its nuclear capacity, will continue be in a strong situation with respect to "dependence" on nuclear power. In a world that would require a minimum of European consultation on such important issues, it is logical that national concerns continue to dominate the discussion.

3.4.2 Energy mix of EU Member States and international comparisons (2011)

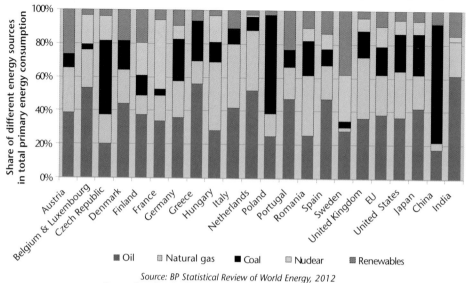

Source: BP Statistical Review of World Energy, 2012
Data collected and collated for the Robert Schuman Foundation, © FRS

As with the USA, Europeans primarily use oil and gas to meet their energy needs while nuclear and renewable play a residual role. Germany and the United Kingdom reflect this model. France is characterized by the central role of nuclear energy not found elsewhere among its partners, except to a lesser degree in Sweden. Conversely, in Sweden, renewable energies play a significant role that is not yet the case in France. Due to their available solar resources, Spain and Portugal rank higher in renewable energy.

3.4.3 Greenhouse gas emissions (1990 - 2010)

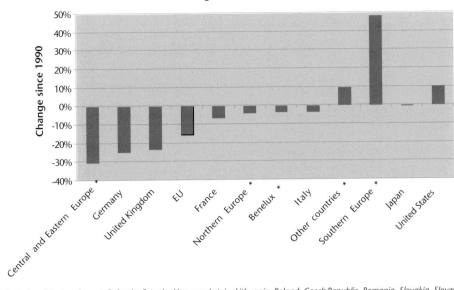

* Central and Eastern Europe: Bulgaria, Estonia, Hungary, Latvia, Lithuania, Poland, Czech Republic, Romania, Slovakia, Slovenia;
Southern Europe: Spain, Greece, Malta, Portugal; Northern Europe: Denmark, Finland, Sweden; Other countries: Austria, Ireland

Source: UNFCCC
Data collected and collated for the Robert Schuman Foundation, © FRS

Over the past 20 years, the EU has managed to reduce its emissions of greenhouse gases by 16%, while Japanese emissions have remained steady and emissions in the USA have increased by 10%. Eastern Europe has been at the forefront of this change with a reduction of 31%, followed by Germany and the United Kingdom where emissions have declined by 25 and 24%, respectively. Despite its environmental credentials, northern Europe has fallen far short of that performance (-4%) and has done worse than France (-7%). In this "battle", Europe is able to mobilize the resources of the European market to conduct trade in emissions credits, making it possible to exchange CO_2 quotas.

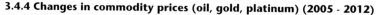

3.4.4 Changes in commodity prices (oil, gold, platinum) (2005 - 2012)

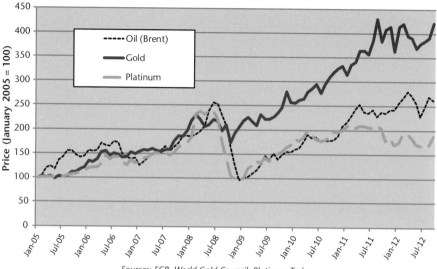

Sources: ECB, World Gold Council, Platinum Today
Data collected and collated for the Robert Schuman Foundation, © FRS

In the medium term, raw material costs are a decisive factor in the growth rate of the economy. Having returned to its pre-crisis levels, the price of oil was fluctuating in a floating band (around 110/115 dollars per barrel) as of late 2012. Crude oil prices are dependent on the decline in the growth of the global economy, the development of renewable energy and a greater supply of oil and shale gas. Professionals expect a decline in the medium term: December 2013 futures are trading at $101 per barrel. However, this underlying trend may face supply shocks of a geopolitical nature. Recent changes in energy markets are profoundly transforming the demand pressure from the USA on world prices. In terms of metals, platinum price movements fit the trend towards stabilization near the current level due to weak demand from western economies. The price of gold barely declined during 2008-2009 and saw a very strong recovery in 2010-2011, both as a refuge and as an instrument for hedging against financial tensions and expectations of inflation. According to the theorem stated by Raymond Barre upon the ending of dollar convertibility in the 1970s, the increase in the price of gold is essentially a phenomenon of a monetary nature.

3.4.5 Impact on production costs of gas and electricity prices (2012)

	Gas price (industry)		Gas price (households)		Electricity price (industry)		Electricity price (households)	
	euro/gigajoule				euro/kWh			
	2012	Change since 2000*	2012	Change since 2000*	2012	Change since 2000*	2012	Change since 2000*
Austria **	n/a	n/a	14.2	82%	0.09*	62%	0.14***	52%
Belgium	9.2	107%	15.2	104%	0.10	29%	0.16	36%
Bulgaria	10.0	187%	11.4	103%	0.07	67%	0.07	73%
Cyprus	n/a	n/a	n/a	n/a	0.22	147%	0.23	177%
Czech Republic	9.0	198%	15.3	327%	0.10	120%	0.12	160%
Denmark	9.9	116%	15.1	69%	0.08	64%	0.13	83%
Estonia	9.8	237%	10.9	178%	0.06	39%	0.08	69%
Finland	10.9	140%	n/a	n/a	0.07	81%	0.11	69%
France	10.5	145%	14.7	110%	0.08	43%	0.10	6%
Germany	12.0	152%	13.2	91%	0.09	33%	0.14	21%
Greece	n/a	n/a	n/a	n/a	0.10	76%	0.11	89%
Hungary **	8.3	202%	12.5	320%	0.10	92%	0.13	115%
Ireland	9.8	172%	14.3	96%	0.13	95%	0.18	132%
Italy **	8.2	99%	12.3	39%	0.11	65%	0.11	-7%
Latvia	9.9	186%	11.2	213%	0.11	156%	0.11	134%
Lithuania	12.5	197%	11.7	153%	0.11	106%	0.10	95%
Luxembourg	14.0	183%	14.4	153%	0.10	42%	0.15	39%
Malta	n/a	n/a	n/a	n/a	0.18	167%	0.16	165%
Netherlands **	7.5	84%	11.6	106%	0.08	26%	0.13	39%
Poland	9.4	67%	10.6	100%	0.09	77%	0.11	56%
Portugal	11.1	61%	16.3	19%	0.11	63%	0.11	-7%
Romania	5.3	130%	3.9	-2%	0.08	106%	0.08	21%
Slovakia	10.6	99%	11.9	95%	0.13	86%	0.14	37%
Slovenia	14.8	210%	17.2	212%	0.09	44%	0.12	44%
Spain	10.0	148%	15.9	74%	0.12	81%	0.15	64%
Sweden	12.5	146%	17.8	133%	0.08	114%	0.13	106%
United Kingdom	8.2	133%	13.8	108%	0.11	65%	0.16	52%
EU	**9.0**	**49%**	**12.0**	**41%**	**0.09**	**39%**	**0.13**	**26%**

* Change from 2001-2005 for the countries for which 2000 data are not available; ** 2011, *** 2008

Source: Eurostat
Data collected and collated for the Robert Schuman Foundation, © FRS

Across the EU, energy costs rose sharply over the past twelve years, while economic growth was lower than in the rest of the world. The divergence of these two trends is a challenge and increasingly important for Europe which seeks to maintain its standard of living and competitiveness. Since 2000, the price of gas for industrial use has increased by 49% and the price of electricity by 39%. However, this average is somewhat misleading for the major industrial countries since gas prices have more than doubled in the Czech Republic (+198%), Germany (+152%), Spain (+148%), France (+145%), the United Kingdom (+133%) and Belgium (+107%) while nearly doubling in Italy (+99%) and the Netherlands (+84%). The price of electricity for industry grew more moderately, up 43% in France and 33% in Germany. In fast-growing countries without nuclear electricity, prices have increased more significantly: +120% in the Czech Republic, 81% in Spain, 77% in Poland and 65% in Italy. In 2012, industry in France, Sweden, Finland and Germany benefited from an average price per kWh below €0.10, while industrial prices in Italy were 10% higher and prices in Spain, 20% higher.

Households have also experienced significant increases in energy prices. Over the last 12 years, gas prices have doubled in major European countries: 110% in France, 106% in the Netherlands, 100% in Poland and 91% in Germany. The rate of increase was lower in some countries of southern Europe: 74% in Spain, 39% in Italy and only 19% in Portugal. The price of electricity borne by households grew only 26% since 2000. Germany was close to the average (21%) but increases were higher in many countries: 106% in Sweden, 83% in Denmark, 69% in Finland, 64% in Spain and 56% in Poland. In France, the increase was very low (6%) while in Italy, household electricity prices actually decreased (-7%).

4. The Budget of the EU: the Necessary Means

4.1.1 Financial framework of the EU (2007 - 2013)

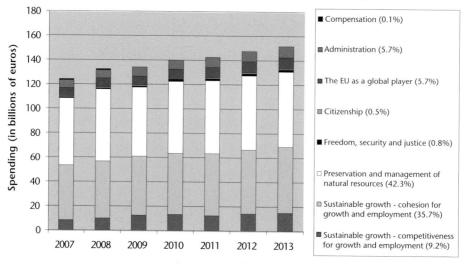

Source: European Commission
Data collected and collated for the Robert Schuman Foundation, © FRS

The European financial framework for the period 2007-2013 represents the projected expenditures for the EU. The total amounts to 1.23% of EU GDP, which is far below the means of a federal state. The expenditure of the US government, for example, reached 18% of GDP. The financial framework covers three main areas of intervention:

– Structural policies, including through the ERDF (European Regional Development Fund). This is the channel that supports the development of the most fragile regions of the EU. It plays a key role for members from Eastern Europe who, because of the impact of their communist regimes from 1947 to 1989, have significant disadvantages. The ERDF also assists countries in southern Europe. These policies contribute a substantial part of their economic development. In the current economic crisis in this region, these resources remain an important factor for economic and social stability.

– Management of resources, including agriculture, through the Common Agricultural Policy (CAP) has long remained the most active EU policy and is the second major axis of intervention for the framework. Agriculture represents only 1.5% of GDP and there is pressure by many governments to control expenditures in this area; for countries in eastern Europe, such as Poland, and for many countries in southern Europe, the CAP remains too important and change will be resisted.

– Measures to promote competitiveness and employment, in particular through the European Social Fund (ESF) constitute the third major component of European fiscal policy.

For the period 2007-2013, the financial framework totalled €925 billion, with €148 billion allocated for 2012.

The European Council meeting of November 22-23, 2012 failed to arrive at an EU budget for the 2014-2020 period.

4.1.2 Distribution of EU budget financing by revenue type (2012)

Total: 132.7 billion euros

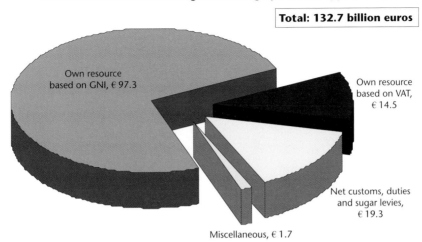

Source: European Commission
Data collected and collated for the Robert Schuman Foundation, © FRS

The EU does not tax directly; resources consist of contributions from Member States. In 2012, these resources amounted to €132.7 billion.

These resources are mainly of three types:

– GNI (Gross National Income) own resources are the main source of EU funding, providing 73% of the total;

– Customs duties, agricultural levies and sugar levies constitute 14.5% of the total. Established in 1970, they are collected by states from the relevant economic actors. With the reduction of customs duties under international trade agreements, these resources have been reduced.

– VAT own resources represent nearly 11% of the total: there is a 1% levy on a harmonized VAT base. This rate was reduced to 0.5% in 2004, and the basis used has been capped at 50% of a state's GDP since 1999.

Since 1984, the United Kingdom has received compensation in the form of a discount originally intended to compensate for the smaller share of agriculture in the British GDP relative to its European partners. The British discount is offset by its partners at the level of their contributions to the resources of the Union. For the 2007-2013 period, the discount amounts to €31 billion. Because its GDP has become higher than the average of its partners, the British situation suffers growing criticism from its partners.

4.1.3 EU budget allocated to the common agricultural policy, the environment and rural development (2012)

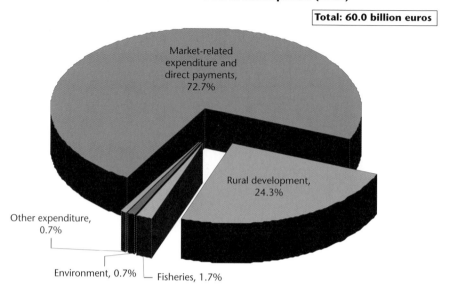

Total: 60.0 billion euros

Market-related expenditure and direct payments, 72.7%

Rural development, 24.3%

Other expenditure, 0.7%

Environment, 0.7%

Fisheries, 1.7%

Source: European Commission
Data collected and collated for the Robert Schuman Foundation, © FRS

With approximately €60 billion, expenditure on natural resources and primary agriculture represents 40% of EU budgetary resources. As the original policy was strongly supported by EU agricultural countries, including France, it not only ensured European agricultural self sufficiency but helped the EU become a major exporter. A limited agricultural country like Germany has become a leading player thanks to the CAP. At a time when rising global demand is strong due to the impact of emerging countries, Europe can turn agriculture a into major comparative advantage which originated 25 or 30 years ago as a political objective rather than a defensive one. Transformations in the global economy have logically blurred the divisions between "les anciens" who support the CAP and "les modernes" calling for a transfer of resources to more "technological" areas.

4.1.4 EU budget allocated to cohesion policy (2012)

Total: 52.7 billion euros

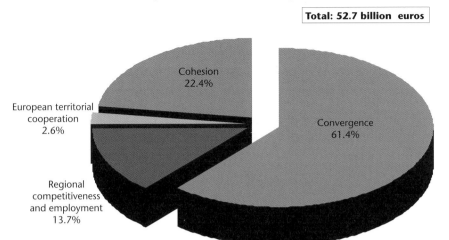

Source: European Commission
Data collected and collated for the Robert Schuman Foundation, © FRS

Spending on "cohesion" items amounted to €54 billion in 2012. Cohesion spending is both economic and social. Activated through the ERDF, the ESF and the Cohesion Fund, this category clearly represents a transfer of resources from the most developed countries of the Union to the less developed economies in eastern and southern Europe. For the current process of adjustment taking place in the eurozone, this plays a key stabilizing role in helping to limit fiscal deficits.

4.1.5 EU budget allocated to improving competitiveness (2012)

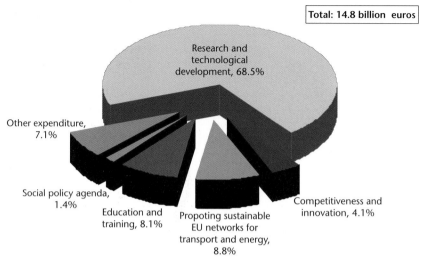

Total: 14.8 billion euros

Research and technological development, 68.5%

Other expenditure, 7.1%

Social policy agenda, 1.4%

Education and training, 8.1%

Propoting sustainable EU networks for transport and energy, 8.8%

Competitiveness and innovation, 4.1%

Source: European Commission
Data collected and collated for the Robert Schuman Foundation, © FRS

In 2012, the EU provided €15 billion to support economic competitiveness, amounting to 10 percent of its budget. This effort is mainly in R&D (68.5%) but it also covered sustainable transport networks, energy and education. The ERDF is the main vehicle for competitiveness spending.

4.1.6 The EU as a global actor (2012)

Total: 9.4 billion euros

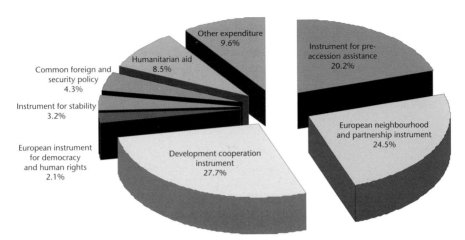

Source: European Commission
Data collected and collated for the Robert Schuman Foundation, © FRS

In 2012, the EU spent nearly €9.5 billion in its role on the international stage. The principal component of this involves foreign aid, which complements and extends the aid activities of Member States. It is also used for neighbouring states, including Arab countries seeking a transition to democracy and more sustainable development.